April 25, 1939.　　W. B. STOUT　　2,155,876
PORTABLE BUILDING STRUCTURE
Filed Nov. 13, 1935　　6 Sheets-Sheet 1

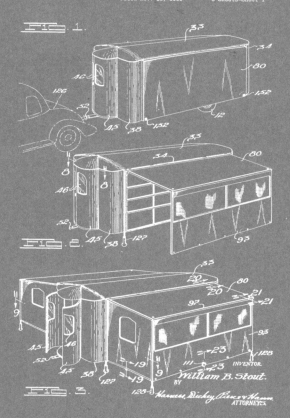

FIG. 1.

FIG. 2.

FIG. 3.

INVENTOR.
William B. Stout.
BY
Harness, Dickey, Pierce & Haun
ATTORNEYS.

Fig. 5.

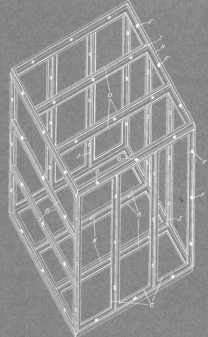

Inventors:
Konrad L. Wachsmann
and Walter Gropius,
by *J. M. Grade,*
their *Attorney.*

Nov. 24, 1959　　R. B. FULLER　　2,914,074
GEODESIC TENT
Filed March 1, 1957　　4 Sheets-Sheet 1

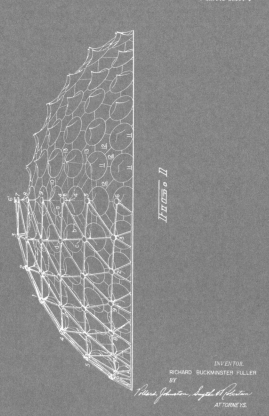

FIG. II

INVENTOR.
RICHARD BUCKMINSTER FULLER
BY
Pierce, Johnston, Smyth & Horton
ATTORNEYS.

May 27, 1947.　　K. L. WACHSMANN ET AL　　2,421,305
BUILDING STRUCTURE
Filed Aug. 10, 1945　　4 Sheets-Sheet 2

Fig. 5.

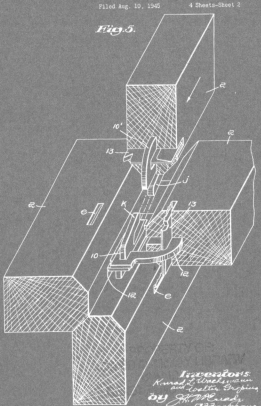

Inventors:
Konrad L. Wachsmann
and Walter Gropius,
by *J. M. Grade,*
Attorney.

HOME DELIVERY

HOME DELIVERY

FABRICATING
THE MODERN DWELLING

BARRY BERGDOLL and
PETER CHRISTENSEN

THE MUSEUM OF MODERN ART
NEW YORK

Published in conjunction with the exhibition *Home Delivery: Fabricating the Modern Dwelling*, at The Museum of Modern Art, New York, July 20–October 20, 2008, organized by Barry Bergdoll, The Philip Johnson Chief Curator of Architecture and Design, and Peter Christensen, Curatorial Assistant, Department of Architecture and Design.

The exhibition is the fifth in a series of five exhibitions made possible by The Lily Auchincloss Fund for Contemporary Architecture and is also generously supported by The Rockefeller Foundation and by Jerry I. Speyer and Katherine G. Farley.

Additional funding is provided by the Foundation for the Advancement of Architectural Thought.

Media sponsorship is provided by *Metropolitan Home* magazine.

Produced by the Department of Publications, The Museum of Modern Art, New York

Edited by Ron Broadhurst
Designed by Naomi Mizusaki, Supermarket
Production by Christina Grillo
Editorial Coordination by Hannah Kim
Printed and bound by Tien Wah Press (PTE) Ltd., Singapore
This book is typeset in Letter Gothic Text and Nobel.
The paper is 130 gsm Nymolla Multifine Woodfree.

Published by The Museum of Modern Art, New York,
11 West 53 Street, New York, New York, 10019-5497

Library of Congress Control Number: 2008925488
Bibliographic information published by the German National Library: The German National Library lists this publication in the Deutsche Nationalbibliografie; detailed bibliographic data is available on the Internet at http://dnb.ddb.de
MoMA/D.A.P. ISBN: 978-0-87070-733-9
Birkhäuser ISBN: 978-3-7643-8862-1

Distributed in the United States and Canada by
D.A.P./Distributed Art Publishers, Inc., New York

Distributed outside the United States and Canada by
Birkhäuser Verlag AG
Basel·Boston·Berlin
P.O. Box 133
CH-4010 Basel, Switzerland
Part of Springer Science & Business Media
www.birkhauser.ch

Front cover:
Pieces of a Lustron Westchester Two-Bedroom prior to installation, Columbus, Ohio, April 16, 1949

Back cover:
The micro compact home being delivered by crane (detail; see page 195)

Printed in Singapore

TABLE OF CONTENTS

FOREWORD

Home Delivery: Fabricating the Modern Dwelling brings for the first time in a half century full-scale structures back to The Museum of Modern Art's campus for an expansive evaluation of the past, present, and future of the prefabricated house. Not since a series of mid-century exhibitions including Marcel Breuer's House in the Museum Garden of 1949, the Exhibition House by Gregory Ain of 1950, and the Japanese Exhibition House of 1955, all integral to history of the plein-air exposition, has MoMA built an occupiable model building to demonstrate contemporary issues to the public. The unprecedented opportunity afforded to the museum by a vacant 18,000-square-foot property in midtown Manhattan—soon to be built upon by Jean Nouvel—was ripe for such a timely and ambitious undertaking.

Deployed on the vacant "west end," as well as in the International Council of The Museum of Modern Art Gallery on the museum's sixth floor, *Home Delivery* illustrates the many paradoxes of the prefabricated house: its commercial ubiquity on one hand and its failure as utopian ideal on the other; the fascination it has held for modernism's leading protagonists; and the role it has played in determining relations between invention and production in modernity. This exhibition takes stock of prefabrication at a distinct moment in the history of architectural practice when all seems poised to change, with architects now being increasingly equipped with the software, hardware, and the public appetite to eliminate the middleman from the equation. With mass customization ever promising to trump mass standardization, the exhibition's five full-scale contemporary works explore this potential by means of five distinct approaches that offer us a glimpse as to what may be next.

It is only fitting for an exhibition that seeks to display the process of architectural production as much as it does the actual product to engage the projects in *Home Delivery* through an active multimedia lens including film, architectural models, original drawings and blueprints, fragments, photographs, patents, toys, sales materials and propaganda, and, of course, the works themselves. This diverse collection of material, brought together from three continents, illustrates how the prefabricated house has been, and continues to be, not only a reflection on the house as a replicable object of design but also a critical agent in the discourses of sustainability, affordability, and design innovation.

Home Delivery: Fabricating the Modern Dwelling is the fifth and final in a series of contemporary exhibitions sponsored by the Lily Auchincloss Fund for Contemporary Architecture, following *Un-Private House*, *Tall Buildings*, *Groundswell: Constructing the Contemporary Landscape*, and *On-Site: New Architecture in Spain*. We are also deeply grateful to The Rockefeller Foundation, Jerry I. Speyer and Katherine G. Farley, the Foundation for the Advancement of Architectural Thought, and *Metropolitan Home* magazine for their support of the exhibition and publication. Barry Bergdoll, The Philip Johnson Chief Curator of Architecture and Design, organized *Home Delivery* with Peter Christensen, Curatorial Assistant. Their efforts have offered us the opportunity to consider this engrossing thread in the history of architecture through the prism of contemporary architecture.

Glenn D. Lowry,
Director, The Museum of Modern Art

INTRODUCTION
BARRY BERGDOLL

OPPOSITE, **FIG. 1** Buster Keaton in *One Week* (1920).
BELOW, FIG. 2 Marcel Breuer, House in the Museum
Garden, The Museum of Modern Art, New York. 1949.
Construction view.
BELOW, FIG. 3 Marcel Breuer, House in the Museum
Garden, The Museum of Modern Art, New York. 1949.

009

Home Delivery pays homage to the tradition of exhibition houses so integral to the history of innovation in modern architecture and famously associated with the garden of the Museum of Modern Art, where the museum last displayed, over a half century ago, model houses to offer full-scale experiences of a new wave of thinking about modern living environments.[1] At the same time it sets out, in anticipation of the sixtieth anniversary of the merger in 1949 of the Museum's Departments of Architecture and of Industrial Design, to redress a historical oversight—a prejudice even—of the Department of Architecture in its near systematic avoidance of the topic of prefabrication, or, more accurately, industrially produced, off-site building, one of the great preoccupations of most of the key protagonists of the modern movement between the world wars and a recurrent topic of innovation, exploration, and sometimes spectacular failure since the mid-twentieth century (fig. 1). The viability and affordability of factory-produced housing has long been proven as more and more modular units blend into the urban and suburban fabric.[2] What might the next generation look like?

Marcel Breuer's House in the Museum Garden (figs. 2, 3), commissioned in 1948 and exhibited to record crowds in the summer of 1949, stands as one of the most influential of all exhibitions mounted by the Museum in its more than seventy-five years of exhibiting architecture. Launching a series that ran for the next three seasons, the House in the Museum Garden, the joint idea of Philip Johnson and Peter Blake, embraced the technique of full-scale demonstration houses employed for so long in world's fairs and building exhibitions and even—most pertinently—in the marketing strategies of home builders. If photographs of Breuer's cedar-sided butterfly-roofed House in the Museum Garden have become iconic images in the history of architectural exhibitions, and not only at MoMA, few are aware that a major impetus for this ambitious undertaking was the popularity of a nearby prefabricated, all-metal demonstration house fabricated by the Lustron Company.

Certainly there had been earlier projects for full-scale buildings in the Museum Garden, so the idea of using the sculpture garden as an outdoor architecture gallery, in the tradition of such museums of vernacular life as Skansen in Stockholm, the Village Museum in Bucharest, or Colonial Williamsburg, was not without precedent. In 1940 John McAndrew, architect of the Museum's first sculpture garden and Curator of Architecture, had planned a full-scale Usonian House as an integral part of Frank Lloyd Wright's first retrospective in the

Museum's new building on Fifty-third Street, designed by Philip Goodwin and Edward Durell Stone.[3] This would probably have been the first time a model house would be built in the United States outside the context of a world's fair. The house too would have been MoMA's belated contribution to the series of full-scale houses on display at the popular New York World's Fair in Flushing Meadow Park of 1939–40. One year later, on the eve of America's entry into the war, Buckminster Fuller was invited to exhibit in the garden a full-scale Dymaxion

Deployment Unit, a mass-produced distillation of his 1927 Dymaxion House, which Philip Johnson and Henry-Russell Hitchcock had rejected for the seminal 1932 International Style exhibition (fig. 4). That same year Stone and John Fistere, an architectural critic, were invited by *Collier's Magazine* to design the "House of Ideas" at Rockefeller Center, a project that sought to introduce natural redwood and plywood as exterior and interior building materials respectively. But it was in the atmosphere of the explosion of new housing in the decade after World War II that the House in the Garden series was born. Its peers were not so much other museum houses (although the Walker Art Center's "Idea House" was certainly an example[4]) as the sales models provided by Levitt & Sons and Lustron.

As the creative force behind the first major exhibition mounted by the new Department of Architecture and Design, Breuer endeavored to develop a sophisticated yet viable alternative to the Cape Cod cottage model that, through Levittown and countless other developers, became the stereotypical image of the house in the suburbs after 1945. Breuer was optimistic that, with a favorable press and the powerful taste-making strategies of MoMA, he might affect a subtle revolution in taste. In selling the house to museum administration, Peter Blake laid out the philosophy behind its profile in relation to its "competitors": "There has been almost what amounts to a conspiracy among magazines and their advisors in not telling the public about building costs. It is proposed that this house shall compete in cost with any small, singly-built, architect-designed country house. Of course we cannot compete, in the museum, with mass-produced housing such as Levitt builds on Long Island, or the advertised costs of prefabricated houses."[5] The most innovative feature of the house was not the vertical cypress siding, the butterfly roof with internalized guttering system, or even the great sheets of glass, but rather the idea of a house that might grow with the family without losing any of its status as a work of architectural art.

It is against this background that the Museum introduces to its vacant lot a selection from the vast range of research underway in contemporary prefabrication. *Home Delivery* both occupies a gallery for traditional architectural display—plans, drawings, models, fragments, and photographs enhanced by film and computer animation—and takes advantage of a one-time chance to use the museum's soon-to-disappear "west end" vacant lot at the Sixth Avenue end of the MoMA campus to stage an outdoor exhibition of contemporary approaches to prefabrication in single and mutli-family dwellings. The show explores new relationships with design that also promise to make matters of sustainability, ecological fabrication, and customization through digital design and manufacturing tools into features of the daily environment. Despite their radically different stylistic expressions, both Larry Sass's Digitally Fabricated Housing for New Orleans—with its digitally mastered, yet optional, gingerbread ornament—and Douglas Gauthier and Jeremy Edmiston's formally ambitious BURST*008 house explore the latest in CNC plasma cutting of modern composite timber to update the tradition of the American pre-cut kit house. Both exploit computer calculations for ordering and cutting material to achieve minimum waste. Both can achieve enormous economies if realized at sufficient volume of production—a perennial goal of prefabrication. Oskar Leo Kaufmann and Albert Rüf refuse the divide between the two traditionally competing schools of thought in prefabrication—flat-pack panel systems and modular construction—revealing how the two systems, in everything from conception to shipping to assembly, can achieve greater flexibility, with room for individual customization, be it on the part of the designing architect or the client. Richard Horden and Haack + Höpfner's micro compact home—the result of decades of research—renews Le Corbusier's fascination with the ocean liner cabin or train compartment as a prototype for the efficient modern dwelling, combining this model with that of the complete living units featured in Emilio Ambasz's *Italy: The New Domestic Landscape* (1972).[6] Horden, however, achieves new efficiencies in energy so that the building can function completely off-grid. Finally, Kieran Timberlake Associates updates Archigram and the Metabolists' visions for a building of interchangeable parts with their Cellophane House, conceived according to the necessities of a culture of diminishing natural resources rather than the culture of mass consumption that fed the ironic utopias of the 1960s. Inside with the exhibition's digitally fabricated walls emerges the suggestion that a formal universe of great diversity, inventiveness, and richness awaits the next generation of prefabricated houses. Not only is prefab on everyone's lips in 2008, but it is poised to make great advances in coming years, both unleashing creative intelligence and tackling the daunting problems facing cities and settlements worldwide.

notes

1   Beatriz Colomina, "The Exhibitionary House," in *At the End of the Century: One Hundred Years of Architecture*, ed. Russell Ferguson (Los Angeles: Museum of Contemporary Art, 1998).

2   In 2008 New York architect Alexander Gorlin is completing nearly 1,500 units of affordable modular housing in East New York, Brooklyn.

3   Peter Reed and William Kaizen, eds., *The Show to End All Shows: Frank Lloyd Wright and the Museum of Modern Art, 1940*, Studies in Modern Art, vol. 8 (New York: Museum of Modern Art, 2004).

4   Alexandra Griffith Winton, "'A Man's House is His Art': the Walker Art Center's Idea House Project and the Marketing of Domestic Design, 1941–47," in *The Modern Period Room: The Construction of the Exhibited Interior 1870 to 1950*, eds. Penny Sparke, Brenda Martin, and Trevor Keeble (London and New York: Routledge, 2006), 87–111.

5   Museum archives.

6   Emilio Ambasz, ed., *Italy: The New Domestic Landscape, Achievements and Problems of Italian Design* (New York: Museum of Modern Art, 1972), 170–200.

FIG. 1 Page from *Toward an Architecture*, Le Corbusier (1923).

HOME DELIVERY: VISCIDITIES OF A MODERNIST DREAM FROM TAYLORIZED SERIAL PRODUCTION TO DIGITAL CUSTOMIZATION

BARRY BERGDOLL

A question in the new spirit: I am 40 years old, why not buy myself a house: for I need this tool; a house like the Ford I bought (or my Citroën, if I'm a dandy).

— Le Corbusier, *Toward an Architecture*, 1923

Human housing is a matter of mass demand. Just as it no longer occurs to 90 percent of the population to have shoes made to measure but rather buy ready-made products that satisfy most individual requirements thanks to refined manufacturing methods, in the future the individual will be able to order from the warehouse the housing that is right for him. It is possible that present-day technology would already be capable of this, but the present-day building industry is still almost completely dependent on traditional, craftsmanly construction methods.

— Walter Gropius, "Wohnhaus-Industrie," 1923

As Le Corbusier and Walter Gropius independently recognized in 1923 the history of off-site fabrication of buildings and the history of an architectural culture of prefabrication are distinct. The first is a long economic history of the building industry that can be traced back at least to antiquity, as we know from the discovery of a shipwreck in the Bay of Tunis laden with all the structural and sculptural elements for erecting a classical temple in Rome's North African colonies, a procedure evoked in Pliny's Letters.[1] The latter is a core theme of modernist architectural discourse and experiment, born from the union of architecture and industry, and marked as much by the creation of an image of modern living as by the exploration of new materials and techniques. The discourse is as much about reforming or changing perceptions, attitudes, and taste as it is about altering fundamentally the relationship of the architect to production and to the client. The modernist obsession with the automobile, from its first appearance off Henry Ford's assembly line in 1907, was immediate; but the analogy of the car and

the house as products of a similar rationalizing design process of standardized parts and types is one that gained currency in the 1920s, spearheaded by Le Corbusier's famous alignment of proposals for solving the housing crisis with mass production of cars (fig. 1) and with techniques of Taylorized assembly in the plates of *Toward an Architecture* (1923), and taken up soon in the Bauhaus, in Ernst May's great housing projects for Frankfurt in the 1920s, and ultimately even by the Tennessee Valley Authority, which produced over ten thousand housing units in the early 1940s.[2]

Over and over again modern architects posed the question: If factory production has made such a revolution both in the production of once hand-crafted objects such as clothes, shoes, and household products, as well as in modern mobility—automobiles, planes, and ocean liners—then why is the culture of building so resistant to transformation? Eighty-five years later, as prefabrication again is commanding the attention and the talents of designers, theorists, and critics from the

FIG. 2 Cover of *Dwell* magazine (April/May 2005).
FIG. 3 reiser + umemoto, "Vector Wall" project for *Home Delivery*, 2008.

013

shelter press, spearheaded by *Dwell* magazine (fig. 2) and employed in the effervescent parametric digital architectural design of younger architectural firms (fig. 3) and in leading architectural schools, there is an equivalent huge cultural divide between those who are creatively engaging with exploring new relations between architecture and production and the steady, almost reflexive, success of manufactured housing, which by most accounts captures nearly a third of all U.S. single-family housing starts but is invisible to, and all but impervious to, design culture.[3] In Japan, the modernist dream of house factories has long ago triumphed, but whether it be at Sekisui House, the country's leader, or in the factories of Toyota Home, the aim is to produce reassuring façades and layouts inexpensively. These manufacturers take great pride in the fact that once the houses leave the ultra-rationalized assembly lines of the factories, where assemblies and sub-assemblies rival the most modern car production, few consumers or passersby in a Tokyo suburb can distinguish a factory-made product from a traditional "stick-built" suburban house, western or Japanese in style. As the promised revolution of mass customization becomes a reality—made possible by new systems of CNC cutting, which are changing the relationship between the designing hand and material production—it is worth recalling that customization is by no means a new discourse, even if the computer has changed the parameters. Nor has rapid manufacturing eliminated all the challenges and paradoxes that have confronted the history of allying architecture more closely with product design than with the traditional stone yard and building site, from anxieties about branding the all-sacred "home" to the challenges of different site conditions and landscapes.

PREFABRICATION BEFORE MODERNISM

Centuries before a theory of prefabrication was developed, parts of buildings were produced in off-site workshops and later in factories. This occurred in the nineteenth century as a largely pragmatic approach to deploying soldiers in distant field operations and rapidly equipping colonies with the rudiments of western comfort—cast-iron churches for the whole Christianizing world, wooden houses for Australia and New Zealand, sheet metal houses for the French Caribbean, German, and Belgian houses for the last colonial gains in Africa—or of meeting the housing demands of the fortune seekers in the California gold rush. It was also during this period that the Red Cross was one of the earliest clients of the German house manufacturer Christoph & Unmack, for whom Walter Gropius and Konrad Wachsmann later invented construc-

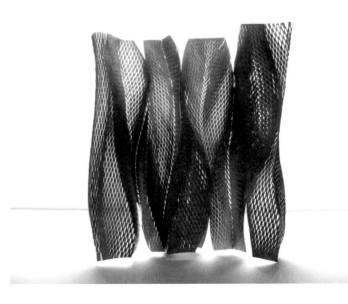

FIG. 4 Eugène-Emmanuel Viollet-le-Duc, plan for a vaulted hall. 1864.

component parts of a building could be fabricated in a builder's yard or workshop prior to their assembly on the actual building site. In other words, men sought to devise construction processes that would shift the major components of labor . . . to the controlled, and increasingly mechanized conditions of the factory. This transfer from ad hoc building to planned multiple production is one of the fascinating break points in the curve of architectural evolution."[4] By 1833 H. Manning of London was marketing cottages for export with claims that assembly could be completed in a day, while in 1840 John Hall of Baltimore published a system that could be moved by a single horse. In *Space, Time and Architecture* (1941) Sigfried Giedion constructed a veritable modernist mythology around the American balloon frame—"its invention practically converted building in wood from a complicated craft, practiced by skilled labor into an industry"[5]—noting that the balloon frame was in use "for some sixty to eighty per cent of all the houses in the United States" by the end of the nineteenth century.[6]

This was a situation that already alarmed leading theorists of the Gothic Revival in the nineteenth century, whose preoccupations had as much to do with thinking about new labor and ethical issues in the relationship between the drawing board and the building yard as they did with the search for a mastery of medieval form for the moral amelioration of society. In his seminal and influential *Lectures on Architecture* (1858–72), French Gothic Revival theorist Eugène-Emmanuel Viollet-le-Duc illustrated projects for integrating prefabricated cast iron elements into otherwise stone and brick buildings (fig. 4) and ruminated on the problems of a growing divergence of the cultures of an industrializing construction industry and a tradition-bound world of design:

> The fact is that there is an utter discordance between the practice of architecture and modern machinery; the novel means afforded to architects are a source of embarrassment to them, not the occasion of inventions and adaptations deduced from new principles. Not well knowing how to make use of means whose notoriety they do not venture to disregard, they only adopt them by way of super addition . . . Our modern architects are like parvenus who have come all at once into possession of a large fortune and do not know how to adjust their expenditure with that discretion which belongs only to accustomed opulence. We must not disguise from ourselves the fact that, in respect to the adoption of novel materials and machines, everything remains to be done in the domain of architecture; nothing has been seriously attempted.[7]

tion systems. Even before the Industrial Revolution, building elements, such as bricks and precut lumber, were often accumulated away from the building site, independent of any specific architectural design. The use of precut wooden elements for the construction of temples was common in Japan by the twelfth century and for houses in Russia and Scandinavia by at least the eighteenth. As prefabrication historian Gilbert Herbert argues, it was "during the nineteenth century, for the first time in the long history of 'man the builder' [that] serious and sustained attempts were made to devise systems whereby most of the

FIG. 5 N. G. Rood, patent for a portable summer cottage. 1882.

015

These words anticipate the central preoccupation of avant-garde architects in the 1920s, that is, the relationship of form-making to the possibilities of industrialized production, particularly with regard to American Taylorism, Fordism, and other theories of scientific management.[8]

FROM MATERIALS TO SYSTEMS

By the turn of the twentieth century, architects and inventors had developed prefabricated houses of nearly every material—timber, concrete, sheet metal, and cast iron—all meant to be produced in great number, many subject to patent (fig. 5), some even published in the period's architectural press, with new techniques of steel engraving making it possible to replicate models. Commercialized wooden systems, including Swedish models offered locally as well as on the

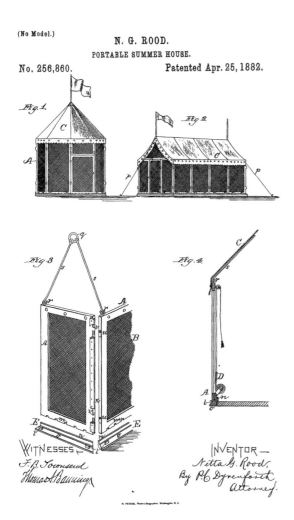

British and German markets by 1900, and systems of wooden panels, such as Karl Hengerer's "Tektonhaus" system in Stuttgart,[9] remind us that there was already a prefabrication boom before the advent of modernism. As early as 1860 French inventors began exploring systems of concrete panels that could be shipped to tropical climates—one recorded example was shipped to the Caribbean island of St. Thomas. In the English exhibition at the Paris *Exposition universelle* of 1878 architect Richard Norman Shaw together with builder/developer W. H. Lascelles took a gold medal for a Queen Anne–style house made of red tinted concrete panels set in a half timber frame, even though *The Builder* was quick to criticize them for failure to achieve an innovative style based on new materials and techniques. Further, the race for patents was to raise new questions about what invention meant in architectural terms: Was invention an expression of the genius of the architect in aesthetic terms as it had been handed down by the laurels of academies and salons, or was it to be submitted to the legal criteria for a new invention vested in patent law? In the latter case, construction and the means of production would be determinant and the architect would be as much an inventor as an artist, the search for form increasingly harnessed to the logic of production in its evolution from mechanical labor to machine production (and, in the last twenty years, to computer-driven machinery).

It is interesting in this regard to compare three patents for replicable systems of concrete houses developed in the decade between 1905 and 1915 on either side of the Atlantic. In 1906 Thomas Alva Edison, sometimes credited as the world's record holder for the number of patents granted (over a thousand), developed his remarkable "Single Pour Concrete System," a vision of concrete construction reliant more on the casting principles of iron facades than on the panel system, which took its analogies from timber construction. Like French inventor and builder François Hennebique's contemporary concrete apartment house on the rue Danton in Paris, Edison's house was indistinguishable in its style and overall form from dwellings in the contemporary taste, the constructive revolution visible only to an eye trained to the fact that the masonry house was completely free of masonry joints. Otherwise the houses, even replicated in multiples in Union, New Jersey, could easily be mistaken for the period's developer bungalows, that is, until the winter arrived. Edison's patent consisted primarily of a system that exploited fast curing concrete to pour the house, including staircases, decorative details, bookshelves, and in some cases, pianos, from a single mold (a remarkable foreshadowing of Rachel Whiteread's

plaster cast of a Victorian interior). The emerging modernist notion of the free or flexible plan was nowhere to be found in this method, which more or less cast in concrete the period's broad taste in houses. Almost contemporary with Edison's efforts, the architect Grosvenor Atterbury developed a revolutionary system of concrete panels—destined to have a long and checkered history for the rest of the century—given convincing demonstration in his work for the garden suburb of Forest Hills Gardens, developed under the auspices of the Russell Sage Foundation between 1909 and 1912 in Queens, New York (figs. 6, 7). Atterbury designed not individual houses but rather a system of some 170 standardized precast concrete panels. Assembly of these heavy elements was by crane, but the most significant innovation lay in the fact that the panels were cast with integral hollow insulation chambers, one of the first examples of an attempt to incorporate complex systems required by modern buildings into the construction process. The system was much admired by Ernst May in the late 1920s, when he put in place the ambitious industrialized house building system in Frankfurt, which included a specially outfitted hall for preparing the panels for shipment to the great ring of new garden settlements to be constructed around the city. It also inaugurated the idea that to devise a prefabricated building system was in essence to redesign architecture itself, rather than to fulfill an individual commission. Not surprisingly Frank Lloyd Wright began to experiment with prefabrication in these same years, both in the hundreds of drawings for his "American System-Built Houses" and in his writings, which looked as much to nature as to industry for inspiration in developing a rationalized system in harmony with his notion of the democracy of individuality.

The third patent using concrete in these years, usually considered to be a watershed break with all past tradition, was Le Corbusier's design in 1914 of the so-called Maison Dom-ino, intended to rebuild the north of France and Belgium after the first waves of the destruction of World War I. In many ways Le Corbusier's was the least resolved of these three independently conceived and radically different prefabricated concrete systems. But while it was a serious patent, the continuing escalation and stagnation of the war prevented even a single such frame from being fabricated. Nonetheless the Maison Dom-ino became the foundation block of a whole theory of architecture, first for Le Corbusier's own development of architectural *Purisme*, a technique of collage of rationalized concrete frames and freely invented forms, and then for a whole school of modernist space-making. By 1920 the small company Le Corbusier had set up, the SEIE, or *Société d'entreprises industrielles et d'études*, which even included a small concrete factory, had gone bankrupt. His attempt to follow an Edisonian model of mounting a laboratory for industrial experimentation, focused on the issues of prefabricated dwellings, would be displaced into developing the Dom-ino as the veritable primitive hut of a new system of architecture, one that provided a rule derived from industry, technique and the rhythms of production, but which would also be the framework for invention. It was, in essence, a replacement in modern industrial terms for the systems of proportion and abstract number that had governed architecture and architectural training since the Renaissance in favor of new building blocks of an architecture born of industrial logic, but one quickly tempered by the development of Le Corbusier's theory of proportional control through regulating lines.

Whereas patents had, up to that point, be they in the oldest of industrialized materials, timber, or the newest, industrialized concrete, sought largely to use industrial methods to achieve convincing replications of the forms, plans and standards of existing houses that they might compete for buyers, Le Corbusier's Maison Dom-ino was to launch a radical new way of thinking about architectural space. "If we wrest from our hearts and minds static conceptions of the house and consider the question from a critical and objective point of view, we will come to the house tool, the mass-production house that is healthy (morally, too) and beautiful from the aesthetic of the work tools that accompany our existence."[10] The first challenge, Le Corbusier proclaimed in response to the French Loucheur law calling for 500,000 low-cost housing units, was, as he put it famously in *Toward an Architecture*, to open "eyes that do not see" to the necessity and the beauty of factory-produced houses delivered to, rather than painstakingly constructed upon, their sites. Also revolutionary was the pursuit of a patent to assure his authorship of a concept that was not strictly architectural, though it was a building block for his own later elaboration of the "five points of a new architecture." The five points, set down in 1927 as a response to German attempts at dry-mounted prefabrication at the Weissenhofsiedlung housing exhibition, were nothing short of a paean to the liberty, i.e., customization, such standardized factory-made units would allow. The following year Le Corbusier joined with the *Redressment Français* movement, launched in 1927 by Ernest Mercier, publishing a pamphlet *Pour bâtir: standardiser et tayloriser*, articulating a tension between freedom and order, which he thought could be mediated by architecture as an art and as a system of industrialized building (fig. 8).[11]

GROPIUS FROM AEG TO BAUHAUS

Walter Gropius was no less determined than Le Corbusier to temper the means of production with the search for architectural form and underlying order, a quest that both he and Le Corbusier had embarked upon in the studio of Peter Behrens. It was to Behrens's patron, Emil Rathenau, head of the German AEG (General Electrical Company) and fellow Werkbund member, that Gropius proposed in 1909, only two years after Ford launched his first assembly line, to create a company for a "General House Building Corporation on Artistically Unified Principles,"[12] an attempt to synthesize two of Behrens's primary concerns in those years: the search for an underlying geometry for all formal research and the quest for an alliance between art and industry. While the title sug-

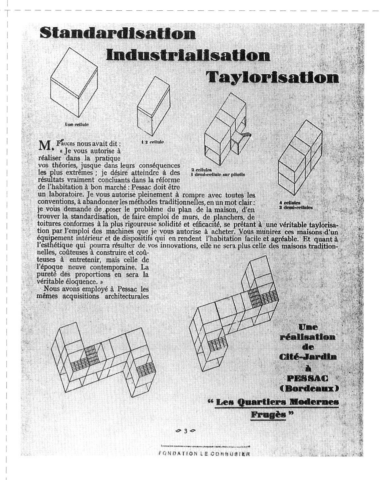

gests that Gropius's priority was to preserve the role of the architect as artist, he was equally concerned—taking up one of the central issues being debated in the Werkbund—with the consumer of the house, since prefabrication implied that the house would no longer be the product of a relationship between an architect and a client but between an architect and multiple consumers. "The idea of industrializing house construction can be realized by repetition of the same component parts in every building project. By this means the mass production can be made both profitable for the manufacturer and inexpensive for the customer," he explained, and went on to suggest that the factory-produced house would leave open not only a terrain for artistic invention but also for personal desire: "The possibility of the assembly of these interchangeable parts satisfies the public desire for a home with an individual appearance."[13] The hope for at least limited customization within a set of established types accompanied the dream of prefabrication from the very outset. And this report would continue for the next

FIG. 9 Row House Type 4, published in the Bauhaus Book Series.

FIG. 10 Walter Gropius, Toerten Siedlung, Dessau. 1926–27.

sixty years to guide Gropius's quest to create a system of construction where efficiencies were achieved without sacrificing the conversation between architect, client, and builder out of which building took form (fig. 9). It was the driving force behind the Baukasten that Gropius, with the collaboration of the Hungarian architect Fred Forbat, developed at the Weimar Bauhaus in 1923 and publicized the following year in the third of the Bauhaus Book Series, *An Experimental House at the Weimar Bauhaus.*[14] Gropius worked with the classical concept of the "Type," more a *gestalt* than a production ideal, and sought through mastering the means of production to achieve a flexible system still open to individual desires and free will, utterly convinced that "from the artistic point of view as well the new building procedures must be affirmed. The assumption that an industrialization of house building would result in building forms becoming ugly is totally erroneous. On the contrary, the unification of building elements would foster the healthy consequence that new houses and city districts would be imbued with a unified character. Monotony, as in British suburban houses, is not to be feared, provided that the basic requirement is met to typify only building components while leaving the larger building volumes subject to variety."[15] Monotony was not wholly avoided however in the first realization of the system, some years later, after the Bauhaus had moved to Dessau and begun to model its thinking more and more on the production methods

already in place at the nearby Junkers aircraft factory.[16] While choices would need to be made in anticipation of, or at least in response to, the period's burgeoning sociological study of the dwelling and of the consumer, when it came to building working-class housing—such as Gropius's famous Toerten Siedlung at Dessau of 1926–27 where the layout was determined by the layout of rail tracks for delivering panels (actually produced on-site here) and the turning radius of construction cranes for hoisting them into place (figs. 10, 11, 12)—Gropius elaborated an open-ended system in which architect and middle-class client could create together a building that would express their respective individuality within the constraints of the dimensions of the parts and the syntax of construction. Such was the hypothesis of the system of steel frame construction with dry assembly panels that Gropius exhibited in 1927 at Stuttgart's Weissenhof. By the late 1930s he was working with Hirsch Kupfer- und Messingwerke AG, a copper manufacturer, to develop prototypes for a factory-made house of copper panels over aluminum foil insulation, a project he continued to refine until 1932, when it was shown at the second German Building Exposition, in Berlin. The scheme then became part of an early, and some would say, cynical contribution to the role prefabrication research would play in Israel's building history, with its ongoing housing shortages and shifting patterns of settlement.[17]

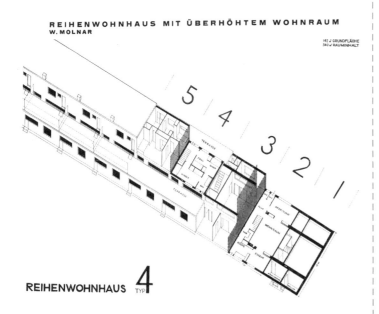

FIG. 11 Walter Gropius, Toerten Siedlung, Dessau. 1926–27.
Site plan with rail-track delivery system.
FIG. 12 Walter Gropius, Toerten Siedlung, Dessau. 1926–27.
Isometric view.

FIG. 13 Marcel Breuer, Bambos Houses I, II, and III. 1927.
Rendering.

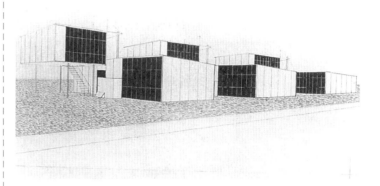

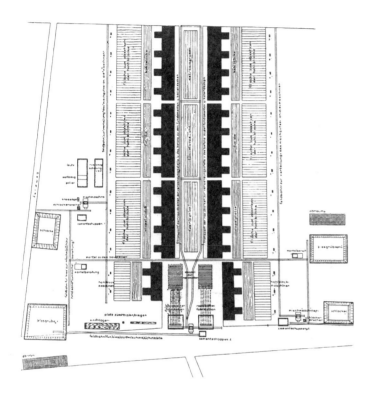

As the Copper Houses were exported to Palestine, the main lines of research in prefabrication emigrated even farther afield with the rise of Hitler. Hannes Meyer, who had turned the Bauhaus decidedly toward a rationalized productivist model—"building is a technical not an aesthetic process . . . Pure construction is the mark of the new world of forms"[18]—and Ernst May both moved to the Soviet Union, where studies of factory production of housing were under way. Gropius and his protégé Marcel Breuer headed west, via England, to the United States. Already in 1928, when Breuer—having developed several prefabricated prototypes in Dessau, including the never realized Bambos Houses (fig. 13)—left the Bauhaus to set up his independent practice, the *Frankfurter Zeitung* reported that "in order for his work to get ahead he must be able to experiment on a large scale. He hopes to find a better chance for close connections with industry when he is working as a freelancer."[19] Gropius, who explained upon resigning the directorship of the Bauhaus that he would concern himself "almost exclusively with research on industrial building methods . . . in particular steel homes,"[20] set off in quest of the secrets of the New World's advances in the industrialization of construction. Despite the fact that America had pioneered off-site fabrication techniques—first in the balloon frame and then from the 1890s with precut timber kit houses sold by specialized companies like Aladdin and by such department stores as Sears (see p. 48) and Montgomery Ward, and was even parodied in Buster Keaton's *One Week* of 1920 (see p. 8, fig. 1)—it ultimately disappointed the head of the Bauhaus. Not only were steel homes nowhere to be found, but as he admitted in a letter to a friend, "I thought that in the United States housing industry I would find a man comparable in stature to that of Henry Ford in the automotive industry."[21] It was not until 1932 that General Houses Corporation began to market a pressed steel house, priced between $3,000 and $4,500.

If anyone might have laid claim to being the Henry Ford of housing it was the self-styled inventor R. Buckminster Fuller, who began to develop his ideas of a "Dymaxion House" and a mass-produced autonomous "Dymaxion" bathroom unit as early as 1927. Fuller understood the necessity for industry to encourage research into the production of lightweight building materials and systems in order to address the demands of transport and assembly. His genius was to explore the integral systems of a building with reference to other design issues. Throughout his career Fuller was interested in the role of geometry in the creation of tensile strength in structures, but no less in thinking of the heating, ventilation, and luminosity issues that could be solved through architectural design rather than by mechanical additions to the body of architecture. His architecture, more than Le Corbusier's, was truly architecture as a living machine, and his geometry was conditioned by structure and statics rather than vision and culture. Working with grain silos, Fuller explored issues of heating and convection to design shapes that would tend toward natural heating and cooling. He was also the first to imagine the use of aluminum—still a relatively expensive material—as a means to achieve a transportable prefabricated house. Most radical was suspending the entire house from a single mast, an idea developed subsequently by the Bowman Brothers, by George Fred Keck, by Richard Neutra, and by Bodo Rasch in Germany. But as Burnham Kelly pointed out nearly a quarter century later, Fuller's ideas were so radical in the 1920s, when there was no housing shortage to speak of in the U.S., that it was not until the housing crisis of the post–World War II years that his system garnered a certain respect and not simply attention: "At the time his house was introduced, Fuller writes, he extrapolated curves of industrial progress, of housing demand and supply, of invention gestation, of the range and frequency of per capita travel, and concluded that the house, with all the improvements in technology that could take place in the meantime, could not be industrially produced for some 21 to 22 years, until 1948–49."[22]

FROM MILITARY DEPLOYMENT TO POSTWAR BOOM

With the demise of Weimar Germany, where Martin Wagner and Ernst May had been poised to make prefabricated housing into large-scale policy in Berlin and in Frankfurt, FDR's America seemed to many the closest thing in the Western world to a progressive social experiment on the national level, all the more so during the years before the United States entered World War II. Far from arriving in the land of free enterprise and laissez faire, the Bauhaus émigrés arrived in a country unusually open to sug-

gestions of new relationships between architect, industry, and consumer, spearheaded by the creation in 1937 of the Federal Housing Administration and by extensive research into industrialized building methods, sponsored by the Pierce and Bemis foundations. Historians of American federal housing policy have long argued that the innovative housing programs of the New Deal fell victim to increasing public and Congressional hostility as mobilization for war began. But around 1941 and 1942, the Defense Housing program experimented with European-style housing developments with the express aim of providing models for private development, a rare example of federal policy attempting to lead rather than follow the market, and along with it came a whole series of investigations into peacetime uses of prefabrication. Though the Public Buildings Administration would earn the nickname Public Barracks Administration by the end of the war, under the leadership of New Dealer John M. Carmody the opening years of the program saw commissions going to a number of the recent émigrés from Germany and Austria, including Neutra, Gropius, Breuer, and Oscar Stonorov, who worked briefly with Louis Kahn.

"The eyes of the world are upon us," Carmody told Gropius and Breuer in 1941, encouraging them to do a "first class job" on defense housing at New Kensington, Pennsylvania.[23] The schedule would only permit twelve days to produce preliminary drawings, perspectives, and a model, to be followed by another eighteen days for working drawings and specifications. With so little time to develop the project, by then nicknamed Aluminum City Terrace, it was out of the question to exploit the opportunity as a full-scale experiment in the prefabrication methods that Gropius had explored in Germany. But Gropius and Breuer were nonetheless eager to develop a prototype, since it was the distinct policy of the federal government that the defense projects were to serve as models for private development. Their design used a maximum number of standardized parts, pushing the Federal Works Agency toward a logic of prefabrication even though the agency had not called for factory-produced housing. The 250 units were divided into six types: one- and two-story simplex, duplex, and triplex units. The site planning marked a sharp break from the long lines of housing determined by the logic of German railroad tracks. Exploiting Corbusian pilotis, they were able to place standard units on a difficult site of sinewy hills and ravines, allowing maximum flexibility at minimum cost (fig. 14). Breuer referred to the planning approach as "an ungeometric setting of free rhythm," and it was quickly taken up by others, notably by Saarinen in defense housing at Center Line, Michigan. It is indeed an approach to planning with prefabricated logic that has come into

FIG. 14 Walter Gropius and Marcel Breuer, Aluminum City
Terrace, New Kensington, Pennsylvania. 1941. Site model.
FIG. 15 Levittown, New York. Aerial view, 1957.

021

its own again in recent years with computer software that allows for staging and construction sequence studies that give as much freedom in site planning as in architectural composition.

Optimistic, like many, that the war would soon come to an end and that a whole new horizon would open for alliances between architecture and industry in a postwar building boom, Breuer threw himself again into questions of prefabrication, devising two prototypes in his own studio for which he tried repeatedly to find an industrial partner. He developed a framework for a new industrialized housing prototype with his Plas-2-Point house, which he called a "radically new" approach both to living and occupying the land, and which was one of the first projects to consider the outer skin of the building as a system of tensile strength in itself, a forerunner of the experiments in single-shell (monocoque) construction that would emerge by the late 1950s with advances in the plastics industry. Monsanto—who would sponsor their famous "House of the Future" at Disneyland in 1957—claimed in an advertisement that Breuer had been inspired by the skeletal frame of bombers in the production of this lightweight timber house that might be delivered to almost any site. Thanks to Monsanto's advertising, Breuer received inquiries from numerous developers and contractors readying themselves in 1944 for postwar prefabrication, but for the most part these were premonitory of the conservative taste that would reign in postwar housing beginning with Levittown (fig. 15), where a veritable military organization was employed to build in situ houses of nearly identical appearance from precut elements. "We are wondering if this design would lend itself to exterior treatment that would not be too different from the accepted, conventional small house," was a not atypical query that summed up the reception of unconventional designs in prefabrication during the immediate postwar period.[24]

Working with Konrad Wachsmann, who had already built a prefabricated log house for Albert Einstein at Caputh, near Potsdam, in the early 1930s,[25] Gropius made great headway between 1943 and 1948 creating the Packaged House system for the General Panel Corporation, the most innovative feature of which was that the same panels could be used for floors and ceilings as well as for walls. For Wachsmann as well as for Gropius this was a great step forward because it limited the number of parts that needed to be fabricated and delivered while increasing the possibilities for design flexibility, so that, ironically, the smaller the deck the greater the freedom in deploying it. As in so many dry-mounted systems, the research focused on the joint, in this case a three-way joint, the element to which Wachsmann devoted the most

research and for which he filed several patents. Despite the complete failure of the system to make money, Gropius still believed in the promise of mass-produced housing: in response to a reporter for the *New York Times* who asked in 1947 if it was not a good thing that at least in the realm of the house one could create a refuge from standardization and industrialization, Gropius noted that between 1913 and 1937 the average cost of a house in America had increased 193 percent, while the average cost of the car had fallen by 60 percent, concluding, "The coming generation will certainly blame us if we should fail to overcome those understandable though sentimental reactions against prefabrication."[26]

It seemed that the United States was poised to enter into peacetime factory production of housing on the scale of the booming car industry. The wartime economy resulted in the production of more than 200,000 prefabricated houses by more than seventy companies, some of them producing at a rate of 1,000 units per month, resulting in nearly 12 percent of the housing market in those years.[27] The porcelain-enameled steel Lustron house is but the most famous of these, with nearly 2,500 units produced in six models and as many colors between 1948 and 1950. While it was a spatially rigid system with little room for architectural innovation or variation, the Lustron—adapted from the White Castle prefabricated roadside restaurants and Standard Oil gasoline stations in the 1930s—had a remarkable but short-lived success. Nearly 20,000 orders had been received by the time the company was forced into bankruptcy in 1950; most of them would go unfulfilled.[28]

It is interesting to juxtapose the complex Lustron system, with its myriad parts, against the remarkably simple and flexible system developed by the French *architecte-constructeur* Jean Prouvé in the same years. From the 1930s, when he had developed a small weekend demountable house with Eugène Beaudouin and Marcel Lods out of folded sheet metal, Prouvé had been experimenting with factory-produced temporary shelter. After the war his attention turned to developing a more complex structural system in which the distinction between frame and infill was progressively eroded.[29] From the simple principle of his *portique*, a piano-tuner shaped upright whose name is reminiscent of the building block of the classical temple, Prouvé introduced a sheet metal design in which the ridge pole of the house provided the basic spatial envelope to which a series of panels provided at once enclosure and rigidity. Conjugated in "Tropicale," "Coloniale," and "Metropole" variants, it was a system that could be adapted to vastly different climates, sites, and scales through modular expansion or pavilion-like additions. A model cluster was built at Meudon, near Versailles, sponsored by the innovative French Minister of Reconstruction Eugène Claudius-Petit, who in the same years stood behind Le Corbusier's development of a heavy prefabricated prototype in the Unité d'Habitation in Marseilles.[30] But even in France Prouvé's success was limited. Few houses were built outside the experimental site of Meudon, and only three of Prouvé's tropical houses were ever mounted in the clever system of airplane delivery

that he hoped would raise the standard of living in decolonizing Africa. By 1964 William J. Levitt would even export his housing system to France, where its popularity would quickly outpace Prouvé's bold prototype.

By the early 1960s in the U.S. Paul Rudolph, who embraced the boom industry of the mobile home even as he deplored the planless installation of them on the edge of towns across America, provocatively declared that the mobile home would be "the brick of the 20th century," an ideal he took to the urban scale in megastructure projects of the 1960s but which he realized only once in his now demolished Oriental Masonic Gardens, a social housing project in New Haven of 1970. The mobile home, later rebaptized "manufactured housing" for legislative reasons, was produced in escalating numbers, but architects for the most part steered well clear. From the early 1950s, nurtured by the prefab-oriented Case Study Houses program created by John Entenza to sponsor research into industrialized building for individual houses, Charles and Ray Eames gave powerful impetus to the use of prefabricated elements in their own Pacific Palisades house (Case Study House No. 8) of 1949, where they organized parts taken from catalogues into a rationalized collage. While the 1950s and 1960s saw a proliferation of new prefabricated systems for inexpensive houses during the postwar explosion of suburban development—including Carl Koch's Techbuilt Houses of 1953 (fig. 16) and William Berke's Deck House system of 1959—the real legacy of the Eameses' sensibility was to emerge during the following decade in the British High-Tech movement, notably in Richard and Su Rogers's seminal Zip-Up house system of 1968 and in the experimental designs of the Japanese Metabolists.

FIG. 17 Kisho Kurokawa, Takara Pavilion, Osaka World's Fair.
1970. Detail of prefabricated joint.
FIG. 18 Kisho Kurokawa, Takara Pavilion, Osaka World's Fair.
1970. Construction process.

023

Approaches to prefabrication in housing followed the dividing lines of the cold war. Prefabricated systems became almost universal by the mid-1960s in the countries of the Eastern Bloc, developed largely from such German prototypes as the Splanemannsiedlung of 1927 in Berlin-Lichtenberg and the experiments with mass production techniques studied by Martin Wagner in the waning years of the Weimar Republic. From the mid-1950s the Soviet Academy of Architecture insisted that architecture be practiced as a technical rather than aesthetic pursuit, declaring prefabricated reinforced concrete to be in the true spirit of the times and ordering, "Architects into the Factories," as the reigning propaganda slogan had it. Under Khrushchev this was elevated into an industrially organized program of mass housing conceived on a continent-wide scale. The testing grounds for ideas came in 1956–57 with the design and construction of the Ninth District of Moscow, Noyve Cheremushki, under the direction of Nathan Osterman. This in turn was reexported to much of Europe (and in the 1960s even to Cuba), and in particular to the German Democratic Republic. The production of dwellings "better, faster, and cheaper" became official party doctrine and many architects emigrated to the West, since in essence a catalogue of types—some ninety—for almost all buildings to be erected by the State had been established within a few years. By the time the Berlin Wall came down in 1989, the entrenched panel construction system, or *plattenbau*, had become synonymous with the monotony of daily life and of the suppression of individual aspiration throughout the former Soviet Bloc and in the former Soviet Republics. Yet there were numerous exceptions, only some of which have recently gained scholarly consideration and renewed appreciation. In Cuba, in particular, such exemplary projects as Las Terrazas, where the concrete panel system was developed for low-tech hand assembly to achieve an unusual flexibility in both programmatic arrangement and compositional subtlety, or in Yugoslavia, where the Jugomont system, a fascinating hybrid with distinctions between parallel structural walls of large-scale concrete elements and lighter metal façade systems capable of partial on-site construction that could be customized and varied in material, was developed, resulted in architectural innovation and subtlety rarely associated with the Soviet panel system.[31]

Meanwhile in the West, with the exception of a few spectacular examples such as Moshe Safdie's prototype for a new urban village in the heavy modular concrete system of Habitat '67 in Montreal, or the astounding work of Zvi Hecker, notably his Ramot housing project in Israel (where prefabrication was to see a flurry of experimentation),

heavy prefabrication either became routine, as in much French new town development, or largely lost inventive steam. Innovation in the 1960s came in two independent lines of research: the quest for a frame system that could accommodate a variety of technologies, materials and even, at the urban scale, programs; and the line of research pioneered in Japan by the Metabolists and given its principle demonstrations in Kisho Kurokawa's Nakagin Capsule Tower, now threatened with demolition in Tokyo, as well as his Takara Pavilion at the 1970 Osaka World's Fair (figs. 17, 18). The British Archigram group, well represented in this exhibition, took up the Metabolist idea with zest and

humor, offering at once utopian solutions for plug-in cities and wry commentaries on the rapidly emerging society of consumption. Less well-known is the remarkable Metastadt-Bausystem (Metacity building system) developed between 1969 and 1970 by the Munich architect Richard J. Dietrich and deployed in vastly reduced form and conceptual simplification at Wulfen near Dortmund in 1975.[32] Within a complex steel frame that could accommodate modules and programs at varying scales, Dietrich projected a form of urban density in an open expandable system that could span highway junctions and leave the ground free while creating a dense megastructure above grade, a system not without parallels to those imagined in the late 1960s and 1970s in the U.S. by Paul Rudolph in a very different stylistic idiom.

The other line of research was the continued exploration of monocoque assemblies, taking inspiration from the airline industry. New materials were deployed to create an architecture with an external skin, be it of aluminum, plastic, or fiberglass, that is also a structural system capable of carrying substantial loads. Prouvé had explored this as early as the 1930s and developed it in a hybrid system at Meudon, but the glory days of monocoque research came with the explosion of new materials in the 1960s and the expansion of the aerospace industry, which offered an image of lightness to counter the heavy precast concrete prefabrication that had hitherto characterized the period. Ionel Schein, notably in his All Plastic House in France, was a pioneer, but numerous examples were developed, perhaps none capturing the public imagination as vividly as the Futuro House by Finnish architect Matti Suuronen, developed essentially as a vacation home for remote locations to which it could be delivered by truck or helicopter. Along with it came, as in many megastructures, the idea of the home as another ephemeral and disposable object, with a shelf life, destined either to be moved to a new location or replaced and updated. One of the most robust and innovative lines of research into monocoque construction, continued over the course of nearly three decades, is that of Richard Horden, whose seminal Yacht House of 1983 takes both its lightweight imagery and its program for an efficient renewal of the modernist ideal of living in a minimum rationalized space from the most advanced boat design.

PREFAB AFTER POSTMODERNISM

Although heavy slab construction lent itself to postmodern ornamental imprints in everything from Ricardo Bofill's great French housing projects at Marne-la-Vallée, outside Paris, and at Montpellier in the late 1980s, as well as in the contextualizing return to historic fabric in the late *plattenbau* work in East Germany, such as the Nikolaiviertel in Berlin, new research into prefabricated housing was essentially thrown out with the modernist bathwater in the 1980s.

A renewed explosion of interest in prefabrication over the last two decades has developed in multiple forms and constituencies, with the most diverse research resulting in pragmatic solutions based on manufacturing and shipping strategies as well as opening whole new territories of digital innovation that reconstitute the very relation between designing and making. Rare are architectural moments with overlapping populist and academic wings, but since 2000 *Dwell*, under successive editors Karrie Jacobs and Alison Arieff, emerged as one of many magazines that have capitalized on and channeled the wide-scale renaissance of a taste for the modern. With an admittedly retro orientation toward "mid-century" modern, the magazine rapidly became the rallying point for a generation of younger house designers inspired to revive the ideals of prefabrication in new projects such as Charles Lazor's FlatPak (fig. 19), Rocio Romero's LV House, and Michelle Kaufmann's Sunset Breezehouse.

Parallel to this phenomenon is the rapid rise of digital production within the design and construction industry, along with the optimism that both the new efficiencies and the new possibilities for mass customization will provide a radically new generation of off-site fabrication. Here the potential of building fabrication to achieve the level of precision expected of design objects, together with new formal and structural experimentations through digital parametric design can open prefabrication to customization not only for consumer preference, but for climate, as well as site and manufacturing conditions.[33] Scott Marble and Karen Fairbanks summed up the potential most eloquently in their Flatform proposal, commissioned for this exhibition: "What distinguishes CNC (computer numerically controlled) technologies for architecture is the opportunity it affords to reposition design strategically within fabrication and construction processes such that what architects actually produce—drawings—shifts from loose representations of buildings to highly precise sets of instruction and data that drive manufacturing processes as part of a coordinated and integrated description of a building."[34] While Kieran Timberlake Associates, represented here with Cellophane House, have claimed that the new age of mass customization is the threshold of a world totally alien to that of Le Corbusier, Gropius, and Wachsmann, one cannot read their recent manifesto *Refabricating Architecture,* calling for a new harnessing of information technology and computer-driven

FIG. 19 Charles Lazor, FlatPak, Minneapolis, Minnesota. 2005.
FIG. 20 Ernst Neufert, Building Machine, 1943. Rendering.

025

fabrication, without thinking of Viollet-le-Duc's appeal to architects of 150 years ago cited at the beginning of this essay.[35]

In some of its most academic applications, the intense focus on digital parametrics, with its virtually limitless capacity for innovation, runs the risk of pursuing a new type of form for form's sake, with the designer preoccupied by algorithms of design rather than the logic of making. Those researches that offer the most promising prospects for a design in which the alliance of new ways of making—including means of calculating the greatest amount of material use with the minimum amount of waste, as well as the greatest potential for algorithms to promote individual creativity—carry with them the potential to posit a prefabricated architecture suited to an era of extreme risk and challenges, from overpopulation to drastic climatic change. At the present moment the great danger is that the computer and its algorithmic prowess become an end in itself, a digital-age version of Ernst Neufert's Building Machine (fig. 20). The contemporary infancy of parametrics in which digital conception often leads to a great deal of hand assembly—as in the beautifully conceived BURST*008, included here,

or other recent small-scale CNC projects—is a condition to be overcome if a fruitful marriage between parametric design and the industrialization of high-quality housing is to be achieved. Yet at the same time that discrepancy suggests the possibility of technology transfer in a global environment in which countries, such as India for instance, with its paradoxical juxtaposition of vast capitals of information technology with vast supplies of hand labor, can reap the benefits of these new techniques. The challenge for the next generation is to pursue a deeper engagement with the techniques of fabrication and an expansion of the range of issues that the new experimental impulse is poised to tackle. The history of standardization is rife with lessons to be learned, not disregarded, even as the conditions of designing in a digital environment and of making in a globalizing world are reconfiguring the very space in which this practice takes place.

notes

1 H. Vergnolle, "La Préfabrication chez les Romains," *Techniques et Architecture* 9), no. 7/8 (1950): 11ff.

2 Christine Macy, "The Architect's Office of the Tennessee Valley Authority," in *The Tennessee Valley Authority: Design and Persuasion*, ed. Tim Culvahouse (New York: Princeton Architectural Press, 2007), 40.

3 Colin Davies, *The Prefabricated Home* (London: Reaktion Books, 2005), 87.

4 Gilbert Herbert, *Pioneers of Prefabrication: The British Contribution in the Nineteenth Century* (Baltimore and London: The Johns Hopkins Press, 1978), 1.

5 Sigfried Giedion, *Space, Time and Architecture: The Growth of a New Tradition* (Cambridge, Mass.: Harvard University Press, 1941), 269.

6 Ibid., 268.

7 Eugène Emmanuel Viollet-le-Duc, *Lectures on Architecture* (London: Sampson Low, Marston, Searle & Rivington, 1877 and 1881) 2: 105–6.

8 Jean-Louis Cohen, *Scenes of the World to Come: European Architecture and the American Challenge, 1893–1960* (Paris: Flammarion; Montreal: Canadian Centre for Architecture, 1995). See also Jean-Louis Cohen and Hubert Damisch, *Americanisme et modernité: l'idéal américain dans l'architecture* (Paris: EHESS, Flammarion, 1993).

9 The examples in this paragraph are discussed by Kurt Junghanns in his authoritative *Das Haus für Alle: Zur Geschichte der Vorfertigung in Deutschland* (Berlin: Ernst & Sohn, 1994), 42–43.

10 Le Corbusier, "Mass Production Housing," in *Toward an Architecture (Vers une Architecture)*, trans. John Goodman (Los Angeles: Getty Research Institute, 2007), 259–60.

11 See Mary McLeod, "Le Rêve Transi de Le Corbusier: L'Amérique (Catastrophe Féerique)," in Cohen and Damisch, *Americanisme et modernité*, 209–25.

12 Walter Gropius, "Programm zur Gründung einer allgemeinen Hausbaugesellschaft auf künstlerischer einheitlicher Grundlage m.b. H.," 1909. See Winfried Nerdinger, *The Architect Walter Gropius: Drawings, Prints, and Photographs from the Busch-Reisinger Museum, Harvard University Art Museums, Cambridge, Mass., and from the Bauhaus-Archiv, Berlin* (Berlin: Mann, 1985). See also Gilbert Herbert, *The Dream of the Factory-made House: Walter Gropius and Konrad Wachsmann* (Cambridge, Mass.: MIT Press, 1984) and Michael Grüning, *Der Wachsmann-Report, Auskünfte eines Architekten* (Basel: Birkhäuser, 2001).

13 English translation from Sigfried Giedion, *Walter Gropius, Work and Teamwork* (London: The Architectural Press, 1954), 74.

14 Adolf Meyer, ed., *Ein Versuchshaus des Bauhauses in Weimar* (Munich: Albert Langen, 1924, third in the series of Bauhausbücher, directed by Walter Gropius and L. Moholy-Nagy; reprint, Weimar: Universitätsverlag der Bauhaus-Universität Weimar, 2003).

15 Ibid., 13.

16 See Walter Sheiffele, *Bauhaus Junkers Sozialdemokratie: Ein Kraftfeld der Moderne* (Berlin: form + zweck Verlag, 2003).

17 See Gilbert Herbert, *The Berlin Connection: The "Palestine Prefabs" of the 1930s* (Haifa: Center for Urban and Regional Studies, Technion Institute for Research and Development, 1979), and also Friedrich von Borries and Jens Uwe Fischer in this catalogue.

18 Hannes Meyer, "Die neue Welt," *Das Werk* 13, no. 7 (1926): 205–24. Here quoted from English translation in Arton Kaes, Martin Jay, and Edward Dimendberg, *The Weimar Sourcebook* (Berkeley: University of California Press, 1994), 447.

19 Quoted in Isabelle Hyman, *Marcel Breuer, Architect : The Career and the Buildings* (New York : H.N. Abrams, 2001), 57.

20 Reginald R. Isaacs, *Walter Gropius: Der Mensch und Sein Werk* (Berlin: Gebr. Mann Verlag, 1984), 500.

21 Ibid., 507.

22 Burnham Kelly, *The Prefabrication of Houses: A Study by the Albert Farwell Bemis Foundation of the Prefabrication Industry in the United States* (New York: John Wiley and Sons, with the Technology Press of MIT, 1951), 27–28.

23 See the excellent study by Kristin M. Szylvian, "Bauhaus on Trial: Aluminum City Terrace and Federal Defense Housing Policy During World War II," *Planning Perspectives* 9 (1994): 229–54. The letter cited here is taken up on page 239.

24 Letter from the GBH-Way Homes Company dated November 22, 1944 to Breuer, Marcel Breuer Archives, Syracuse University, Box 47.

25 Dietmar Strauch, *Einstein in Caputh, Die Geschichte eines Sommerhauses* (Berlin: Philo, 2001).

26 Quoted in Giedion, *Gropius*, 77.

27 Colin Davies, op. cit., 23.

28 Thomas T. Fetters, *The Lustron Home: The History of a Postwar Prefabricated Housing Experiment* (Jefferson, N.C.: MacFarland & Company, 2002).

29 There is a huge Prouvé literature since the seminal 1981 exhibition at the Museum Boijmans van Beuningen in Rotterdam with its excellent catalogue, *Jean Prouvé constructeur* (Rotterdam and Delft: Museum Boijmans van Beuningen, 1981).

30 The best source in the ballooning Prouvé literature is Christian Enjolras, *Jean Prouvé, Les maisons de Meudon, 1949–1999* (Paris: Editions de la Villette, 2003). For further Prouvé literature see the bibliography in this volume.

31 Vladmir Mattioni, "The JU 61 System of Bogdan Budimirov, Zeljko Solar, and Dragutin Stilnovic," in *Project Zagreb, Transition as Condition, Strategy, Practice*, eds. Eve Blau and Ivan Rupnik (Barcelona: Actar; Cambridge, Mass.: Harvard University Graduate School of Design, 2007).

32 I am grateful to Florian Breiphol for bringing this system to my attention, for his diploma work on the Metastadt-Bausystem written at the KHB, Weissensee, Berlin, 2006, and for his contribution to this catalogue.

33 Branko Kolarevic, *Architecture in the Digital Age: Design and Manufacturing* (New York and London: Taylor & Francis, 2003).

34 Marble Fairbanks proposal to The Museum of Modern Art, 2007.

35 Stephen Kieran and James Timberlake, *Refabricating Architecture: How Manufacturing Methodologies are Poised to Transform Building Construction* (New York: McGraw-Hill, 2004).

FIG. 1 Fredrick Blom, rendering of prefabricated estate. 1830.

027

SCANDINAVIA: PREFABRICATION AS A MODEL OF SOCIETY

RASMUS WÆRN

If anything, wood distinguishes Nordic architecture.[1] And wood maintains an inherent potential for prefabricated construction. Trees are virtually ready-made beams and pillars. Log houses can be made and moved to less sylvan sites; planks can be cut to size in workshops and then packed and marked according to their position; pieces of wood can be glued together into large elements, designed to make a beam or a complete building.[2] The history of prefab in Scandinavia—and in this cultural entity I also include Finland—can be written in three chapters: the pioneer age, the mass-production age, and the customization and design age. Over the course of this history, the Finnish avant-garde took greatest advantage of the technology, but Sweden and Norway made the first experiments in prefabrication.

The first Scandinavian to recognize the potential for manufacturing prefabricated houses on an industrial scale was a Swede named Fredrik Blom, born in 1781, a polymath, an architect, and a colonel in the Corps of Naval Engineers. He thought of the wall as a series of parts that could be built up and taken down as the occasion demanded. As a military man, he envisioned a system of constructing movable buildings as barracks, but in practice his output mainly comprised houses, often summer homes, for the well-to-do (fig. 1). Mobility may have been Blom's prime concern, but the popularity of his houses owed to their appearance of solidity. Blom offered his customers individual building components—complete walls, a wall with a door, a wall with windows, etc.—that were then joined together with iron ties. Some 140 houses were produced by 1840—smooth, classical-style buildings that attracted attention all over Europe. Prefabrication became something of a sensation in the early days of industrialization, and few could rival Blom in the deployment of prefabricated wood.

Blom's houses were handcrafted, but the emerging sawmilling industry was quick to mechanize the idea. The Stockholm firm of Siwers and Wennberg began exporting movable houses to California in 1849, and the Norwegian exhibition at the 1889 World's Fair in Paris focused on portable homes for export, though the Norwegians never reached the scale of production of the Swedish. Houses were marketed through catalogues that were a commercial variant of the pattern collections that served as architectural sourcebooks throughout the nineteenth century. The pattern books themselves were progenitors of prefabrication, introducing to the masses new building typologies. The realization of these pattern-book houses largely depended on customization, but soon their industrial manufacture would be reality.

MASS-PRODUCTION AND STANDARDIZATION

A great housing shortage beginning in 1917 broadened the demand for prefabrication to accommodate the masses, and the industry was soon standardized and mechanized in both Norway and Sweden. In the 1920s the city of Stockholm began leasing at affordable terms plots on which tenants, usually blue-collar workers, could build their own homes. The city provided standard drawings to maintain quality and to give the new developments a uniform character, and the state government soon began publishing collections of these drawings, making them a nationwide standard. This unassuming, often tradition-based system of housing construction was in many ways superior to the German "dogmatic […] and almost unreserved acceptance of standardization for all building material" or Le Corbusier's "almost devout adulation of mechanical equipment," to use the words of Hans O. Elliot, a pioneer in the development of Swedish construction standards.[3]

Overall mass production in Scandinavia was driven by the house building industry. The first catalogue of prefabricated homes for delivery anywhere in Sweden was published by the Borohus company in 1924, after which the industry grew rapidly: by the end of the 1930s there were more than twenty manufacturers of "catalogue houses." The sawmills in

FIG. 2 Alvar Aalto, AA-System Houses Type 14. 1939. Elevation.

the densely forested provinces produced between four and five thousand buildings per year. The majority were houses and villas, but gymnasiums, factory buildings, churches, and hotels were also manufactured.

Untouched by the war, Swedish industry was able to assist Finnish reconstruction efforts with the manufacture of two thousand prefabricated wooden homes after the Winter War of 1939–40. The houses were built in Sweden but designed in Finland, where a more radical aesthetic developed. Before the war, Alvar Aalto had already designed a wooden house type for the workers at the A. Ahlström company, the so-called AA-System Houses (fig. 2). Aalto, familiar with the latest American prefab technology after his sessions at the Massachusetts Institute of Technology, played an important role in reconstruction efforts that focused on standardization and he designed Finland's first house production factory in 1940. In 1942 a Reconstruction Bureau was established under the leadership of Aarne Ervi and Viljo Revell, both of whom had formerly worked in Aalto's studio. The use of standardization had now been broadly investigated, but the demand for prefabricated houses was still relatively modest.

The end of the war altered the scene—the demand for houses was greater than ever. In addition to addressing its own housing shortage, Finland paid part of its war debt to the Soviet Union in prefabricated houses. And despite Sweden's more efficient methods of production, Norway imported homes from the more aesthetically daring Finland. Norway needed a hundred thousand units immediately, but their small-scale industry hindered the proposed expansion, as did mechanical problems with joints and fittings encountered when erecting buildings during hard winter conditions.

There is good reason to suppose that Sweden at this time was the world's leading manufacturer of wooden prefabs. More than 50 percent of all new wooden houses were prefabricated by approximately sixty to seventy different companies. In 1947 alone 17,500 prefabricated houses were produced in Sweden, which can be compared with pre-1941 output in the United States totaling some 18,000. While the U.S. would increase this figure by more than twenty times in the postwar years, the rational principles characterizing this production would also be explored in Sweden. The manufacturers favored pragmatic solutions and eliminated special architectonic features, such as corner windows, which would compromise value.

However, in Sweden designing prefabricated houses was not regarded as purely a matter for engineers. In 1947, under the title "The New Empiricism, Sweden's latest style," the English *Architectural Review*

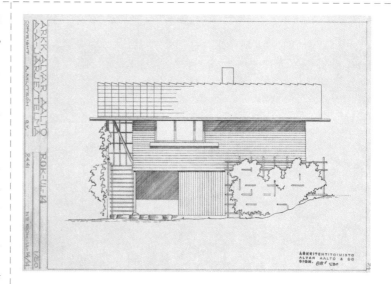

published architect Sven Markelius's own villa, located on the outskirts of Stockholm. As head of the standardization commission initiated by the Swedish government, Markelius had developed the principle that mass production of houses should be based on standardized parts, not standardized houses. While the latter scenario could very well lead to "unsuitable uniformity and dreary similarity," a system of parts would allow greater variety and scope of design. Markelius's own house, built in 1945, became the showroom example of the "system house," which Svenska Cellulosa Aktiebolaget and other manufacturers attempted to introduce to the market. But these efforts to promote a new building type ultimately failed, despite the manufacturer's advertised assurance that "a practical man should be able to erect the house in two hours with his wife's assistance."

But Markelius's work on standardized building did have a future. His close friend Aalto spearheaded the development of standardization in Finland, and the uniform 100-millimeter planning module soon became standard throughout Scandinavia. The only country that did not fully accept construction standardization was Denmark, which was still firmly rooted in traditional methods. Additionally, during this time prefabrication was still equated with wood construction, and sparsely forested Denmark kept to brick and mortar.

EXPERIMENTATION AND EDUCATION

Part of the reason why prefabricated building developed under the aegis of single-family housing was strong union opposition to the transfer of jobs from the construction industry to manufacturing, restricting such a shift to projects of smaller scale, i.e., residential projects. Added to this, short production runs encouraged experimentation. Leading architects were enlisted to launch various construction kits, often through competitions published in the now expanding range of design periodicals. The 1940s and 1950s were characterized by a curiosity about prefabrication similar to that which occurred during prefab's inception in Scandinavia some hundred years earlier. Individual architects experimented with new technical solutions. The radical Erik Friberger took rationality to great lengths in the houses he designed and built in Gothenburg between 1949 and 1952. The inner walls were movable, all wiring and plumbing was concealed, and the house had absolutely no radiators thanks to the circulation of warm air in the attic, which heated the ceiling.

Prefabrication had become a broad concept ranging from precut timber to construction modules composed of prefabricated elements. Builders and engineers as a rule wanted to move prefabrication into ever larger units, while architects typically advocated smaller modules, in a manner similar to the Finnish couple Kaija and Heikki Siren, who developed the old precut technology further. In Sweden the National Power Board developed a system of slabs that could be moved and erected wherever new hydropower stations were to be constructed so that during the construction period the site would contain entire communities accommodating five hundred workers, complete with homes, a shop, a post office, a first aid station, and a community center. The system was modeled on American prototypes, with each construction component scaled for easy loading onto a truck.

Modular principles also encouraged bolder design. In 1955 prominent Swedish architect Ralph Erskine designed a circular weekend cottage of three-millimeter sheet steel for the manager of an engineering works. The house, consisting of sixteen prefabricated sections, was later to be reproduced in large numbers. On its own the steel igloo is fascinating, but the mass effect would have been devastating.

The egalitarian ideals of the 1960s encouraged uniform solutions. A broader prosperity opened a market for holiday homes, a type well suited for experiments in prefabrication. Almost every progressive Scandinavian architect developed prefab schemes. Most of them remained prototypes. One radical exception was the Futuro House, designed by the Finn Matti Suuronen in 1968. The plastic UFO landed in holiday resorts, on military grounds, and in housing developments, making its architect world famous.

The Futuro House was an exception in the history of Finnish architecture, which has otherwise been associated with a contextually sensitive brand of modernism rather than with high-tech adventures. Some of the finest examples of this sensitivity were the various prefab systems developed by architects Kristian Gullichsen, Kirmo Mikkola, and Juhani Pallasmaa. In general, the column-and-beam system, influenced by both traditional Japanese architecture and contemporary steel construction, was applied to single buildings as well as to open systems such as the Moduli 225 project, based on a frame measuing 225 by 225 centimeters. In artistic terms this system was the peak of wooden prefab in Scandinavia, but its flat roofs were poorly adapted to Scandinavian winters.

The 1960s also saw the implementation of standardized architecture in Denmark. Arne Jacobsen developed Kubeflex and Kvadraflex, two systems of cubic volumes. His fellow countryman Jørn Utzon designed Espansiva, a puzzle-like wood system that could form large units of varying function. All three systems could be expanded to create whole villages, but none left the prototype phase. During the same period, Swedish experiments were restricted to initiatives from state committees, such as a cost-efficient traditional cottage system developed in 1965 called Tvären, in which its prefabrication was not at all expressed in its design.[4]

By this time, in all parts of Scandinavia, even those architects who did not experiment with industrial construction methods restrained themselves by minimizing variation in dimensions. Working with modules was a reaction against the exaggerated individualism of the old masters like Aalto by a younger generation, such as the Norwegian architect Sverre Fehn, who always used standardized lengths.

PREFABRICATION AND POLITICS

Prefabrication became a core in the general housing policy that the Scandinavian countries adopted to a greater or lesser extent in the 1960s. Consistent use of prefabricated sections was considered to be not only the most economically feasible but also the only politically acceptable solution to the production of affordable housing: for instance the Swedish minister of finance complained at the wastefulness of employing highly paid manpower to produce drawings for practically identical buildings. Around 1960 building standardization achieved its first real breakthrough when practically all new housing was planned using multiples of 300 millimeters. Prefabrication was still a marginal phenomenon, but when in 1965 the state proclaimed a mas-

FIG. 3 HSB-BORO catalogue. C. late 1940s–early 1950s.

sive ten-year construction program, this made possible the large-scale serial production of concrete wall and roof-beam units. Construction companies devised systems of their own which soon transformed the architect's job into a matter of picking and mixing pieces. Soon the urban planner also had to submit to the demands of construction systems for rational production. Modular building reflected the 1960s view of society, imagining that everything could be broken down into functions, which could then be assembled into ready-made solutions. This view eventually led to a backlash that stigmatized the architect as an enemy of the people.

As the 1960s drew to a close, "catalogue homes" dominated the market for detached houses, as opposed to individual or systematized houses designed by architects. As the mass produced homes became more and more individualized, suburban communities grew visually chaotic. But the abundance of variation was merely superficial. Site regulations and provisions rigidly defined the planning of a "good home." The proportions of these low and broad houses were often problematic, but they managed to address a common taste with lessons learned from new holiday destinations and dispatches from America. With prefabrication methods of some sort used in 85 percent of private homes by the 1980s, the integration of these disparate structures had become a quandary: on the one hand the individual home must not be too eccentric if it is to be viable in a broader context; on the other hand, stereotypes seldom appeal to the individual consumer. Manufacturers reacted by illustrating their catalogues with lone buildings, where the natural landscape was their only neighbor (fig. 3).

TWO CAUSES, TWO EFFECTS

Despite its prominent role in the modern history of Scandinavian building, prefabrication has for a long time been looked down on as something less than architecture, the history of which has always favored particular buildings rather than general solutions. But prefab has nevertheless consolidated its role, for two reasons. First, the fashioning of detailing, which has always been a part of responsible architecture, has been taken over by the products industry. Ready-made products are everywhere, they are more advanced than one-off designs, and they are better built. Second, the uniform building systems employed by construction companies are now more developed, and although lower quality is still a consequence of lower costs, the fact remains that mass production of housing without using prefab systems is no longer economically feasible.

But parallel to this, prefabrication maintains other virtues. When Taschen published its comprehensive book on the Case Study Houses in 2002, those who had admired the non-rhetorical and rational aesthetics in contemporary low-budget architecture suddenly had a bible. Extravagant without being exclusive, raw without being hostile, the quasi-industrial approach of the Case Study Houses appealed to architects pursuing lower budgets through less expensive materials as well as to wealthy or "creative-type" homebuyers who responded to their pared-down aesthetic. The handcrafted was replaced by mechanized design for the "cut-and-paste" generation, and the credibility of prêt-à-porter rose at the expense of the tailored. Today, fashion from H&M and serial furniture from Ikea represent reliability, while the building trades continue to lose credibility in scandals concerning poor performance, uncertain costs, and broken promises.

FIG. 4 Juul & Frost Architects, "Better Cheaper Dwellings"
project, Køge, Denmark. 2004–8.

031

This was an opening for the product industry that led to two different concepts: First, there appeared a new opportunity to assume a role in developing residential design concepts so that the personal would be expressed in the selection of products. Prefabricated houses are no longer anonymous but brands, offering one safe choice. Several new companies, such as Pinc House and Arkitekthus in Sweden, offer fixed, branded designs, some signed by well-known architects. As a light version of this concept, construction company Skanska produces a house made of standardized and mass-produced units that is marketed through the ubiquitous brand Ikea. Second, there emerged the opportunity for the product industry to refine the concept of customization so that the production system would offer a wide range of designs. An array of components now allows the customer to take part in the design process in the same manner as Gullichsen and Pallasmaa's Moduli 225, Utzon's Espansiva, or Aalto's AA-System Houses once did. The Norwegian architecture firm Snøhetta has worked on a system called Løvetann, with aluminium pillars and panels measuring 4.8 by 4.8 meters, that would bring out the architect in each customer. These timeless principles recall the pioneer projects of structuralism, but what once was intended as a generic solution is now exclusive—and expensive.

Prefabricated systems continue to proliferate. Today Norway, Sweden, and Finland enjoy a large surplus of mature forests, which has spurred the development of new building technologies that employ massive wood elements to create both large-scale and small-scale structures. As a result of these developments, several new prefabricated designs have been launched recently such as a multistory apartment building in Trondheim, Norway, designed by Brendeland & Kristoffersen, and in Finland the precut summer home called PlusHuvilat, designed by architects PlusArkkitehdit, and the prefab permanent home called Laavu (also know as Touch House), designed by noted architects Heikkinen-Komonen, which all employ simple structures to reconcile tastes for both the primitive and for the modern.

All over Scandinavia prefabrication is now supported by the government. A joint venture between the building trade and the Finnish government made their prefabricated concrete industry the leader in Scandinavia by the 1970s, and in Denmark government support has resulted in an extremely simple housing district comprised of factory-made, room-sized volumes designed by the architects Juul & Frost (fig. 4). The Danish Royal Academy of Art now has a department for research in prefabrication, the first of its kind. Mass-production turns the particular into principles: the industry explores all possible uses of natural resources, while for architects prefabricated homes hold a potential similar to that of prints for the artist, that is, as an avenue toward accessibility. Prefab is for everyone.

The third age of prefabrication in Scandinavia is the age of internationalization. What were once small local sawmills that made their money on placeless buildings have now become placeless corporate juggernauts. All major enterprises in the trade are operating internationally: for instance, the first Skanska/Ikea homes were recently erected in Britain. Large-scale production necessarily demands a wider field of operation. Just as the place of a car's production is no longer important to the consumer, it will not take long before globalization strikes the last truly domestic sector—the home.

notes

1. The visible use of wood is remarkably higher in Scandinavia, including Finland, than in any other region in the world, according to *The Phaidon Atlas of Contemporary World Architecture* (New York: Phaidon, 2004).

2. The trade in log houses dates back to at least the beginning of the seventeenth century, when manufactured homes were sold on Russian markets.

3. Hans O. Elliot: "Standardisering av bostadstyper och byggnadsmaterial" (Standardizing of housing types and construction materials), *Nordisk Byggedag* (1927): 93; and "Om typer och typserier av mindre bostadshus" (On types and type series of minor houses), *Byggmästaren* 19, (1926): 229.

4. The initiative came from the head of the National Institute for Building Research, Lennart Holm; the architect was Hilding Lögdberg. The joint venture between Holm, Lögdberg, and the Consumer Institute and the National Housing Board saw only a few buildings erected.

POSTULATING THE POTENTIAL OF PREFAB: THE CASE OF JAPAN

KEN TADASHI OSHIMA

Already in my early beginnings as an architect, I was greatly intrigued and attracted by the Japanese house. Its lightness, its flexibility and pleasing lines impressed me deeply. The restrained order of its standardized building parts appealed to me as the hallmark of a deeply rooted culture adaptable to any new development. The elements for today's industrial prefabrication seem to be inherent in this ancient modular conception, which simultaneously left freedom for a great variety of compositions, avoiding monotony.

I consider it a challenging task for the new generation of Japanese architects to find the fitting links between that flexible, traditional concept of the old craft periods and the new development of an industrial basis. With keenest interest I will watch the architectural contributions to come from my Japanese colleagues.[1]

—Walter Gropius, 1950

Walter Gropius's observations on the potential of developing a diverse and dynamic field of industrial prefabrication in Japan proved to be uncannily prescient through the course of the second half of the twentieth century. Today Japan leads the world in the production of prefabricated houses, which constitute as much as 20 percent of the domestic housing market.[2] Within this context, mammoth manufacturers, including Panasonic and Toyota, working closely with governmental and financial sectors, have actively implemented modern mass production methods to successfully realize Le Corbusier's vision to build the house as a "machine for living." Moreover, individual architects and builders have also long embraced prefabrication by developing prototypes to reach a wider demographic and to increase quality and efficiency. The case of Japan thus begs fundamental questions about the nature of prefabricated house design and construction. Namely, how new is the idea of prefabrication and what are the physical and cultural conditions that led to its success in Japan? What are the advantages and disadvantages of prefabrication and what opportunities does it offer for both manufacturers and individual designers?

By 1950 Gropius's aspirations had in fact already taken root in the defeated nation of Japan to address the realities of reconstruction. The idea of prefabricated construction produced by specialized builders to maximize quality and efficiency was fundamental to building ideals in Japan, and it made particular sense for modern construction. In the 1930s, architect Kameki Tsuchiura (1897–1996) had introduced Gropius's Trockenbau (dry building) prefabricated concrete panel system through magazine articles and in his own house designs.[3] Then, like now, the ideal of maximum factory construction facilitated increased quality and fire safety and reduced required on-site labor. Tsuchiura advocated the use of new materials such as cinder concrete and the panel method within a traditional conceptual framework.

More fundamentally, traditional Japanese residential post-and-beam construction could be considered inherently a system of prefabrication, and the introduction of new modes of production could thus be seen as a modernization rather than transformation of building principles. The Japanese house constructed in The Museum of Modern Art's sculpture garden in 1954–55 (fig. 1) implicitly illustrated the role of prefabrication through its design and assembly.[4] While highlight-

ing the modernity of the classic *shoin* residential building tradition, prefabrication enabled the house by Junzō Yoshimura, based on a seventeenth-century precedent, to be manufactured in Nagoya, Japan, and assembled in Manhattan. It illustrated how building in Japan has relied since ancient times on principles of prefabrication by specialized building guilds that were each responsible for specific pieces that would be prefabricated and assembled on site.[5] As the post-and-beam structure was based on the regularized column spacing known as the *ken*, the infill elements of shoji screens, fusuma panels, and tatami mats prefabricated by individual craftsmen in various locations of Japan could be precisely put together almost like pieces of a puzzle. Moreover, major governmental and religious construction projects in Japan from at least the Nara period (710–794) utilized standardized designs and prefabricated building techniques.[6] The skilled specialized carpenters cut many of the mortise and tenon joints into the pillars and beams according to highly developed techniques off-site and then assembled them on-site.

In Japan during the immediate postwar period, such rational building methods facilitated the construction of prefabricated dwellings to alleviate a housing shortage of 4.2 million units. Early examples were primarily barrack-type structures. Le Corbusier's disciples Junzō Sakakura (1901–1969) and Kunio Maekawa (1905–1986) both actively sought to realize their master's ideals. In 1941 Sakakura began to develop an A-frame "assembly architecture" (*kumitate kenchiku*), and Maekawa pursued his own prefabricated housing scheme, which he named Premos (fig. 2), and produced more than 1,000 units between 1945 and 1952.[7] While maintaining the living unit of the tatami mat as the basis for these minimal fifty-two-square-meter living units, Maekawa incorporated a system of self-supporting three-*shaku* (2.98 feet) honeycomb panels covered by plywood sheeting and used shallow wood trusses to support the roof. By 1947 the architectural profession earnestly pursued the dream of prefabrication with articles promoting "pre-assembled houses," "standard pre-made houses," and "panelized houses."[8] The minimal typical twelve-*tsubo* (427 square feet) houses met the needs of the housing crisis, and made an easy transition from traditional wood frame construction to prefabrication through the use of modules suited to tatami mats and shoji and fusuma screens.

The 1950s also witnessed the emergence of individual minimal dwellings as experimental prototypes for mass production. Architect Kiyoshi Ikebe (1920–1979) drew from his work experiences with Sakakura from 1944 to 1946 and Maekawa as a member of NAU: New Architects' Union.

Ikebe developed a series of numbered case study houses that totaled ninety-eight in which he incorporated now common industrialized elements such as standard steel sash windows. Here he sought to simplify Le Corbusier's Modulor to reach a broader audience in Japan through his own GM (General Module) system, based on simple multiples of two, and subsequently became a pioneer in the industrialization of and modular coordination in housing. In 1952 Makoto Masuzawa (1925–1990), who had worked for Czech-American architect Antonin Raymond (1888–1976), developed his own two-level minimal house (fifteen *tsubo* or 534 square feet) that through its simple, straightforward design was ripe for prefabrication but not realized until after his death.

Following these smaller-scale trials, prefabricated housing in Japan took off as an industry in 1959. Contributing factors included the continuing postwar shortage of housing and skilled craftsmen at this time, complemented by a baby boom and rise in nuclear families.[9] Sekisui House, Daiwa House, National, and Misawa Homes all began production at this time to produce initially basic boxlike homes for flat, densely populated areas of Japan. Early models did not allow for changes in the fundamental structural system, but gradually evolved to models with more complicated roofs, plans, and multi-levels. Manufactured houses developed into two types: a "closed-system" modular type consisting of standardized room-sized units, and an "open-system" of a timber or steel frame and infill panel system (aluminum, lightweight concrete, lightweight ceramic, etc.). Continuing traditional concepts of modular column spacing, these prefabricated houses, many of which had tatami mats, either followed a unit system with typical widths of 2.7 and 3.6 meters or column spacing with a 0.9- to 1.0-meter module.[10] The concept of modular coordination had been proposed by Alfred Farwell Bemis in *The Evolving House* (1936), but would not be nearly as readily embraced in the United States as in Japan.[11] Many of the early interior plans consisted of a series of Japanese-style rooms grouped around a Western-style living room, encased within an eclectic mix of architectural styles ranging from Tudor to neo-Wrightian Prairie Style.

Sekisui House, together with its affiliated company Sekisui Heim (Sekisui Chemicals), which has become the leading prefabricated house manufacturer in Japan, established its reputation through the production of a modular steel box system epitomized by the Sekisui Heim M-1 (fig. 3). Developed with Katsuhiko Ōno, this system reduced cost and labor requirements by maximizing factory production. It was first introduced at the Tokyo International Good Living Show in 1970 and today is inhabited by some 10,000 homeowners. Onetime owner and leading Japanese architectural historian Terunobu Fujimori (1946–) noted that the house offered quality construction, strength to withstand earthquakes and fires, and an economical price despite lacking a pronounced design personality.[12] Beyond this, current models offer extended year warranties, much like a car, and are similarly marketed with extensive customized options. Houses are thus seen more as consumer goods than as long-term financial investments and are expected to last decades rather than generations.

During the 1960s and early 1970s architects of the Metabolist movement embraced prefabrication through their espousal of manufactured elements that could be organically inserted and replaced within various superstructures. Architect Kiyonori Kikutake (1928–) looked beyond Sigfried Giedion's examples of industrially produced kitchens featured in *Mechanization Takes Command* (1948) to build his own Skyhouse (1959) as a concrete superstructure supporting "move-nett" prefabricated kitchen, bathroom, and bedroom units that could be added or subtracted as necessary (fig. 4). Kisho Kurokawa (1934–2007) collaborated with the Taisei Construction Company first to develop toilet capsules for Expo '70 and then to develop a closed system of industrialized building units for export to Southeast Asia as a flexible precast-concrete town house system.[13] These ideas found their apotheosis in Kurokawa's Nakagin Capsule Tower (1968–72), which consisted of two steel-frame reinforced-concrete tower shafts that supported 140 individual prefabricated one-room living units. The project underscored the conception of the home as a manufactured project, although the idea that the units could be replaced like an organism regenerating a cell has not been realized.

In counterpoint to close collaborations between large-scale prefabricated housing manufacturers and banking and governmental agencies such as the Ministry of International Trade and Industry (MITI) and the Ministry of Construction, which has sought to raise the standard of living by constructing safer, longer-lasting houses, the individual architect has actively participated in methods of prefabrication on both a large and small scale. Companies such as Misawa Homes have sponsored housing design competitions since 1968, inviting judges including Jean Prouvé, Kiyoshi Ikebe, Kisho Kurokawa, and Kiyonori Kikutake to bring fresh approaches to prefabrication that are not purely technically based.

Individual architects have subsequently embraced factory produced and assembled materials to address the many irregular lots and complex programmatic requirements for individual clients where typical two-level prefabricated homes designed for flat suburban sites fail. In a majority of these small houses, narrow streets limit the size of prefabricated pieces to the typical 2.5-by-12-meter-long truck beds. Following the ideas of Charles and Ray Eames in their own California Case Study House (1945–49), Waro Kishi reinvented the traditional wooden-frame row house using factory-produced molded cement panels and aluminum sash windows in his design of the Kim House (Osaka, 1986–87), which he could tailor in this and other designs to individual sites and clients to create an "industrial vernacular." Osamu Ishiyama (1944–) by contrast designed highly individualistic dwellings such as the Gen-An and Dam·Dan (both 1975), which use the vernacular building

FIG. 4 Kiyonori Kikutake, Skyhouse, Tokyo. 1959.

035

material of corrugated steel sheets to form what he termed "huts in the age of industrialization." Shigeru Ban, designer of the prefabricated cardboard Paper Arch for The Museum of Modern Art's Abby Aldrich Rockefeller Sculpture Garden in April 2000, built on his previous work in prefabrication including the Furniture House (Lake Yamanaka, Yamanashi, 1995) in which 2.4-meter-high/90-centimeter-wide/45-centimeter-deep bookshelves support the house's flat roof.

The legacy of minimal houses designed by Ikebe and Masuzawa converge in the work of Kazuhiko Namba (1947–), who continues the tradition of numbered experimental houses. In pursuing a series of "box houses" that currently number more than 117, Namba has expanded on "the cube as a module" ripe for perfection through mass production that Bemis had proposed in *The Evolving House*, published just after the author's death.[14] Namba's stated goal in the Box House series is to "achieve the basic performance of an urban house with a minimum number of substances." While standardizing its "open" frame-and-fill

design and construction system to increase performance level and efficiency, ultimately the system is designed to accommodate diverse site and client needs for the varied locations and increasingly diverse client base.[15] Like Masuzawa's minimal house, the Box House maintains the model of a double-height square-plan space designed to accommodate as many functions as possible in the smallest possible volume. The 100-cubic-meter three-dimensional space incorporates stairs with built-in shelves and uses structural tie bars for lighting. Moreover, the southern overhang serves to shade the interior in the summer and allow sun to enter in the winter and heat the earthen floor workspace in this passive solar scheme.

Namba subsequently transformed his strategies for individual box houses to a mass market through the prototypical Aluminum Eco-Material House (1999) and the MUJI House (2005). As a development of Namba's box houses for a mass market, the basically one-room house designed for a family of four uses an industrially produced wooden structural frame akin to traditional Japanese modular proportions with various manufactured "infill" options.

In the twenty-first century, prefabrication has passed through a new threshold of development and diversification in Japan. With a shrinking of the house makers' target middle-market demographic of a nuclear family of four, they are being forced to rethink the future development of their products. The typical two-story model has not been designed for a single occupant, yet studies have shown that some 17 percent are actually single. Moreover the breakdown of the actual cost of typical prefabricated homes remains opaque as it is distributed widely for not only the product and labor, but also for marketing, research, and development.

Nowhere has the dream of a factory-produced house made and marketed like an automobile taken root as strongly as in Japan. Beyond embracing the mechanized factory assembly line first used by Henry Ford to achieve mass production of the automobile, housing manufacturers such as Toyota are developing intelligent hybrid houses that literally link to the owners' cars. Toyota had experimented with precast concrete rigid-frame housing units from 1946 to 1950, but suspended the project when its automobile production started to expand.[16] The Toyota Dream House PAPI, like similar prototypes being developed by Panasonic and others, uses the technologies that it developed in auto manufacturing for the housing industry to achieve high precision through factory production, reduce environmental load, and create an integrated network between the resident and the house, household

appliances, and automobile.[17] Features include intelligent bedrooms in which the light, temperature, and sound are adjusted based on bio-sensors attached to the residents' bodies to promote a full night's sleep. Moreover, a hybrid Prius automobile may be both hooked up to an E-station tower terminal in the garage as well as serve as a reserve "mobile power plant" to supply electric power to the house for up to thirty-six hours.

Today individual architects empowered by computers and new materials are forging new diverse paths to accommodate an increasingly diverse client base. Rather than constantly reinventing the wheel for each residential design, firms such as FOBA (whose name derives from the associate firm FOB Co-op, an import company distributing household goods and fashion items) take a somewhat prêt-à-porter strategy to research and develop specific consistent house typologies that are adjusted to suit specific sites.[18] Architects' new materials for prefabrication include "engineered wood" and aluminum domesticated for use as both a structure and surfaces by architects including Namba and Toyo Ito (Aluminum House in Sakurajosui, 2000). The ideal of the minimal house proposed by Masuzawa continues to serve as a model for prefabricated dwellings that has been reinvented in various ways, such as Hitoshi Abe's "Tall" version, which extends the nine-*tsubo* volume by three meters to increase floor area and reach a new degree of freedom in its modes of habitation.[19] Moreover, developments in digital prefabrication and small-scale prefabrication serve as the basis for a new generation of experimental dwellings. Yasuhiro Yamashita (1960–), with his firm Atelier Tekuto, has brought together frame-and-

fill design to form such projects as his Cell Brick House (Tokyo, 2004) (fig. 5). From the exterior, the house appears to be composed of staggered concrete blocks. However the interior reveals the composition of steel boxes (900 x 450 x 300 mm) that becomes what the architect calls "void masonry." The boxes function simultaneously as the house's structure and as storage units and even as sunshades to reduce heat gain. On a smaller scale, architect Ben Satoh (1966–) has reinvented tradition to create a prefabricated Maple Teahouse (2005) that can easily be transported to sites around the world. In the twenty-first century, prefabrication further offers the potential to achieve sustainability through increased efficiency in the production and use of materials, as well as reduction in actual energy consumption through strategies of natural lighting and ventilation.

The ideal of prefabrication in Japan is thus an open-ended system of building with infinite possibilities rather than a uniform, standardized box. Prefabrication's success in Japan builds directly on its history of coordinated and highly specialized building techniques that could readily be embraced by industrial production through the support of favorable governmental and economic conditions. The necessities of the immediate postwar period and increasing dominance of nuclear families led to the widespread success of prefabricated houses in Japan; however, changing demographics and lifestyles call for its continuing evolution. With new modes of production and a new generation of architects, Gropius's call for "the new generation of Japanese architects to find the fitting links between that flexible, traditional concept of the old craft periods and the new development of an industrial basis" has a renewed importance today and it is "with keenest interest" that we await the architectural contributions from Japan.[20]

notes

1 Walter Gropius, Cambridge, Massachusetts, November 1950, in Koyama Masakazu, ed., *Walter Gropius* (Tokyo: Kokusai Kenchiku, 1954), 4.

2 Shuichi Matsumura, *Kōgyōka jūtaku·kangae* (Thinking about the industrialized house) (Gakugei shuppansha, 1987), 5.

3 These houses include Kameki Tsuchiura's own house, the Takashima House (1934), and the Abe House (1935) by Ken Ichiura. These articles include Ken Ichiura, "Kenchiku seisan no gōritekini tsuite" (Rationalization of building production), *Kenchiku zasshi* 51, no. 633 (1937): 1490–96; and Ken Ichiura, "Kanshiki kōzō no jūtaku" (The house of dry construction), *Kokusai kenchiku* 8 (March 1932), reprinted in *Space Design* (July 1996): 36–37.

4 Arthur Drexler, *The Architecture of Japan* (New York: The Museum of Modern Art, 1955), 262–86.

5 Matsumura, *Kōgyōka jūtaku*, 20.

6 William Coaldrake, "Manufactured Housing: The New Japanese Vernacular," *Japan Architect* (January 1987): 58.

7 "Premos" derived its name from "pre" for prefab, M for Maekawa, O for Kaoru Ono, who was a structural engineer and professor at Tokyo University, and S for the San'in Manufacturing Company. See *Jonathan Reynolds, Maekawa Kunio and the Emergence of Japanese Modernist Architecture* (Berkeley: University of California Press, 2001), 146–49.

8 Nishi Kazuo, "Prehabu jūtaku no dai ikkan wo miru" (Looking at the first period of prefab houses), *"Gendai kenchiku no kiseki" Shinkenchiku*, special issue (December 1995): 146.

9 Renee Mathieu, "The Prefabricated Housing Industries in the United States, Sweden and Japan." *Construction Review* 33 (July–August 1987): 2–21.

10 See Shozō Baba, ed., "Jūtaku no kōgyōka ha ima" (The industrialized house is now), *Shinkenchiku*, special issue (April 1984).

11 Albert Farwell Bemis, *The Evolving House* (Cambridge, Mass.: The Technology Press M.I.T., 1936).

12 Interview, December 6, 2004.

13 Michael Franklin Ross, *Beyond Metabolism* (New York: Architectural Record Books, 1978), 60–73.

14 Albert Farwell Bemis, *The Evolving House*. see Kazuhiko Namba + KAI-workshop, *The Box-Houses: Towards a New Eco-house* (Tokyo: NTT Shuppan, 2006), and Kazuhiko Namba, *Namba Kazuhiko: The Box-Houses under Construction* (Tokyo: TOTO Shuppan, 2001).

15 Kazuhiko Namba, *Namba Kazuhiko: The Box-Houses under Construction*, 7.

16 *Shinkenchiku*, special issue (April 1984): 81.

17 Nakata Senhiko, ed., "A House of Sustainability," *Architecture and Urbanism*, special issue (December 2005).

18 Thomas Daniell, "Architects as 'Housemakers' in Japan," *Architectural Design* 73, no. 4 (2003): 82–89; Toshiko Kinoshita, "Prêt-à-porter no ie zukuri," *Jūtaku tokushū* 180 (April 2001); "Jūtaku wo tsukuru sekai to ikani kakawaru bekika," *Jūtaku tokushū* 192 (April 2002): 18–23.

19 Abe's design is part of a number of reinterpretations of Masuzawa's "Nine-Tsubo House" including "Remix" by Takaharu and Yui Tezuka, "Garage Life" by Kentaro Yamamoto, and "Cellar House" by Rikuo Nishimori created for an exhibition at the Living Design Center in Tokyo in 1999.

20 Walter Gropius, op. cit., 4.

PROJECTS

The following section contains documentation of architectural projects, both realized and unrealized (both placed against a brown background). Additionally, this section contains a select collection of building systems, paradigms, and commissions produced specifically for this exhibition as well as three architectural toys (placed against an orange background). Each of these fifty-eight projects and items is accompanied by a short descriptive text and a selection of elemental images. The projects are sequenced chronologically by their initial design date. Projects whose design spanned numerous years are listed within a date range that includes dates of commercial production when applicable. In the cases of work realized but not replicated or works whose commercial production was terminated, the final date is the date construction or production ended.

Principal architects or architectural firms and collaborators are listed in the heading. When appropriate, project names have been translated into English. Locations of built projects are noted in text, although many projects were not designed to be site-specific.

MANNING PORTABLE
COLONIAL COTTAGE FOR EMIGRANTS

H. MANNING

BELOW Early example of system ("La Trobe's Cottage," Joli Mont, Victoria, Australia).
BOTTOM LEFT Plan.
BOTTOM RIGHT Axonometric views of framing system and completed building.

In 1972 historian Gilbert Herbert published an expansive paper in the *Journal of the Society of Architectural Historians* in which he unearthed the previously obscure history of the Manning Portable Colonial Cottage for Emigrants. Herbert detailed the story of a London carpenter by the name of H. Manning, who built a wood-frame house for his son who was emigrating to Australia. As British emigration to Australia ballooned in the following five years, H. Manning's portable cottage for his son, by unaccounted circumstances, became the prototype for what would become the first documented prefabricated house. An advertisement for "Portable Colonial Cottages" by H. Manning, appearing in the November 27, 1837, edition of the *South Australian Record*, provides the first record of the genesis of the Manning Portable Cottage Company; dozens of portable cottages were sent to Australia in the following years. The cottage consisted of grooved wooden posts embedded and bolted into a continuous floor plate carried on bearers. The posts carried a

wall plate with supported simple triangulated trusses. Various wood panels of standard size clad the frame. While many houses in Australia and other British colonies prior to 1833 had been built with materials shipped from Britain, the Manning Cottage appears to be the first house designed specifically for ease of travel and construction. Included in the shipment was a "small compass" for orientation purposes. Manning stated, "As none of the pieces are heavier than a man or boy could easily carry for several miles, it might be taken even to a distance without the aid of any beast of burthen." The lack of transportation infrastructure in Australia at this time makes this point particularly salient. The fabrication was to occur entirely in the carpenter's shop, requiring no site work apart from the construction of a simple foundation. No joints, cutting, or even nailing were necessary. According to Manning, "whoever can use a common bed-wrench can put this cottage up." Manning's constructive techniques presage prefabrication before there was even

such a word, conceptualizing a rigorous dimensional standardization and coordination: "Every part of it being made exactly of the same dimensions, that is, all the panels, posts and plates, being respectively of the same length, breadth and thickness, no mistake or loss of time can occur in putting them together." The cottage became a commercial success, and Manning developed several models of varying size and cost, testifying to the fact that the houses were provisioned for clients across a range of incomes and to the notion that the prefabricated house could be a measure of status in the colonial setting.

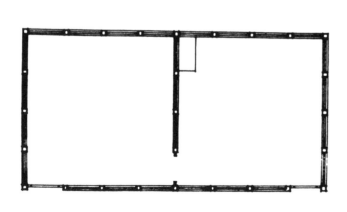

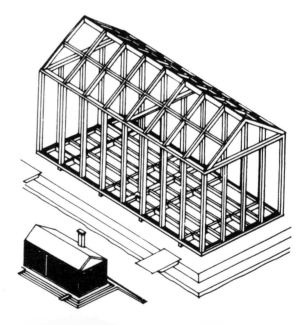

LEFT Axonometric diagram.
RIGHT Erection of large balloon frame structure.

041

BALLOON FRAME
ATTRIBUTED TO AUGUSTINE TAYLOR

The balloon frame method of wood construction is arguably the first incarnation of a prefabricated construction system since it regularized the production of houses into a palette of ready-made units that could be assembled in various configurations rapidly and affordably. The balloon frame is often considered one of the first thoroughly American forms of serial architectural production. It abandoned all lingering traces of European influence, celebrated the abundance of timber in the United States, and abandoned more expensive and labor-intensive materials that were not readily available in North America. Wood construction methods transposed to the United States from Europe had been characterized by elaborate joineries requiring skilled craftsmen largely unavailable in the New World.

The method is primarily attributed to the Chicago builder Augustine Taylor, who developed the system in response to the city's housing shortage. The system eliminated mortised beams and fittings, replacing them with two-by-fours and two-by-sixes set close to one another in increments of approximately one foot spaced horizontally. Studs and cross members were inserted in various configurations and could be increased or decreased in number depending on the anticipated structural integrity needed for the project. Wooden sheathing would subsequently be placed over the frame. Most importantly, the members were held together with manufactured cut iron nails, similar to today's common steel nail. These allowed for the connection of wooden members with greater ease and efficiency over crafted joineries. The entire wall unit could be delivered to a site and simply tilted upright, allowing house construction to occur in a matter of days.

Carpenters who suspected the apparent flimsiness of such a construction system dubbed it "balloon frame," believing it would blow away. The system, however, proved sufficiently strong to withstand tornadoes and other inclement weather with great stability. St. Mary's Church, built in 1833 in Fort Dearborn, Illinois, is believed to be Taylor's earliest use of balloon frame construction. Taylor's system quickly swept the building industry of Chicago and other burgeoning American cities in the Midwest and Florida, where it remains particularly evident today. The system has been infinitely reproduced, altered, and tweaked and remains one of the most common systems for house construction in the United States as well as other countries and regions with abundant timber resources such as Canada and Scandinavia.

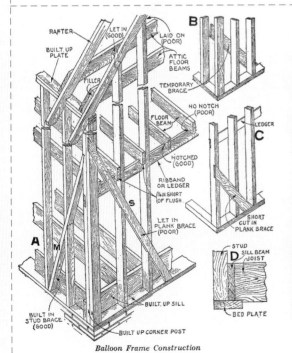

Balloon Frame Construction

SINGLE POUR CONCRETE SYSTEM

THOMAS EDISON

Thomas Edison is rarely thought of as an architect. His astounding roster of inventions tends to overshadow a lesser-known passion of his: cement and concrete. Edison's fascination with cement and concrete began as he was inventing new and improved rotary kilns in 1902. The immense success of both Edison's rotary and long kilns spawned his own cement production factory, known as Portland Cement Works, in New Village, New Jersey. Parallel improvements in crushing and grinding equipment also influenced the rapid increase in production of cement at the turn of the century. While concrete became even more common in commercial and industrial architecture, Edison is one of the first designers to imagine that the material could be used to construct an entire house repeatedly, without a single secondary building material, a system in which even the bathtub and an optional piano would be seamlessly integrated into the global structure.

By this time Edison had already established his reputation as the leading patent holder in the United States, so it is not unusual that his approach to constructing a house would follow in the inventive tradition of patenting replicable objects. Consequently, Edison designed a system that he would later call the "Single Pour Concrete System," in which a series of balloon-frame molds would be brought to the construction site to compose one continuous mold that formed walls and floors alike with designated voids for windows and doors. This scheme is perfectly illustrated in Edison's official patent drawing submission. When the mold was complete a specially designed rotating kiln on wheels with a hydraulic vertical pump system would be brought to the site. The vehicle would then feed the wet concrete mix through a funnel-like opening at the top of the mold, and the mix would slowly settle to the bottom. The pourers would allow the mix to cure in increments of some four feet, lending the finished house a somewhat striated appearance. Edison first experimented with the process on a model, which became affectionately known as the "chicken coop," in his studio. With funding from the wealthy New Jersey manufacturer Charles Ingersoll, Edison built about one hundred houses in and around Union, New Jersey, in 1917; some are still standing.

Edison frequently claimed he was not driven by the search for profit. Instead, he envisioned a system that could harness the increased availability of concrete to address the housing shortage in and around New York City quickly and affordably. Edison himself was from a humble background and paid several visits to the tenements on Manhattan's Lower East Side, reflecting on ways to improve quality of life. The single pour house benefited from certain material advantages, like cleanability, resistance to insects and rotting, and high structural stability in the face of storms. However, the challenge of maintaining a requisite homogeneous mix through each layer proved nearly impossible for Edison and his team and led to severe cracking in many of the houses. The houses had persistent problems in the following years, yet the ultimate demise of the scheme was more likely due to the limited interest of clients. Few people seemed prepared to live in an all-concrete house as it was so completely alien to traditional house construction. Ultimately, Edison's concrete company was disbanded in 1942.

Yet not long after Edison constructed his houses in New Jersey, precast and prestressed concrete became increasingly commonplace, reinvigorating the relationship between the concrete and housing industries. Edison's approach, however, remains as novel an application of concrete today as it did when it was first conceived one hundred years ago and stands as a seminal example of how pioneers outside the profession of architecture contributed highly imaginative proposals to the development of the prefabricated house in the twentieth century.

1,326,854.

Patented Dec. 30, 1919.

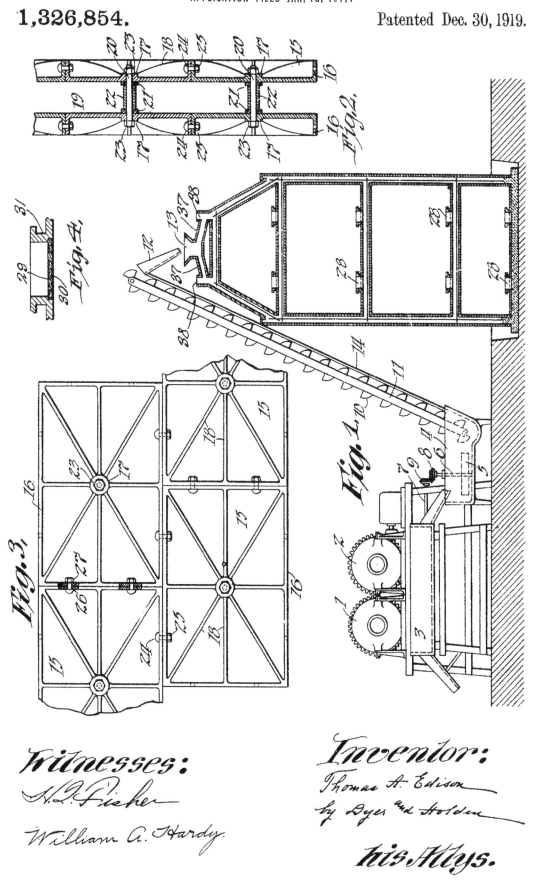

OPPOSITE Patent drawing.
BELOW Construction photo, single pour concrete system.
Philipsburg, New Jersey.

BELOW Single pour concrete houses. Phillipsburg, New Jersey.

SEARS CATALOGUE HOMES
SEARS, ROEBUCK AND COMPANY

For nearly thirty-two years, Sears, Roebuck and Company of Chicago was the most prolific designer and manufacturer of prefabricated housing anywhere in the world. Between 1908 and 1940 the company sold over 100,000 homes through their "Modern Homes" mail-order catalogue. A small army of staff designers created some 447 different models that were rendered for the annual sales catalogue, which promised door-to-door delivery and assembly of every single element of the house. The models ranged from simple one-room structures to elaborate multifamily, multistory units. Even at the time of production, Sears made absolutely no claim that the variety of home designs they were churning out was remotely innovative. Instead, the company emphasized the ability to track market trends in popular home design, affording the client the added benefit of customizing numerous aspects of each house, including hardware and appliances, certain finishes, the ability to mirror an existing floor plan, and even furnishing sets. In fact, Sears would eventually develop an arm of their homebuilding enterprise to include the capacity to process blueprints drawn entirely by unskilled or semiskilled customers, functioning as a clearinghouse to render the rough designs architecturally sound, and sending the customer the raw building materials and an assembly manual in just a matter of months. Furthering the streamlined system, Sears even secured financing and administered mortgages. Although most clients were motivated to order a Sears home purely for its affordability, Sears found enough diversity in their clientele to offer three tiers of home lines whose costs were commensurate with their relative quality: Honor-Bilt, Standard Built, and Simplex Sectional.

Almost all Sears models used the balloon frame technique, bringing the method even greater familiarity across the United States. Sears homes are also notable for pioneering the use of drywall and asphalt shingles and for introducing central heating for residential use. The constructive techniques were largely disguised behind veneers that would hide any trace of how the house was truly built. In a sense, this illuminates a bias against prefabricated building technology and its constructive aesthetic. Despite the fact that the Sears homes were produced en masse, systematically, efficiently, and affordably, the designers and customers alike self-consciously made every effort to bury these qualities underneath an artificial veil of handcraftedness that was remarkably easy to spot. Regardless of the infamy among architecture circles earned by Sears homes, their development as an approach to building is an undeniably epoch-making event that had immense significance to the history of the prefabricated house as well as architectural history in general.

MODERN HOME No. 146

- First Floor Plan -

- Second Floor Plan -

$1,660.00

For $1,660.00 we will furnish all the material to build this Seven-Room Residence, consisting of Lumber, Lath, Shingles, Mill Work, Ceiling, Siding, Flooring, Finishing Lumber, Buffet, Medicine Case, Building Paper, Pipe, Gutter, Sash Weights, Hardware and Painting Material. NO EXTRAS, as we guarantee enough material at the above price to build this house according to our plans.

By allowing a fair price for labor, cement, brick and plaster, which we do not furnish, this house can be built for about $3,960.00, including all material and labor.

For Our Offer of Free Plans See Page 3.

EXTRA large living room with paneled oak beam ceiling, rustic brick fireplace. The doors are veneered oak of the latest Craftsman design with oak trim to match. Large cased openings lead to the reception hall and the dining room. The dining room has paneled oak beam ceiling and modern buffet with seats at each side and large window seats along the windows of the exposed side. Large well lighted reception hall has a bay window and a window seat. This hall leads to an oak open stairway of modern pattern. The unique arrangement of the stairs enables one to reach the second floor from the kitchen or from the reception hall. The cellar stairs are placed directly under the main stairs. The pantry between the dining room and kitchen distinctly separates the kitchen from the rest of the house. A cased opening connects the pantry with the kitchen. The doors, staircase, window seats and interior trim of the first floor are finished in the best quality of oak with clear oak flooring in the reception hall, living room and dining room. The kitchen and pantry floors are made of the best grade of maple.

Note the well arranged second floor plan. Like the rest of the plan, every foot of space is utilized to the very best advantage. Three large airy bedrooms, each with large windows on two sides, giving plenty of light and ventilation, with closets adjoining. Plate glass mirror door in front bedroom. Even the small bedroom or servant's room has light and ventilation from two sides. The entire second floor has selected birch trim with birch six-cross panel doors to match. All flooring on the second floor is made of clear maple. Our architect in planning this house has planned on economy in heating, which can be plainly seen by this economical arrangement.

Clear cypress siding from water table to second story window sills; balance of second story and roof shingled with cedar shingles. Edge grain fir flooring 1⅛ inches thick for porch.

A large roomy veranda with massive stonekote columns. Ornamental Priscilla windows are specified for the attic. Colored leaded art glass over the buffet in the dining room. All windows and doors are of the very latest style.

Foundation is made of concrete block.

Excavated basement under the entire house, 7 feet high from floor to joists. First floor, 9 feet high from floor to ceiling; second floor, 8 feet high from floor to ceiling; attic room, 14x14 feet, 7 feet high from floor to collar beams. Gables and columns are sided with stonekote, the most modern style of construction.

This house can be built on a lot 46 feet wide.

Complete Warm Air Heating Plant, for soft coal, extra	$ 97.37
Complete Warm Air Heating Plant, for hard coal, extra	99.90
Complete Steam Heating Plant, extra	177.44
Complete Hot Water Heating Plant, extra	232.05
Complete Plumbing Outfit, extra	166.30

SEARS, ROEBUCK AND CO. **CHICAGO, ILLINOIS**

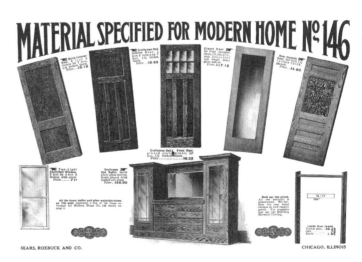

AMERICAN SYSTEM-BUILT HOUSES

FRANK LLOYD WRIGHT

OPPOSITE, FAR RIGHT Perspective, Variation 1.
OPPOSITE, TOP LEFT Perspective, Variation 2.
OPPOSITE, BOTTOM LEFT Perspective, Variation 3.

Just three years after Sears, Roebuck and Company began constructing catalogue homes in bulk, Frank Lloyd Wright designed a markedly different type of house, the "American System-Built Houses" (also known as the "American Ready-Cut System"). Whether Wright was reacting specifically to the cookie-cutter homes being churned out by Sears, and later by other department stores such as Montgomery Ward, remains unclear. But his approach differed in its quest to produce infinite variation rather than set models. He is one of the very first architects of note to tackle the issue of the factory-built house and to contemplate its immense potential in a time of rapid industrialization.

Wright teamed up with the Milwaukee-based construction firm Richards Company between 1911 and 1917, outlining in over nine hundred drawings a systematized housing array where the wood framing, cladding, floor joists, rafters, roofs, moldings, windows, and doors would all be cut precisely in the factory and required no on-site carpentry. The result was decreased construction time and labor costs, offering a fresh alternative to prefabricated houses on the market, none of which was blessed with a recognizable architectural name.

Wright transposed the uniquely American and self-styled prairie house into the blueprint for a housing system that could disseminate his unique architectural vision across the United States. What is so astonishing about the collection of drawings, now held at the Frank Lloyd Wright Foundation, is the fact that no two designs are alike. Wright explicitly indicated that it was the elements that were to be prefabricated, not the overall forms. In one sense, this begs the question of the client's role, a fact that is difficult to decipher because none was ever built. It remains unclear if Wright imagined that he would design a specific house for a specific client, simply keeping in mind a palette of prefabricated ingredients, or whether the sheer mass of drawings was intended to function as a menu of options from which to order directly from a supplier. Despite a marketing campaign, the house never caught the notice of private consumers and it was eventually abandoned as Wright turned his attention to more lucrative commissions. Regardless, the approach was entirely novel and portends a fascination with mass customization that would emerge in Wright's work many years later.

OPPOSITE Patent drawing, 1914.

MAISON DOM-INO
LE CORBUSIER

Developed as war erupted in Europe, Le Corbusier's seminal patent drawing for the reproducible Maison Dom-ino is the summation of the major concepts he developed with the Swiss engineer Max Du Bois that would inform his architectural ideology throughout the 1920s in addition to functioning as the structural basis of the majority of houses he would design until 1935. The structure reinterprets the Hennebique frame—designed by the French engineer François Hennebique in the latter half of the nineteenth century as a generic frame system for houses in which the iron frame was covered with a thick layer of concrete for fireproofing. It uses the structural skeleton as a canvas upon which, as Kenneth Frampton describes it in *Modern Architecture: A Critical History* (1992), "an author can impose stylistic elements." It was one of the first examples within Le Corbusier's oeuvre where he employed regulating lines, a fact which can be seen in the many study drawings produced for the final drawing. The stringent adherence to regulating geometries recalls Palladian designs and other classical devices that seek to "maintain proportional control over the facade." However, Le Corbusier sought to imbue the classical notions of proportionality and harmony with modern-day industrial potential. Later, in *Toward an Architecture* (1923) he would write, "If we eliminate from our hearts and minds all dead concepts in regard to houses and look at the question from a critical and objective point of view, we shall arrive at the 'House Machine,' the mass production house, healthy (and morally so too) and beautiful in the same way that the working tools and instruments which accompany our existence are beautiful." Here Le Corbusier forms a singular expression reconciling classical architectural principles and modern industry.

The prototype itself is open to a vast array of interpretations. Its play on the word *domino* is an amalgamation of the words *domus* and *industry*, denoting the house as a patently standard unit. More importantly it is the visual summation of a project that was never meant to be built but rather anticipates the architect's Five Points, an architectural doctrine that he would articulate more than a decade later in written form. All five of these points were latent in this simple frame: 1) the *pilotis* elevating the mass off the ground; 2) the free plan, achieved through the separation of load-bearing columns from the walls that subdivide the space; 3) the facade, or elevation, is the equally free vertical corollary of the plan, allowing for, 4) the long horizontal ribbon window; 5) culminating in the roof garden, which recovers the area covered by the volume at ground level. As a self-supporting building form only subsequently spatially divided and enclosed, the Dom-ino is comparable to the balloon frame. Like Taylor's invention, Le Corbusier patented a "proto-architecture" that was the point of departure for his own Purist architecture, which he celebrated as deployable in equal measure by other architects. The architect also authored several drawings that imagined potential groupings of the Maison Dom-ino.

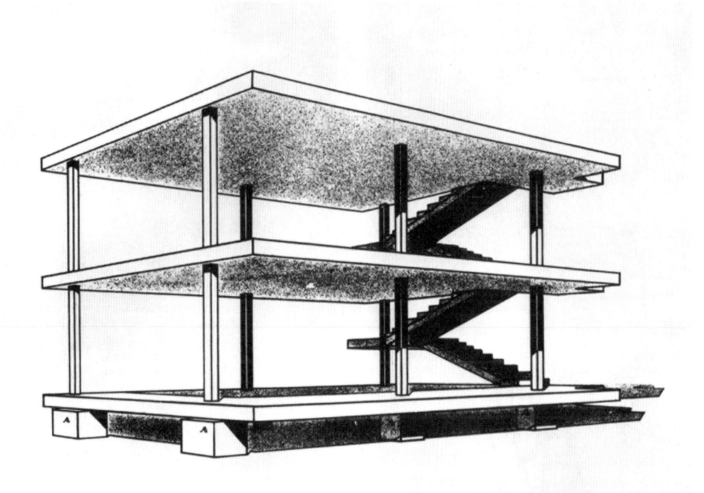

MONOLYTHE—OSSATVRE DE BETON ARMÉ
COVLÉE SANS COFFRAGE
SVR SER POINTS D'APPVI FOVRNIS A.

ERECTOR SET

A. C. GILBERT

The Erector Set is a collection of small-scale metal beams, nuts, bolts, screws, pulleys, gears, flanges, and small electric motors that was the most popular American toy construction set throughout the United States in the twentieth century. Designed in 1911 by A. C. Gilbert and manufactured by his eponymous company, the Erector Set has been produced in a countless variety of kits, typically producing a specific type of structure, in any number of different scales. Unlike LEGO or other modular building toys, the Erector Set is not mimetic of modular construction but rather comprises prefabricated unique parts that come together in a prescriptive fashion. The Erector Set kits most often constructed are scale models of bridges and skyscrapers; however, other kits include formulated homes of a distinctly different nature than their modular toy counterparts such as Lincoln Logs and LEGO.

ABOVE Box cover, 1911.
TOP RIGHT "Landmarks of the World" special edition set fully assembled.
RIGHT Advertisement, 1943.

LINCOLN LOGS (VERSION 1)

JOHN LLOYD WRIGHT

The perennially popular Lincoln Logs were the invention of Frank Lloyd Wright's son, John Lloyd Wright. Regardless of the designer's pedigree, Lincoln Logs are among the most inventive among a myriad of architectural toys developed parallel to prefabricated housing research in the twentieth century. Consisting of notched miniature logs approximately three quarters of an inch in diameter and varying in lengths, the system is analogous to the systematic ways that American log cabins were built. The name is, in all likelihood, derived from the popular association of the log cabin with Abraham Lincoln as well as the possible double entendre of the term "link in," which describes the way in which the logs fit together to create a larger architectural unit. Some argue that the method of interlocking architectural units so celebrated in the system is reminiscent of Frank Lloyd Wright's design for the basement of the Imperial Hotel in Tokyo, where similarly interlocking beams rendered the structure earthquake resistant. John Lloyd Wright's Lincoln Logs make a convincing case that the vernacular log cabin is indeed a system born of a prefabricated way of thinking and making.

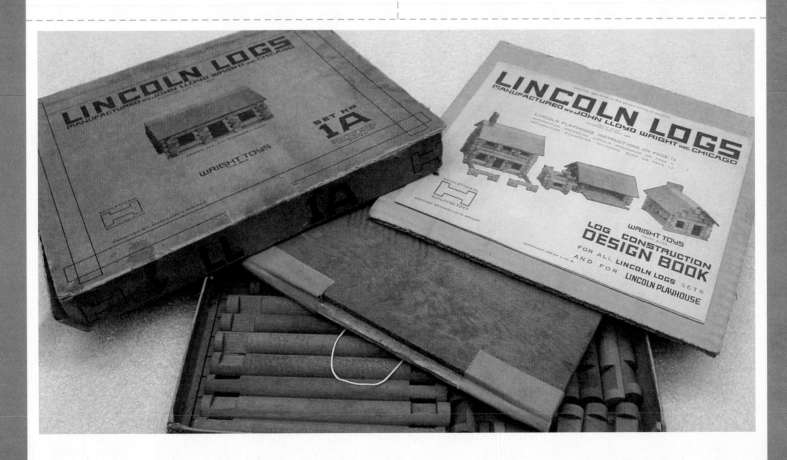

BAUKASTEN
WALTER GROPIUS AND ADOLF MEYER

The seeds of the fascination with prefabrication within the Bauhaus began in unrealized projects conceived during the Weimar years. In 1922 Walter Gropius established an "estate co-operative" that Fred Forbat, a young Hungarian architect, was charged with developing. Between 1922 and 1923, Gropius and Adolf Meyer would develop a system, called Baukasten ("building blocks"), of standard, industrially produced building elements that could function as a variable kit of parts, interlocking to form a near infinite array of configurations. Gropius and Meyer envisioned that architects would guide the client through the system employing a scale model to illustrate possible configurations. Gropius himself described the system as "an oversized set of toy building blocks out of which, depending on the number of inhabitants and their needs, different types of machines for living can be assembled." The material palette included wood, steel, and glass and had the potential to align and combine materials in unexpected, original ways.

Although never built, these prototypical designs served as the point of departure for several of the concrete-panel, industrially produced housing blocks built once the Bauhaus had moved to the industrial city of Dessau a few years later. These marked the Bauhaus's turn toward a philosophy of rationalization to achieve a new unity of art and industry. In 1926, Georg Muche and Richard Paulick designed a steel prefabricated house for the Dessau-Törten housing development that was being overseen by Gropius. In 1927 Marcel Breuer designed two separate steel-framed prefabricated houses, called Bambos I and Bambos II, designed for the younger Bauhaus masters but never built.

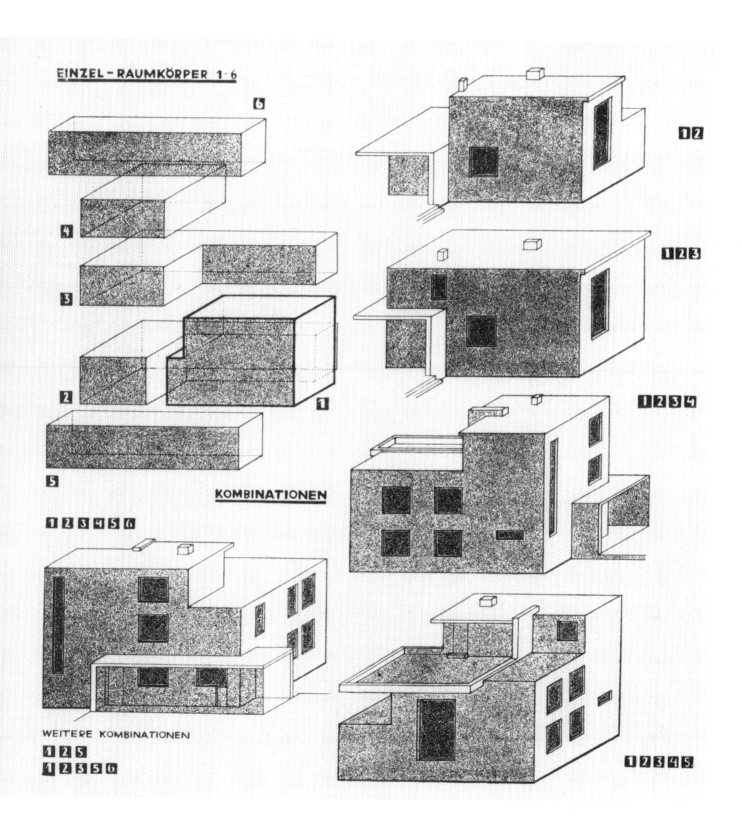

EINZEL-RAUMKÖRPER 1-6

6

4

3

2

1

5

12

123

1234

KOMBINATIONEN

123456

12345

WEITERE KOMBINATIONEN

125

12356

1927

DYMAXION HOUSE
R. BUCKMINSTER FULLER

R. Buckminster Fuller's Dymaxion House remains one of the most critical projects not only on prefabricated housing but on industry and architecture in general. Along with his geodesic dome, the Dymaxion stands as the iconic "Bucky" project, encapsulating a cosmos of far-reaching economic, political, scientific, and architectural theories. Fuller, who, like Thomas Edison, is more commonly viewed as an inventor than an architect, began his research on the Dymaxion in 1927, seeking to ameliorate what he perceived as a myriad of failures in current homebuilding techniques. First and foremost, Fuller believed that a good house could be produced as systematically as a good car, and that a factory-made house had the potential to change the way in which peoples across the globe lived. While mass-produced kit houses were scarcely new in 1927, factory-made houses that openly celebrated their means of production were. Fuller envisioned a material palette identical to that of the car, and placed paramount importance on ease of shipment and assembly. Homebuilding was no longer to be the work of architects or builders, but rather the work of machines and an ever-industrializing global economy.

While systematization was at the core of Fuller's objectives, so too was a subsequent autonomy from industry and infrastructure. In both built prototypes Fuller adopted or designed mechanical systems that vastly reduced resource use. Fuller's concern with efficient design anticipates the sustainability movement by decades; he sought to demonstrate that autonomous ways of life in an industrialized society were not only theoretically viable but also practical and attractive. These conceptual underpinnings determine every formal aspect of the project.

Fuller's first such formal stroke in the design of the Dymaxion was its low-slung dome roof, which was inspired by vernacular tropes, such as grain silos in Siberia and yurts in Central Asia. These provided ample evidence of natural ways to maintain cool temperatures through a vertical heat-driven vortex that would suck cooler air downward into the dome if it was properly ventilated with a single overhead vent as well as with peripheral vents. The roof was hung from a central vertical stainless-steel strut, set on a single foundation with radial beams that supported the floor. Wedge-shaped fans of aluminum sheet metal formed the roof, ceiling, and floor. Each structure was assembled at ground level and then winched up the strut. Each element was discrete and consequently easily fabricated, packaged, and shipped.

Of particular note were the bathroom and wet unit, which greatly reduced water use by means of a "packaging toilet," "fogger" showerhead, gray water system, and efficient horizontally agitated laundry system. One could bathe with less than one cup of water per day. Fuller went on to patent a stand-alone version of the bathroom system in 1938, which consisted of a continuous metallic drop-in unit that could supplant the fixtures of porcelain bathrooms and introduce a level of industrial-grade hygiene into any home. A plastic replica of the bathroom was commercially available intermittently until the 1980s. A vacuum turbine provided electric power.

The two Dymaxion houses that were prototyped—the "Barwise" House and the "Danbury" House—would never be inhabited. However, they were purchased by investor William Graham after the venture failed. In 1948 Graham constructed a third hybridized version of the Dymaxion House for his family, who continued to live there into the 1970s. This house, along with its component prototyping parts, was donated by the Graham family in 1991 to the Henry Ford Museum, where it was painstakingly reconstituted to its initial design and remains on exhibit today.

Why the Dymaxion never went into production is a subject of continuing debate. The inflexibility of the system to adapt to households of varying sizes, programs, and economic means is often cited, as is the disregard for site-specificity and any contextual architectural idiom, not to mention a general fear of modernist forms for houses. Fuller, however, would not be crestfallen, as he transferred his research after World War II to the Wichita House, a project that would continue to develop the technological concepts of the Dymaxion House.

BELOW LEFT Elevation, axonometric section, and plan composite.
BELOW RIGHT Watercolor elevation, axonometric, and plan composite.
OPPOSITE, TOP LEFT Deck tensioning pattern.
OPPOSITE, BOTTOM LEFT Plan, illustrating geometries and regions.
OPPOSITE, RIGHT Conceptual sketch.

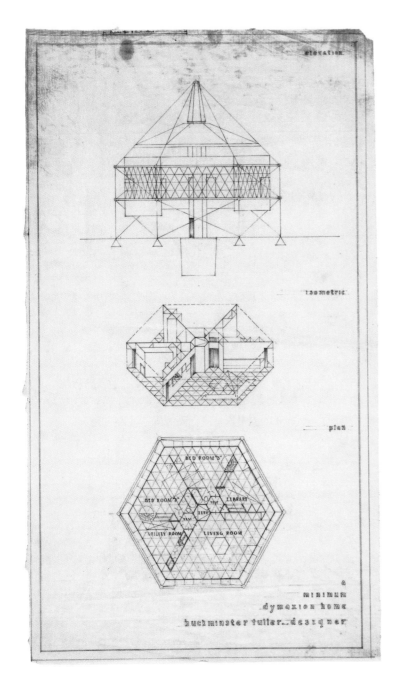

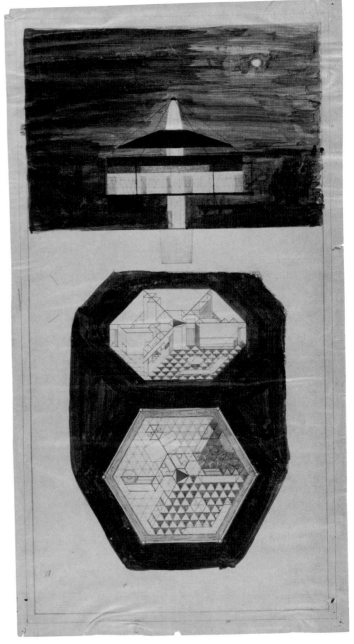

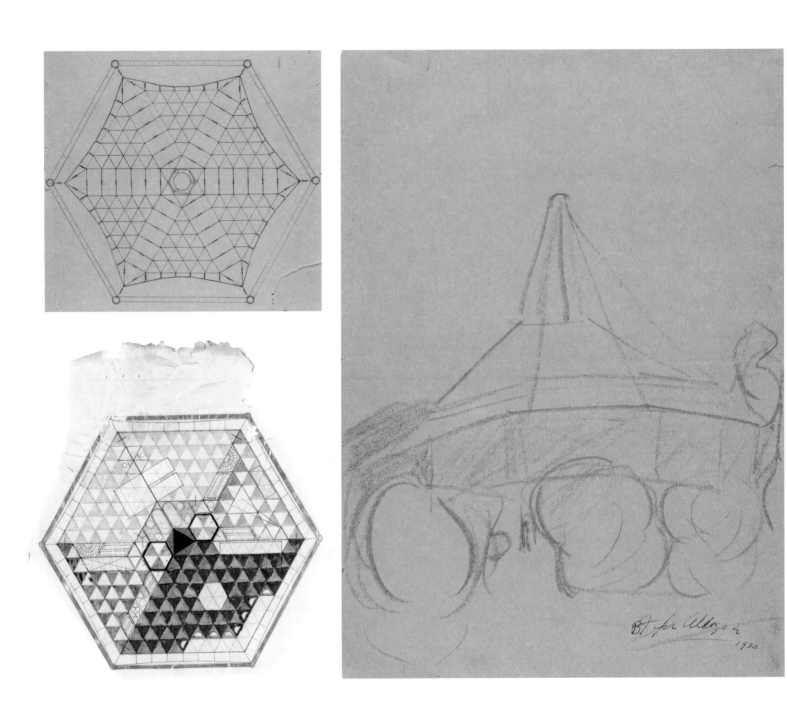

COPPER HOUSES
WALTER GROPIUS ET AL.

OPPOSITE, TOP Model.
OPPOSITE, BOTTOM Plans of variations.

Haifa, in northern Israel. On a slope of Mount Carmel stands a multistory, dark-green structure, its entire exterior faced with copper. Built in the mid-1930s, it once served as a pension for Jewish refugees from Germany. Today it houses four families that only recently emigrated from Russia.

In Eberswalde, a city 70 kilometers northeast of Berlin, there are also greenish black houses made of copper. In one of them live Sabrina and her boyfriend, Steve, both unemployed. Their house was built according to designs by Walter Gropius in 1932. They find the interior perfectly nice but would prefer to tear it down because it's so ugly on the outside. They have no idea why it is a protected monument.

What do these houses have to do with each other, and what story do they have to tell?

Due to the housing crisis in Germany during the 1920s, the Eberswalde-based firm Aron Hirsch and Son, a global player in the copper and brass industry, became interested in the business of mass-produced housing. It acquired a patent for transportable, insulated metal walls, developed by the architects Friedrich Förster and Robert Krafft, and set up a special division to manufacture prefabricated copper houses. Various types of houses were designed. Their exterior walls and roofs were made of copper, insulation was provided by aluminum foil and asbestos roofing paper, and the framing was of wood. Their interior walls were sheet metal ornamented with intricate patterns. The whole structure consisted of prefabricated, easily transportable elements, which could be assembled within twenty-four hours on site. In 1931 a small model subdivision was erected not far from the factory in Eberswalde. The houses, technologically quite modern but aesthetically eclectic, were given flowery names: "Copper Castle," "Source of Life," "Spring Reverie," "Jewel," "Sunshine," "Fairy Tale in Copper," and "May Morning." At the 1931 Colonial Exhibition in Paris the six copper houses Hirsch displayed were awarded a Grand Prize.

In the same year Walter Gropius was hired to refine the existing models. In 1932 he presented two of the prototypes he had developed at the Second German Building Exposition, held on the Berlin fairgrounds and displaying the slogan "Sun, Air, and Housing for All!" Boasting that with regard to "technology and organization" he had helped to make the Copper House eminently marketable, Gropius claimed credit for several improvements, including "corrugated sheet-copper for the outer walls, aluminum instead of steel for the inner, a simpler corner joint and an altered appearance." Gropius, who by then was signing himself as director of the copper house division, sought to contact possible investors and customers both within Germany and abroad. He envisioned large housing projects with as many as fifty to two hundred copper houses. Various domestic firms were interested, as well as developers and planners in the United States and the Soviet Union. But in 1932 the Hirsch company went bankrupt. When René Schwarz, Aron Hirsch's son-in-law, then set up the copper house division as an independent undertaking he ended the collaboration with Gropius and concentrated on marketing the villa-style models "Favorite" and "Copper Pride." The sales pitch emphasized the speed with which the houses could be erected rather than their modest price: theoretically they could be assembled in only twenty-four hours.

Then in January 1933 the National Socialists came to power, and suddenly a new market for the copper houses arose: Jewish émigrés to Palestine. Beginning in March 1933, the company placed advertisements in the *Jüdische Rundschau*, the Zionist Federation's weekly newspaper. They touted the company's products as offering "first-class privacy, hygienic living, [and] superb investment" and urged readers to "buy copper houses for Palestine." In August 1933 the company put out a special catalogue, with models designed specifically for the Palestine market, called "Haifa," "Jerusalem," "Tel Aviv," and "Sharon." The largest model, with a living space of 2,800 square feet, was called "Lebanon." Soon a branch of the German Copper House Company was opened in Haifa. At least fourteen houses found their way to the British Mandate of Palestine, but the copper houses did not catch on any more than did other types of economic dwellings.

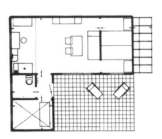

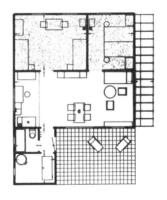

ALL KUPFERHAUS

DAS IDEALE EINFAMILIENHAUS

HIRSCH KUPFER- & MESSINGWERKE A.-G. BERLIN

HARDENBERGSTR. 43 / FERNSPR.: SAMMEL-NR. C1 STEINPLATZ 8091 / FÜR FERNVERKEHR: SAMMEL-NR. C1 STEINPLATZ 4536

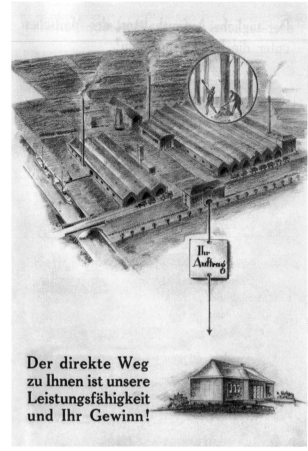

Ihr Auftrag

Der direkte Weg
zu Ihnen ist unsere
Leistungsfähigkeit
und Ihr Gewinn!

Höhenschnitt eines zweigeschossigen „Allkupferhauses"

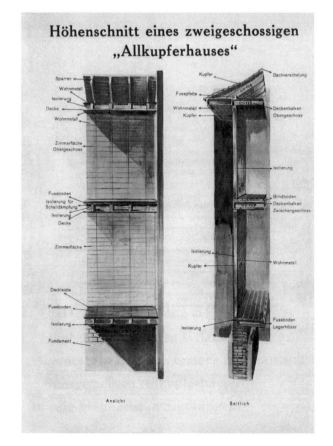

Ansicht

Seitlich

Farbenmuster für unsere Innenwände

MANDELBRAUN · KORALLENROT · BEIGE ROSÉ

RESEDAGRÜN · NILGRÜN · ELFENBEIN

BERGBLAU · PASTELLBLAU · BEIGE

E I N I G E   B E I S P I E L E

Reliefmuster für die Innenwände

DIAGONAL · ENGLISCH · JAPANISCH

OBLONG · KACHELMUSTER · DECKENMUSTER

When the National Socialists began to rearm, copper came to be in short supply, and its export was forbidden. It is said that the last copper house delivered was immediately melted down on arrival in Tel Aviv, the value of the copper being greater than the cost of the house. The further history of the German Copper House Company remains somewhat vague.

Copper houses erected in Germany were also threatened by Germany's war of expansion and annihilation. In 1942 all homeowners were required to notify the authorities of any structural elements made of copper. In some cases the copper was removed and turned over to the armament industry. Other owners, unwilling to sacrifice their homes for the sake of "total war looting," disguised their copper houses by painting them white.

Today, few people know the story of the copper houses. Since 1984, when Gilbert Herbert wrote *The Dream of the Factory-Made House*, no major study has been published. Herbert himself never saw the copper houses in what was then East Germany. Inasmuch as the copper houses are relatively unspectacular structures in terms of aesthetics, they have as yet found little notice in standard histories of architecture. This may be in part because although technologically advanced, they are conservative in design and by no means fulfill the claim to the "unity of art and technology" advocated by Gropius. They have nothing to do with the radiant, white modernism of such World Heritage sites as the Bauhaus in Dessau or the White City of Tel Aviv. On the contrary, they are almost black. They are architectural documents of German and Israeli history. Recorded in the copper houses are stories of the expulsion and annihilation of German Jews, of the barbarity of modern times, but also of the salvation of the *Alijah*. It is precisely this ambiguity that constitutes their special value.

—Friedrich von Borries and Jens Uwe Fischer

BELOW LEFT AND RIGHT Construction photos
of the Copper Houses at the Second German Building
Exposition, 1932.
BOTTOM LEFT Interior view.
BOTTOM RIGHT Exterior view

LEGO

OLE KIRK CHRISTIANSEN

LEGO, the ubiquitous modular construction building block for children, is among a handful of architectural toys that represent in microcosm full-scale prefabricated building technologies. Invented by a Danish carpenter, Ole Kirk Christiansen, in 1932, LEGO was initially manufactured in wood. Expanded to plastic in 1947, it took on the form we are familiar with today. Originally named the "Automatic Binding Brick," the traditional LEGO block is constructed as a hollow box with a series of round studs centered on an 8-millimeter grid. The studs on one block lock into holes of a reciprocal dimension on the bottom of another LEGO block. A collection of just eight 2-by-4 bricks of the limited palette of five colors can produce over eight trillion configurations. Numerous architects have been inspired by LEGO and its amazing array of constructive possibilities, including contemporary practitioners such as Bjarke Ingels and Kengo Kuma. LEGO is part of The Museum of Modern Art's permanent collection.

BELOW LEGO set.

KECK CRYSTAL HOUSE

GEORGE FRED KECK

The 1933 Century of Progress Exposition capitalized upon Chicago's reputation as the most architecturally progressive city in the United States by committing a very large portion of the mammoth exposition to contemporary architecture. A handful of architects and manufacturers was charged with designing housing prototypes that would conceptualize ways in which new technologies could change the housing industry, particularly of the prefabricated variety. The most audacious of the houses, all built at full scale, was George Fred Keck's Crystal House. Keck had a keen interest in the burgeoning International Style, which had been identified and promoted in an exhibition and book produced a year earlier by Henry-Russell Hitchcock and Philip Johnson at The Museum of Modern Art. The house both reflected this interest and arguably canonized a distinctly new housing type: the glass house. Equipped with a four-point manifesto, Keck defines not only a formal typology but also many architectural issues that were completely new. The first point discusses the open plan in relation to cost effectiveness; the second references the house as the servicer to its inhabitant, not vice versa; the third focuses on the importance to one's health of passive heating and the modulation of natural light; the final point outlines the need to design within the boundaries of mass production without relinquishing the "opportunity for individual expression" tastefully and affordably.

Completely glazed on all sides, the house's three levels were supported by an exterior prefabricated steel truss frame that allowed for a completely open interior plan. All glass panels and mullions were of standardized sizes, a provision that, despite the fact that the house was built as a one-off, implied future potential for prefabricated manufacturing and assembly. Keck described the house as one of a number of "laboratory houses [that] were designed not primarily to be different or tricky but to attempt seriously to determine whether better ideas and designs for living could be found." He went on to comment, "probably the most important function of the Crystal House was to determine how a great number of the people attending the exposition would react to ideas that entirely upset conventional ideas of a house." While the house did succeed on that level, it was not a commercial success and was never replicated. Nevertheless, the house's influence on architects generations later remains palpable. The house was one of five from the exhibition that were relocated to the residential enclave of Beverly Shores, Indiana, where it still stands.

GOOD HOUSEKEEPING STRAN-STEEL HOUSE

H. AUGUST O'DELL AND WIRT C. ROWLAND, ARCHITECTS

Good Housekeeping magazine combined forces with the Stran-Steel Corporation and the Detroit-based architectural partnership of H. August O'Dell and Wirt C. Rowland to fabricate one of the more innovative houses presented at the Chicago Century of Progress Exposition's *Houses of Tomorrow* display in 1933. The partnership cleverly married three parties with complementary functions: O'Dell and Rowland would provide the design, Stran-Steel would provide raw materials and fabrication techniques that would largely inspire the design strategy, and *Good Housekeeping* would lend its reputation as a modern lifestyle trendsetter. Collectively they would fashion a house that would appeal to clients interested in a self-styled and experimental prefabricated modern dwelling, a steel-framed, two-story boxlike volume with smaller volumes flanking either side, the upper level in the middle section being entirely dedicated to a large recreation room. The 1,300-square-foot house sold for a mere $7,500 (about $110,000 in 2008) and was one of the few houses from the exposition later replicated for fabrication. The baked iron enamel modular panels cladding the steel skeleton were until this date entirely unknown to the realm of housing, being more traditionally associated with domestic fixtures like bathtubs and kitchen appliances. The steel frame consisted of newly designed steel beams developed by Stran-Steel. These were the first such beams to have greater flexibility than wood beams while also being lighter and stronger, each beam connecting to the other by interlocking joints rather than on-site welding, which would have increased cost and assembly time. A specially designed nail penetrated the girders and held both the wallboard and exterior enamel panels in place. The house, as proved over the exposition's duration, was highly weather resistant and entirely fireproof. With rounded corners and exterior frieze, the house was more akin stylistically to its Art Deco contemporaries than to the majority of exhibition houses in line with the International Style. Despite its stylistic connection to Art Deco, the material palette of the project was strictly industrial. Along with the Keck Crystal House and three others, the original exhibition house was relocated to Beverly Shores, Indiana, where it can still be seen.

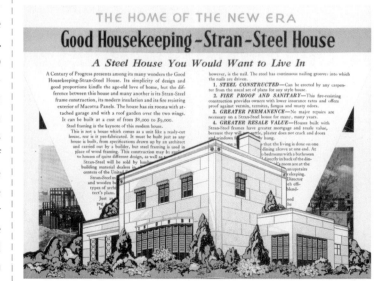

JACOBS HOUSE
FRANK LLOYD WRIGHT

The Jacobs House is the most idiosyncratic yet successful example of a series of more than fifty small homes that Wright designed in the latter part of his career, collectively known as the Usonian houses. More a concept than a category, the houses represent a major epoch of Wright's career where, riding high on the critical success of Fallingwater and the Johnson Wax Building, the architect made a deliberate decision to shift his focus back to one of his earliest preoccupations: affordable housing. For Wright, the affordable house in America had been constantly disappointing, rarely embodying the imagination and inspiration that good architecture, regardless of cost, could afford. Wright had proven, time and again, his expertise on large-budget homes, but the modest budget market had proven more impenetrable. From a set of drawings for affordable homes published for *Ladies' Home Journal* in 1901 to the dozens of designs employing his "American System-Built Houses," Wright's modest houses had received less fanfare.

Wright designed the Jacobs House in Madison, Wisconsin, for journalist Herbert Jacobs, his wife, and their young daughter in 1936. It is considered both the catalyst for and pinnacle of the Usonian period of Wright's career, bringing to the fore both design and construction parameters that would characterize all future Usonian houses. After citing the project's cost of $5,500 (about $80,000 in 2008), Wright told *Architectural Forum* in 1938: "Mr. and Mrs. Jacobs must see themselves in somewhat simplified terms. What are the essentials in their case, a typical case? It is not necessary only to get rid of unnecessary complications in construction, necessary to use work in the mill to good advantage (off-site prefabrication) . . . At least this must be our

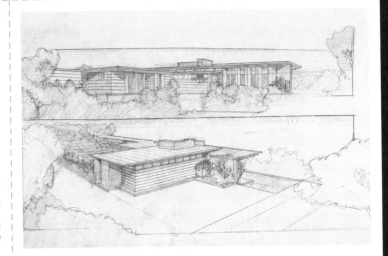

economy if we are to achieve the sense of spaciousness and vista we desire in order to liberate the people living in the house . . . it would be ideal to complete the building in one operation as it goes along, inside and out." Consisting of a single story laid out in an L-shaped plan embracing a private yard, the house achieved these goals through three primary innovations, which would be employed in all subsequent Usonian homes: "board and batten" walls, a planning grid, and a new underfloor heating technology. With the exception of a select few points of masonry, load bearing columns, and walls, the entire building envelope consisted of modular sandwich panels and glazing that was prefabricated off-site and applied to both the exterior and interior, improving upon the "System-Built" by eliminating the need for stucco

and applied decoration. The planning scheme consisted of a 2-by-4-foot rectangular grid that served as the basis for all modular elements both in plan and elevation. Wright's ingenious "floormat" system circulated steam between the flooring and the ground plane or the basement, eliminating the need for radiators and greatly reducing utility costs, setting a significant precedent for centralized HVAC systems.

The name "Usonian" refers to a term coined by American writer James Duff Law and attempts to describe a particular "New World" character of the American landscape, devoid of influence from any previous architectural idiom. While Wright would go on to build numerous other notable Usonians, the Jacobs House remains the most significant, not only for being the first, but also for being one of the most durable and least expensive.

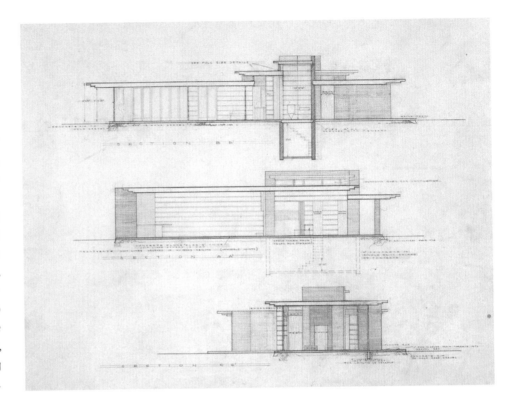

QUONSET HUT
OTTO BRANDENBERGER FOR THE
GEORGE A. FULLER COMPANY

The Quonset hut is perhaps the most ubiquitous prefabricated structure born out of a period of war. More an evolution of another wartime typology—the British-built Nissen hut of World War I—than an architectural innovation, the Quonset hut was first built at Quonset Point, Rhode Island, one of many naval bases established by the Allied forces during World War II. The U.S. military enlisted the services of the George A. Fuller Company, one of the largest construction contractors in the United States and builders of such iconic projects as the Flatiron Building in New York and the Lincoln Memorial, to design a simple, repeatable, and inexpensive structure that could be deployed as housing across naval bases on the Atlantic seaboard and the Pacific rim. Otto Brandenberger, the only architect on staff at Fuller, led the project.

The original design, known as the T-Rib Quonset hut, was a 16-by-36-foot semicylindrical structure with an 8-foot radius, framed with steel members and sided with corrugated steel sheets. The ends of the structure were capped with preassembled plywood faces punctured with openings for a door and windows. The interior contained insulation that was installed on-site, pressed wood lining, a tongue-and-groove floor, and crude overhead lighting running along the central spine of the ceiling. The structure cost approximately $800 ($12,000 in 2008) to build. While exceptionally affordable, the living conditions were tight and dark, and thus the Quonset hut garnered something of a dubious reputation among the general public.

By war's end, variants on the original T-Rib model were to be found all over the coastal United States. Today, Quonset huts are more frequently used as private dwellings, and adaptations have made them signifi-

No. 1655   Seabees Erect A Quonset Hut At Camp Endicott, R. I.   *Official U. S. Navy Photo*

cantly cheerier. In certain parts of the United States, particularly Alaska, they are the most common vernacular building form. In 2006 the Quonset hut was the subject of an exhibition at the Alaska Design Forum in Anchorage.

OPPOSITE, TOP Homoja Naval Village, Annapolis, Maryland, c. 1944.
OPPOSITE, BOTTOM Postcard depicting the assembly of a hut.
ABOVE Naval personnel in front of hut in Adak, Alaska, 1943.

BELOW Blueprint for redesigned Quonset Hut, 1941.
BOTTOM Isometric drawing of common hut.
RIGHT Interior view of hut, Adak, Alaska, 1943.

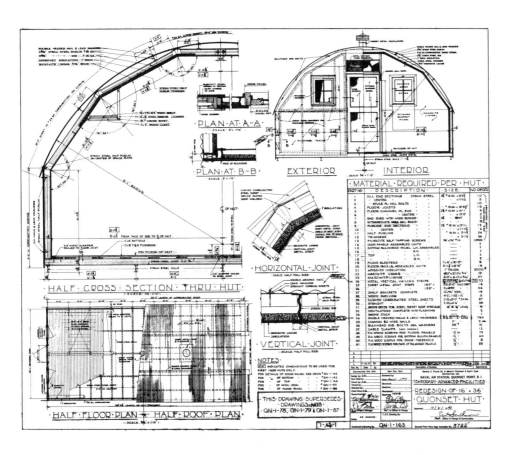

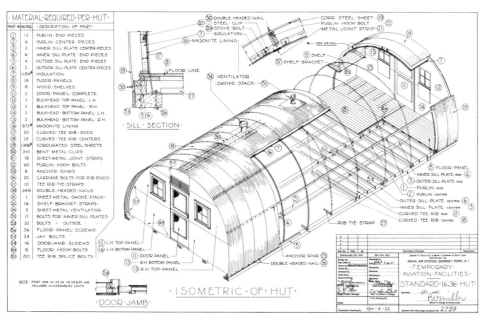

PACKAGED HOUSE/ GENERAL PANEL SYSTEM

KONRAD WACHSMANN AND WALTER GROPIUS

BELOW Illustration of unloading and construction process.
BOTTOM Illustration of trucking system.
OPPOSITE Gropius and Wachsmann inspecting test house, Queens, New York, 1946.

Rather than representing a revolution in prefabrication, Konrad Wachsmann and Walter Gropius's Packaged House represents the zenith of the wood-frame, panelized houses that were, by 1942, fairly common on both sides of the Atlantic. What is more relevant is the nature of the partnership between two influential architects with their own distinct interests in collaborating on such a project. Despite the cachet of its authors, the house, like so many before and after it, would ultimately fail as a commodity, remaining influential today by virtue of its conceptual underpinnings, rather than for its commercial success.

Escaping internment in Germany virtually penniless in 1941, Wachsmann arrived at Gropius's American home in Lincoln, Massachusetts, homeless and without work. Gropius, an old friend, was in a position to help as he was both practicing and teaching at Harvard and had recently severed ties with his longtime collaborator, Marcel Breuer. He provided Wachsmann with a place to stay, draw, and discuss architecture late into the evening. Gropius endorsed Wachsmann's desire to embark on a charrette for an industrialized housing system, which they eventually called "The Packaged House." Gropius would later acknowledge that his role was more that of facilitator and mentor, providing Wachsmann with the financial and intellectual resources to pursue the project, including patenting the system in 1942. Wachsmann, on the other hand, was at the helm on the drawing board, feverishly setting his mind to the task of producing a set of twenty-four drawings that functioned as the blueprint not only for a housing system, but for an entire house-making corporation. In many ways it was the light at the end of the tunnel for Wachsmann in the very dark days of the height of World War II. The project seems to have offered Wachsmann his most exciting design opportunities since his important explorations in prefabrication, his house for Einstein at Caputh, near Potsdam, completed in 1929, and timber houses produced for the Berlin Building Exhibition in 1931.

Wachsmann had already produced some drawings in exile in France and he spent his first several weeks in the U. S. converting the drawings from meters to feet and inches in the hopes of making the project commercially viable in the United States. The system had no ideal arrangement, and Wachsmann chose not to draw any definitive house models. Instead he developed a palette of ten different types of 40-by-120-inch panels laid out in 40-inch three-dimensional space-frame panels forming all horizontal and vertical surfaces. The panel system overall was not of sufficient originality to gain the patent that Gropius sought. It was, in fact, the X-shaped wedge connectors that linked each panel vis-à-vis a set of metal plates housed in the panel edge that proved to be the inventive, and consequently commercially noteworthy, element of the system. The wedge, which was essentially flat, replaced the

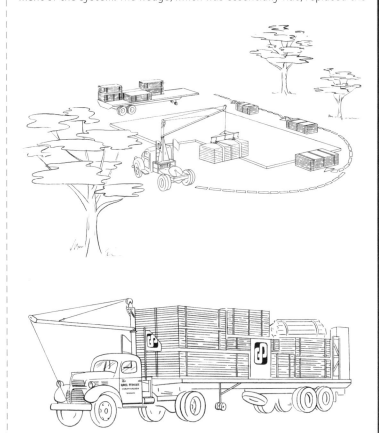

BELOW Model of delivered pieces stacked and erected.
OPPOSITE, TOP Plans and elevations for three variations.
OPPOSITE, BOTTOM (clockwise) Type A rendering and elevations; Type B rendering; frame connection system; sectional perspective.

standard Y-shaped connector that, because of its three dimensionality, proved harder to manufacture and easier to damage. Wachsmann prepared a set of remarkable and refined drawings that he would eventually depart with as the relationship between house-guest and host became increasingly strained. Gropius and Wachsmann parted amicably, and Wachsmann continued to consult Gropius as he pursued investors in New York City for what he now called the General Panel System. The two held very different conceptions of the system's potential. Gropius believed that the technological progress that enabled a system such as the Packaged House was, essentially, an immutable force that inevitably had to be har-

nessed by humans to achieve their own goals. Gropius, considered a humanist by many, saw the machine as a potentially dehumanizing force that man had to control. Wachsmann, who is quoted as saying, "Tomorrow is everything," had a very different perception of technology as a liberating force in architecture. The debate of technology's role in architecture continues today and is uniquely embedded in the fabric of this modest proposal for a prefabricated house.

Teetering on bankruptcy, Wachsmann found investors and, after much scrambling, mounted a prototype in Somerville, Massachusetts, in 1943. Although praised by critics, the house failed to gain reliable investors. Finally, in

1946 the Celotex corporation of Burbank, California, acquired both the design and a former airplane engine factory, forming the General Panel Corporation. A plan to produce 8,500 houses per year in a burgeoning post-war housing economy proved unsuccessful when the facility's equipment failed to provide the proper tolerances needed for the system to work, ultimately affecting output and, consequently, the bottom line. In 1952 the corporation went bankrupt, and the "dream," as Gilbert Hebert labeled it in his 1984 book, of the Packaged House would become yet another failed endeavor in the history of the prefabricated house.

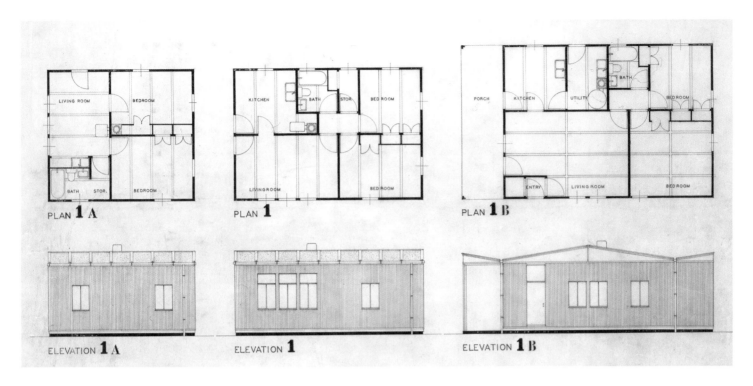

PLAN **1**A

PLAN **1**

PLAN **1**B

ELEVATION **1**A

ELEVATION **1**

ELEVATION **1**B

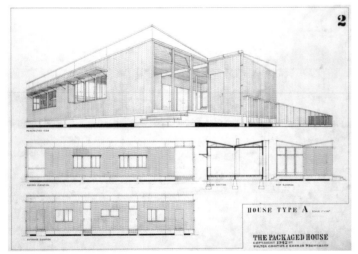

HOUSE TYPE A

THE PACKAGED HOUSE
COPYRIGHT 1942 BY
WALTER GROPIUS & KONRAD WACHSMANN

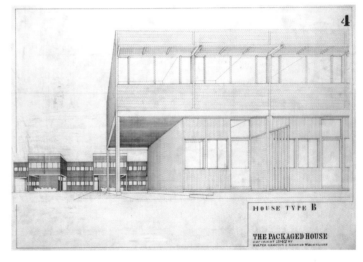

HOUSE TYPE B

THE PACKAGED HOUSE
COPYRIGHT 1942 BY
WALTER GROPIUS & KONRAD WACHSMANN

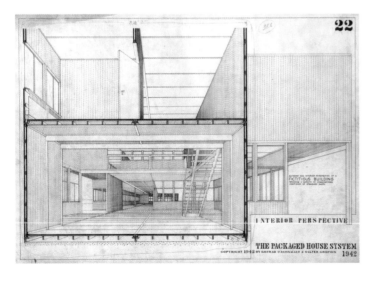

INTERIOR PERSPECTIVE

THE PACKAGED HOUSE SYSTEM
COPYRIGHT 1942 BY KONRAD WACHSMANN & WALTER GROPIUS 1942

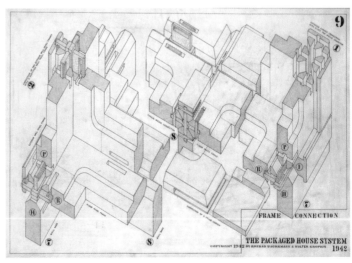

FRAME CONNECTION

THE PACKAGED HOUSE SYSTEM
COPYRIGHT 1942 BY KONRAD WACHSMANN & WALTER GROPIUS 1942

OPPOSITE Interior view of test house.
BELOW, TOP ROW Primary architectural joint; foundation system seam; foundation system corner.
BELOW, MIDDLE ROW Panels organized for construction; foundation; construction phase 1.
BELOW, BOTTOM ROW Construction phase 2; construction phase 3; construction phase 4.

YANKEE PORTABLES

MARCEL BREUER

BELOW Plans for three variations and rendering.
OPPOSITE, TOP Type A elevations, rendering, and plan composite.
OPPOSITE, BOTTOM Assembly diagram and schedule.

In the early 1940s Marcel Breuer returned his attention from site-built houses to prefabricated housing. Breuer had studied projects for pre-fabrication at the Bauhaus in the 1920s, and now the vitality of mass production in the United States in the 1940s encouraged him to explore its applicability to American timber construction. He sought to create an "American" minimum home that took its cue from the production lines of Henry Ford and the automotive industry, in this case using wood. The result was a "de-mountable," one-story wood-frame house that could sit on a site-poured concrete pylon foundation. The house could be realized in different sizes depending on the number of bedrooms the client would choose: one, two, or three, with living, dining, and kitchen spaces remaining relatively fixed from plan to plan. Interiors were to be finished with plywood and specially designed sliding window-screen units. One of the most remarkable elements of this modest house was an elastic wall joint that afforded a substantial tolerance of potential imperfections within the prefabricated elements comprising the structure. Breuer went so far as to make arrangements with a manufacturer as well as a contractor to assemble the elements in anticipation of potential interest from the United States National Housing Agency, which was initiating major efforts to deploy prefabricated homes across the country. Although it remained unbuilt, Breuer's proposal for defense workers' housing in Wethersfield, Connecticut, also for the National Housing Agency, was a reissue of the Yankee Portables with the notable stylistic change of a butterfly roof, which, as Isabelle Hyman points out in *Marcel Breuer, Architect* (2001), made the latter proposal significantly more expensive. Initially dubbed the "Nomadic Nest," the name Yankee Portables reveals Breuer's interest in the New England "Yankee" traditions celebrated by Sigfried Giedion in his influential *Space, Time and Architecture* (1941).

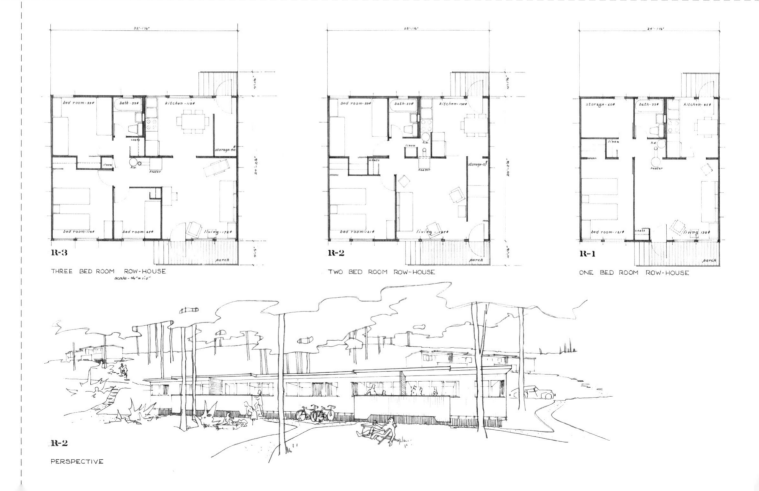

R-3 — THREE BED ROOM ROW-HOUSE

R-2 — TWO BED ROOM ROW-HOUSE

R-1 — ONE BED ROOM ROW-HOUSE

R-2 — PERSPECTIVE

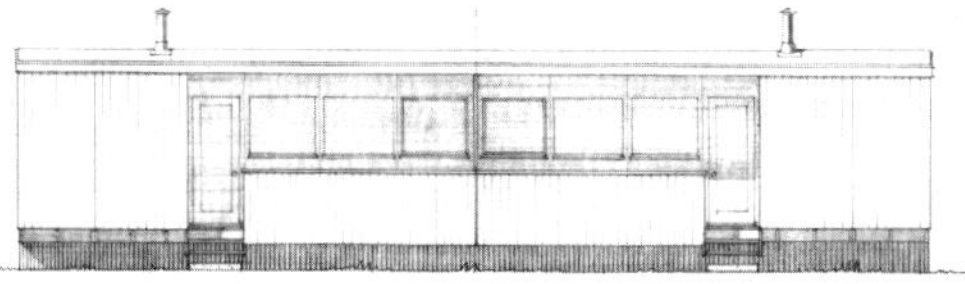

FRONT ELEVATION

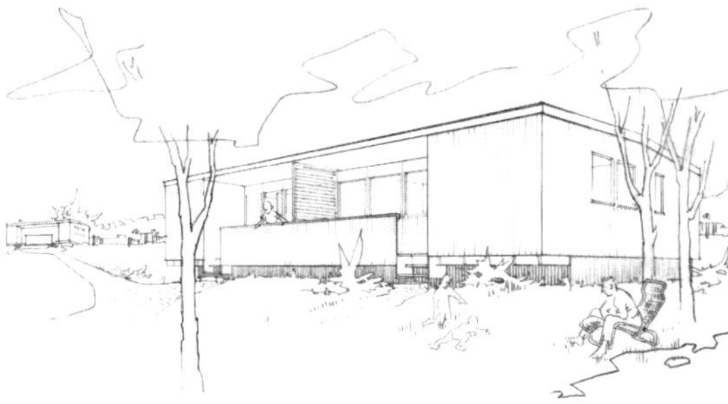

PERSPECTIVE

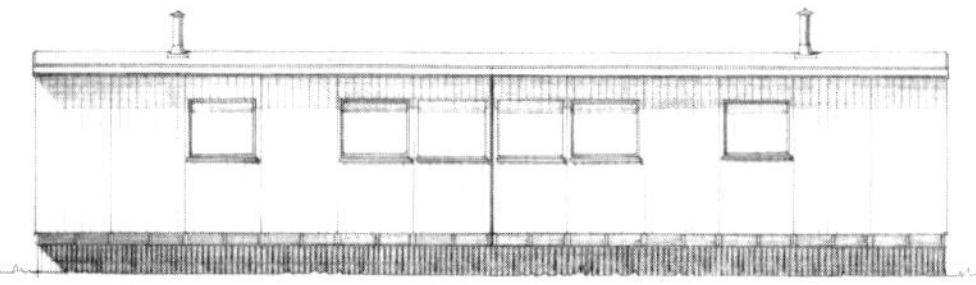

REAR ELEVATION

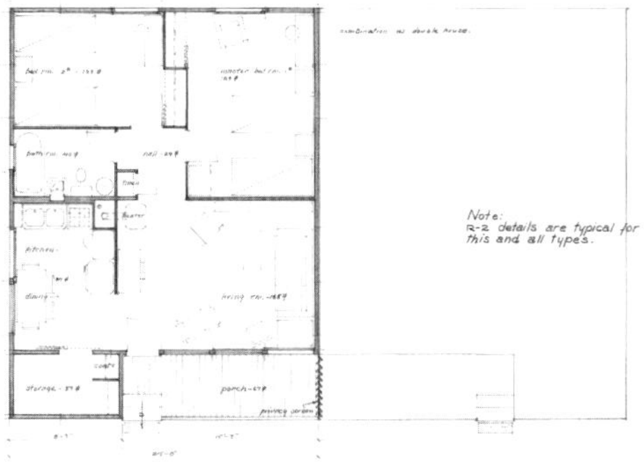
Note:
R-2 details are typical for this and all types.

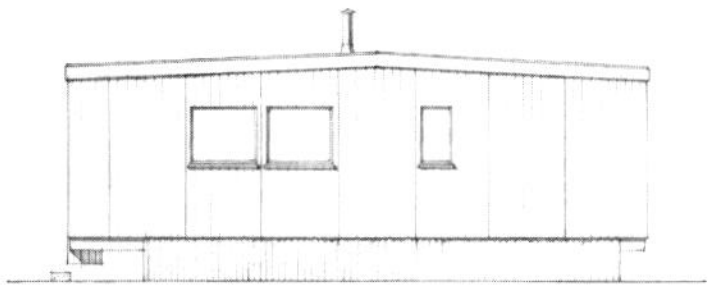

SIDE ELEVATION

PLAN

ASSEMBLY SCHEDULE

1. Cleaning, rough grading, leveling etc.
2. Trenches for sewer, water, gas and installation of piping for same from a point 5 ft. from perimeter of house. Connect piping to utilities. Also install water and gas risers to meter. Soil piping, wastes, traps and all roughing below finished floor level, also installed. Insulate exposed piping to a point 2 ft. below rough grading—.
3. Excavate for piers. Pour concrete footings and piers set bolts in piers.
4. Install 4"x8" girders on piers, and bolt.
5. Install the sub-floor panels over girders and tighten bolts at piers.
6. Place wall panels (bearing) on sub-floor platform, connect 3 or 4 of same by continuous cornice piece, lift and erect panels - bracing at corners with panels of non-bearing walls; fasten wall panels to floor platform by means of continuous sill piece. Install all bearing walls and bearing partitions as above.
7. Erect non-bearing exterior walls; spline of last joint of wall inserted from above.
8. Erect roof panels and secure to bearing walls.
9. Erect 'Plumbing wall panel.
10. Install roofing, edge and ridge piece, facia board and caulk joints between panels of exterior walls.
11. Install soils, wastes and vents in 'Plumbing wall also exposed piping and chimney.
12. Flash vents and chimney at roof.
13. Install window guide frame and sash (shop-painted).
14. Erect interior partitions, shelving, closets, steps to porch, and railing.
15. Final alinement of entire structure. Apply asbestos skirting.
16. Install wiring layout over sub-floor and connect to shop-installed wiring in panels.
17. Paint exterior trim and finish; apply 'field-coat' of shingle stain to finish siding.
18. Install finish floor panels, linoleun in bathrooms base boards and thresholds.
19. Paint first coat on interior wall trim, shelves, etc.
20. Install plumbing fixtures; range, heater, hot water heater.
21. Hang doors (shop-trimmed) and install hardware on the job.
22. Interior paint; second coat.
23. Electric fixtures, switch plates. Test.
24. Floor finish.
25. Porch floor, fly screens for windows and doors.

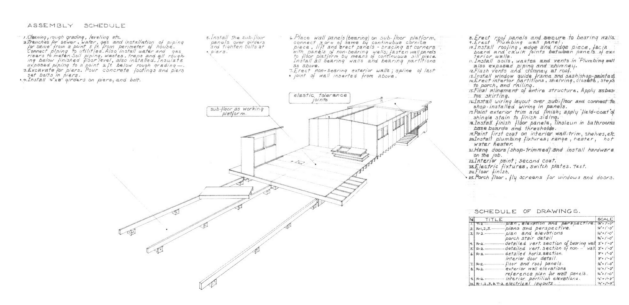

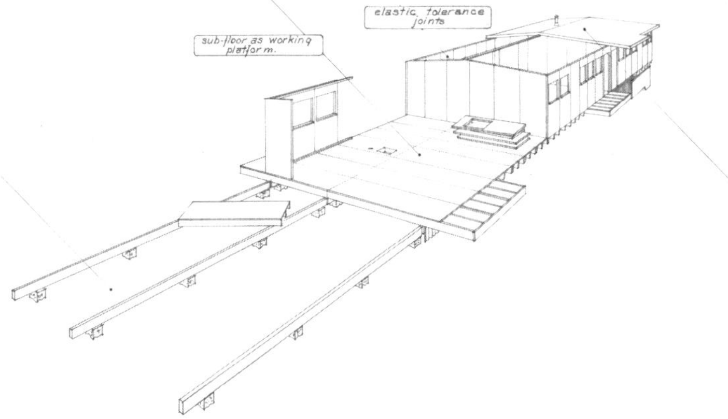
elastic tolerance joints
sub-floor as working platform.

SCHEDULE OF DRAWINGS.

N	TITLE		SCALE
1.	T-2	plan, elevation and perspective.	¼" = 1'-0"
2.	R-1,2,3.	plans and perspective.	¼" = 1'-0"
3.	R-2.	plan and elevations	¼" = 1'-0"
		porch stair detail	¾" = 1'-0"
4.	R-2.	detailed vert. section of bearing wall	3" = 1'-0"
5.	R-2.	detailed vert. section of non- " wall.	3" = 1'-0"
6.	R-2.	detailed horiz. section.	3" = 1'-0"
		interior door detail.	3" = 1'-0"
7.	R-2.	floor and roof panels.	½" = 1'-0"
8.	R-2.	exterior wall elevations	½" = 1'-0"
		reference plan for wall panels.	¼" = 1'-0"
9.	R-2.	interior partition elevations.	½" = 1'-0"
10.	R-1,2,3, & T-2.	electrical layouts.	¼" = 1'-0"

YANKEE PORTABLES

ALL-DEMOUNTABLE HOUSING

MANUFACTURED BY

CUSTANCE BROTHERS INC. LEXINGTON, MASS.

DESIGNED BY

MARCEL BREUER A.I.A. CAMBRIDGE, MASS.

PLAS-2-POINT HOUSE
MARCEL BREUER

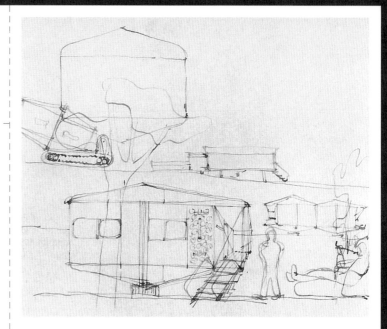

With the Plas-2-Point Breuer continued his investigations into prefabricated housing begun a year earlier with the Yankee Portables project. The house's plywood substructure was to be given a thin coat of liquid plastic by the plastics manufacturer Monsanto, a novel take on traditional sealants that would render the entire structure more durable and easier to clean. Even more inventive was the fact that the structure touched the ground at only two points, anchored to foundation blocks that eliminated the need for any expensive grading or full foundation work. This greatly decreased the amount of time necessary to assemble the house. Connecting the two anchor points was a massive central girder from which radiated a tapered truss system—inspired by the trussing of an airplane wing—on either side. Vertical posts supported another spinal girder, which had a trussing system identical to that of the floor system. Modular plywood panels could be configured in variations to form the roofing, flooring, and interior wall divisions. The house contained two bedrooms, a living room, dining area, kitchen, and terrace. The two anchor points would barely be visible at ground level, giving the entire structure the appearance of hovering above the ground slightly, like an airplane about to land or, perhaps, take off.

Breuer had a model built of the project and used it as part of his design curriculum while teaching at Harvard. His students took active roles in developing the scheme and subsequently building the model under his supervision. Monsanto Plastics published a feature article on the project in the October/November 1943 company magazine, in which Breuer issued a statement on the powerful role that plastics could play in the future of prefabricated housing, remarkable considering that the project anticipates by nearly twenty years other plastic monocoque designs. As with the Yankee Portables, the Plas-2-Point was pitched as postwar housing to officials in Washington, D.C., but the project would never get off the ground, feeding Breuer's increasing frustration with the inability of architects to break into the prefabricated housing market in the United States. In Breuer's eyes, the future of the prefabricated house would unfortunately rest within the hands of "commercial fabricators who don't bother with architecture."

FROM WARTIME PLASTICS-BONDED PLYWOODS... THIS "PLAS-2-POINT HOUSE" FOR POSTWAR LIVING

Architect Marcel Breuer, now professor in Harvard's department of architecture, trained, then taught at the famed Bauhaus. To his credit are the first tubular steel chairs and some of the best examples of contemporary architecture and industrial design here and in Europe.

HARVARD'S Marcel Breuer has pondered the skeleton of a modern bomber ... probed the possibilities of war-born, new plastics-bonded plywoods ... and produced this interesting and original design for postwar prefabrication which he has christened the "Plas-2-Point House."

"Compared with current prefabricated construction," Mr. Breuer estimates, "the Plas-2-Point House would weigh a third as much, cost only 70% as much and, knocked down for shipment, would occupy only 30 to 40% as much packing space. Even fully assembled houses could be trucked short distances from central assembly lines to individual building sites, then quickly anchored to foundation blocks."

Since neither walls nor partitions are load-bearing, the "Plas-2-Point House" is highly flexible. Exterior wall panels might be heavily insulated for cold climates or simply a series of screens for the tropics. They might be built up from Resinox-bonded plywood with a durable, colorful, weather-resistant melamine surface—or even from paper or fabrics impregnated with Resinox and melamine resins.

To save weight, gain production economies and add new notes of color and style, many of the house's fittings and accessories would probably be molded from plastics.

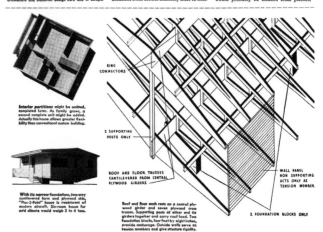

Interior partitions might be omitted, completed later. As family grows, a second complete unit might be added. Actually this house allows greater flexibility than conventional custom building.

With its narrow foundations, two-way cantilevered form and plywood skin, "Plas-2-Point" house is reminiscent of modern aircraft. Six-room house for cold climate would weigh 3 to 4 tons.

RING CONNECTORS

2 SUPPORTING POSTS ONLY

ROOF AND FLOOR TRUSSES CANTILEVERED FROM CENTRAL PLYWOOD GIRDERS

Roof and floor each rests on a central plywood girder and seven plywood cross trusses. Supporting posts at either end tie girders together and carry roof load. Two foundation blocks, four feet by eight inches, provide anchorage. Outside walls serve as tension members and give structure rigidity.

WALL PANEL NON SUPPORTING ACTS ONLY AS TENSION MEMBER

2 FOUNDATION BLOCKS ONLY

OPPOSITE, TOP Conceptual sketch.
OPPOSITE, BOTTOM Article in Monsanto company magazine.
BELOW Model.

WICHITA HOUSE
R. BUCKMINSTER FULLER

Fuller saw new potential to revisit ideas he had investigated with the Dymaxion House in the booming postwar American economy in 1944. With the necessary money and support in place, he moved into the Beech Aircraft Factory in Wichita, Kansas, where he would research an updated Dymaxion and introduce it to the public. Because of the earlier financial failure, Fuller had to convince his investors that what he was researching was, in fact, *not* a prefabricated house. They gave him a two-year lease on the company's plant including all of its labor capabilities, materials, machinery, etc. In turn, Fuller had to hand over right of first refusal over design matters to them. Because of the decline in airplane production, Beech was seeking to break into the housing market, hoping eventually to produce fifty thousand to sixty thousand units per year for $6,500 ($75,000 today), or 50 cents per pound, the first house ever priced by its weight. Fuller was able to claim that the house was not, in fact, prefabricated by toying with a rigid trade definition that identified prefabrication as the "fabrication of semifinished products such as panels and parts that are used at the site as a subassembly." The Wichita House was delivered as a whole. Fuller's system therefore marks a bifurcating moment when two strains of veritably prefabricated construction become evident: the panel system of flat parts (known largely today as "flat pack") and the newer modular system of prefinished pieces.

Formally the house was refined from the hexagonal, faceted face of the Dymaxion to a hemispherical form with a monocoque dome and a

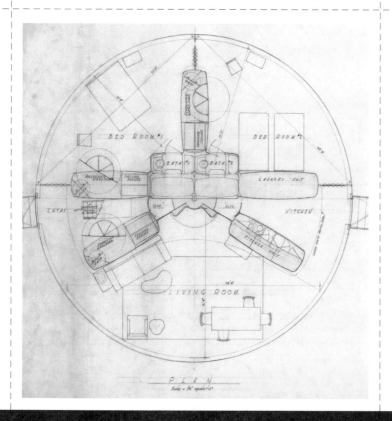

ventilator at its cap. Rather than being suspended a full story in the air, the Wichita House sat just a few inches off the ground. The central mast no longer contained an elevator and laundry facilities, retaining only its function as a utility core. Fuller's monocoque drop-in Dymaxion bathroom, which he had patented, was added to the layout. The critical reaction to a full-scale prototype was significantly more positive than it had been to the Dymaxion. The gentle curves created a more satisfying interior flow; the palette of finishes on the inside were more refined and better constructed. Like the Dymaxion, the Wichita was intended to be a "dwelling machine," and Fuller pursued this notion in lectures and writing, suggesting that industrial design and architecture had never been more compatible. In the end, the Beech Company decided not to produce the Wichita House, convinced that, despite its reception and improvements, the public was still not prepared to inhabit a machinelike object. Fuller and his team had to leave the Wichita plant in 1947. Like the Dymaxion, the Wichita House would enter the annals of replicable utopian homes that would never see the light of day.

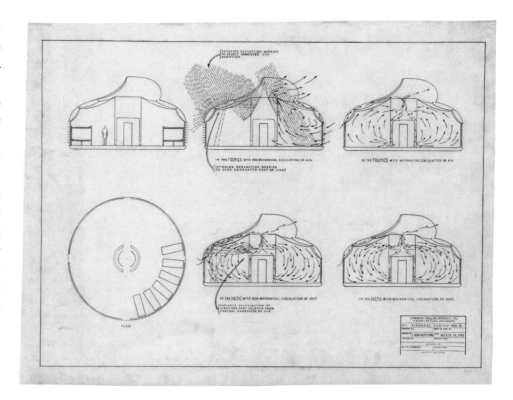

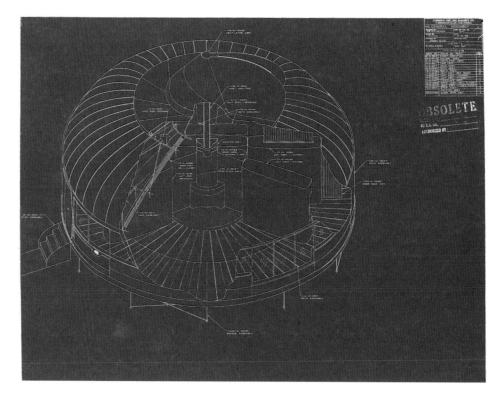

OPPOSITE, TOP Wind studies.
OPPOSITE, BOTTOM Isometric
cutaway construction blueprint.
BELOW Construction photos.
RIGHT TOP Construction photo.
RIGHT BOTTOM Interior view.

CASE STUDY HOUSE NO. 8
CHARLES AND RAY EAMES

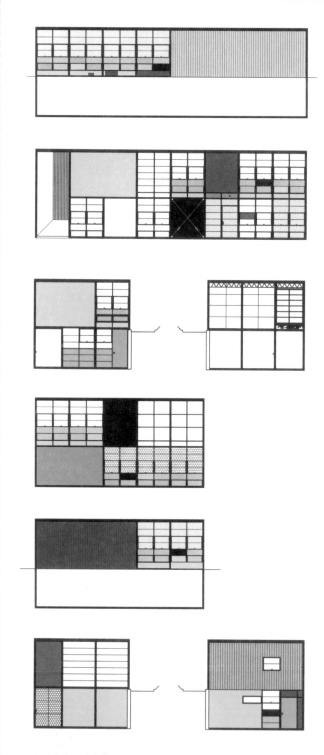

Arts & Architecture magazine's editor John Entenza initiated the Case Study House program in 1945 as an experiment that would commission major architects to reconsider the modern dwelling, largely in reaction to the plethora of model homes being produced by non-architects in the post–World War II building boom. Prefabricated to varying degrees, all of the houses responded to the mission of infusing good design at a good value into the American housing market. The most successful in strategizing a completely innovative system made entirely of off-the-shelf elements was Case Study House No. 8, designed by husband-and-wife team Charles and Ray Eames as their own residence.

Consisting of two detached volumes, one a living quarter and one a work studio, the house demonstrates the possibilities of designing with a finite palette of prefabricated parts: every element was ordered by catalogue or purchased from an industrial manufacturer, including the structure's steel beams and trusses, siding of various materials and colors, glass, asbestos, and Cemesto board, all laid out on a grid that made concern over tolerances obsolete. The architects focused entirely on making the most voluminous space possible with limited resources, evidenced by the 17-foot-high ceiling in the double-height living room. Charles Eames told Entenza that he had asked himself three determinate questions before designing the project: How cheap is space? How industrial is our building industry? How light is steel? To the Eameses, the value of the domicile had less to do with fine finishes and luxurious amenities than with the sheer volume of space one could obtain with the least amount of cash, with the price per cubic foot costing a mere eight dollars adjusted for inflation.

The Eameses did not explicitly design the house for replication, and because the house was designed for themselves it largely reflected their personalities as both designers and people. Nonetheless the system they had designed certainly held the potential to be copied, so long as the client was willing to take matters into his or her own hands.

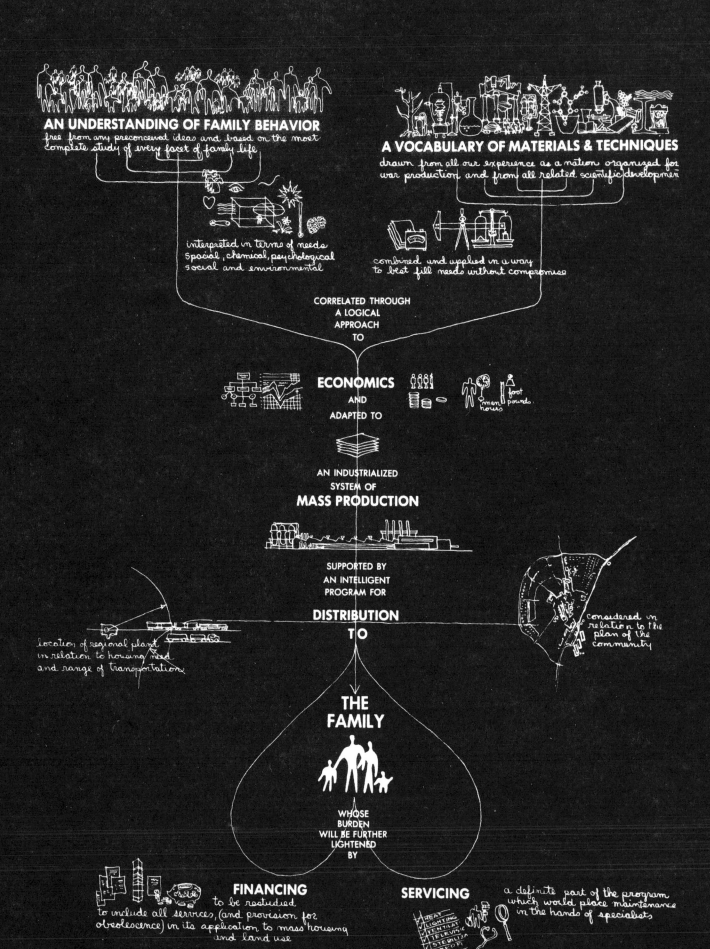

AN UNDERSTANDING OF FAMILY BEHAVIOR
free from any preconceived ideas and based on the most
complete study of every facet of family life

A VOCABULARY OF MATERIALS & TECHNIQUES
drawn from all our experience as a nation organized for
war production and from all related scientific development

interpreted in terms of needs
spacial, chemical, psychological
social and environmental

combined and applied in a way
to best fill needs without compromise

CORRELATED THROUGH
A LOGICAL
APPROACH
TO

ECONOMICS
AND
ADAPTED TO

foot
pounds
man
hours

AN INDUSTRIALIZED
SYSTEM OF
MASS PRODUCTION

SUPPORTED BY
AN INTELLIGENT
PROGRAM FOR

DISTRIBUTION
TO

location of regional plant
in relation to housing need
and range of transportation

considered in
relation to the
plan of the
community

**THE
FAMILY**

WHOSE
BURDEN
WILL BE FURTHER
LIGHTENED
BY

FINANCING
to be restudied
to include all services, (and provision for
obsolescence) in its application to mass housing
and land use

SERVICING

a definite part of the program
which would place maintenance
in the hands of specialists

HEAT
LIGHTING
VENTILAT
TELEVISIO
STERILIZA
DEODR

OPPOSITE Charles Eames's drawing in *Arts & Architecture*, July 1944, diagramming the contents of the article "What Is a House?" which he cowrote with John Entenza.
TOP LEFT Charles and Ray Eames on steel frame.
TOP RIGHT Exterior view.
BOTTOM LEFT Interior view of studio.
BOTTOM RIGHT Exterior detail.

UNITÉ D'HABITATION
LE CORBUSIER

The seminal and much debated Unité d'Habitation in Marseilles is a monumental twelve-story concrete housing block acclaimed as one of Le Corbusier's most accomplished realizations. It represented a massive paradigm shift in the discourse on mass housing in postwar France and elsewhere. Despite a complex interchange of internalized "vertical cities" replete with internal shopping avenues, the structural scheme is deceptively simple. Because steel proved to be too expensive and difficult to control qualitatively, the building is framed by a simple rectilinear precast concrete grid which celebrates its construction by leaving the rough-hewn edges and surfaces formed by the wooden formwork unaltered, an aesthetic that gave rise to the term *béton brut*, or raw concrete. Le Corbusier likened the whole frame to a wine rack, in which the apartments functioned as the bottles. The apartments, which were designed (yet not fabricated) as autonomous units, were simply to be slipped into their respective voids, hugging their opposite neighbor in what has been described as a "scissor section," a solution inspired by earlier research into Soviet systems. Each unit contains a double-height living space with a deep balcony and a direct view of nature that becomes the prominent external characteristic. The notion of the building's skeleton as a "rack" for discrete, autonomous units to be plugged into is a preamble to the megastructures that would emerge in the following decades.

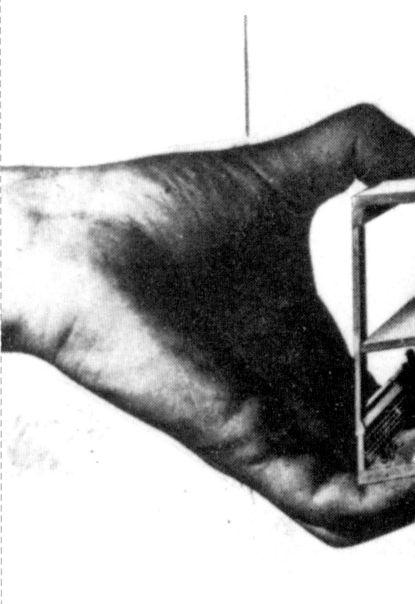

KHRUSHCHOVKAS
UNATTRIBUTED

Taking its name from the post-Stalinist regime of Nikita Khrushchev, Khrushchovkas was the generic name for a low-cost prefabricated concrete panel system developed throughout the Soviet Union to build the massive three-to-five-story apartment blocks that have become infamous, and perhaps emblematic, of a time and place in architectural history. Regardless of appearance, the system proved to be one of the most cost-effective and rapidly deployable prefabricated building systems to date, even among neighbors in Europe with a much longer prefabricated building tradition. Perhaps nowhere else did a prefabricated building system become so intrinsically intertwined with a political epoch.

Following the mass national investment in concrete factories in the 1950s, Vitaly Lagutenko, chief planner of Moscow from 1961 until his death in 1967, developed a research institute dedicated exclusively to the research and development of precast concrete panel systems. It developed, among other plans, a packaged design for a five-story (the maximum number of floors permitted without elevators) apartment block called "K-7." The block was the most ubiquitous of all of Lagutenko's models, with more than sixty thousand such buildings built. Typical apartments within the K-7 type contained either one, two, or three rooms and a bathroom cubicle and ranged from 320 to 640 aggregate square feet. The Khrushchovka system continued to be used throughout the Eastern bloc until the fall of the Soviet Union in 1990.

Adding to its overall efficiency, albeit at the expense of the residents, the Khrushchovkas were conceived as a two-tiered system of "temporary" and "permanent" structures. Temporary Khrushchovkas were built of lesser-grade concrete and with less structural integrity and were intended to be inhabited for no more than forty years, while permanent Khrushchovkas were built with higher-grade concrete and greater attention to detail, predominantly in larger cities. Despite the fact that virtually all temporary Khrushchovkas have surpassed their expiration date, many are still in use. Current plans to demolish these buildings, primarily in Moscow and St. Petersburg, will largely eradicate Khrushchovkas from Russia's urban landscape, a prospect that has, surprisingly, raised the ire of preservationists who value the structures' historical significance.

RIGHT Khrushchovkas (variant), Kiev, Ukraine.

WESTCHESTER TWO-BEDROOM MODEL HOUSE

CARL G. STRANDLUND FOR THE LUSTRON CORPORATION, INC.

In 1945 millions of American soldiers returned home from World War II to face the greatest housing shortage the United States had ever known. As the automobile industry had propelled the nation's economy in the 1920s, economists saw great potential in the housing sector to keep a delicate postwar economy on track. President Truman understood this challenge and created the cabinet-level position of National Housing Expediter, a post that would oversee an unprecedented government initiative to subsidize housing construction, preferably of the quick and inexpensive variety. Prefabricated housing had never had more real potential for viability in the American landscape, and from this initiative numerous "house factories" were born.

Many of these factories continued in the vein of the Sears tradition, prefabricating houses that appeared, at least from a distance, to be handmade, replete with faux brickwork, stucco, and finishes. Carl Strandlund, a Swedish-born inventor of farm tools and holder of over 150 patents, secured from the government $40 million to develop a very different type of prefabricated home. Strandlund envisioned a manufactured house made entirely of steel, appropriating prefabricated building systems that his company, Chicago Vitreous Enamel, had made popular primarily for gas stations. For the Reconstruction Finance Corporation (RFC) the primary appeal was guaranteed business for a steel industry whose livelihood was in question. For Strandlund, the motive was the price point; he hoped the all-steel house would cost significantly less than its wooden, mass-produced counterparts such as those William J. Levitt was projecting for Levittown. A vice president of the Lustron Corporation remarked, "You put down a hammer and a saw

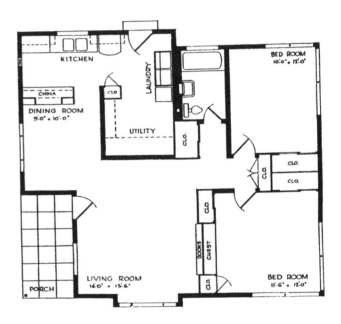

FLOOR PLAN OF LUSTRON MODEL HOUSE

Manufactured By

LUSTRON CORPORATION
CICERO 50, ILLINOIS

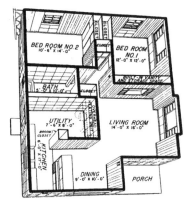

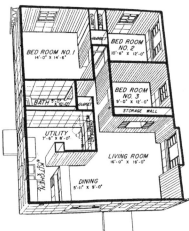

and pick up a wrench." Strandlund acquired a wartime airplane factory in Columbus, Ohio, and retooled many of the machines already on premises to build homes instead of airplanes.

Lustron produced its very first house, baptized the "Westchester Two Bedroom," in 1948. The house, roughly 32 feet square, sat on a concrete foundation poured in place on which a steel skeletal frame would rest, topped by trusses spanning the structure in 4-foot increments. All internal divisions were prefabricated modular units that frequently doubled as shelving, cabinetry, closets, and vanities. The exterior was clad in 2-foot-square porcelain-enameled steel panels, notable for their durability and ease of cleaning. The entire house arrived on a specially designed Lustron truck, packed flat. Assembly took approximately eight days. The formal composition of the house was not particularly novel, but the material palette and remarkably fast assembly set it apart from anything built before it. In a sense, the Westchester was, along with Keck's Crystal House and the Stran-Steel House, one of the first prefabricated houses whose form explic-

itly illustrated its means of construction. It was frankly and proudly an industrial product.

But the initial excitement wore off all too quickly. By 1949, sales were seriously lagging as the houses proved to be 30 to 50 percent more expensive than projected. Instead of producing one hundred per day, the company was realizing only some twenty. Amid growing skepticism from the RFC, one last large check was issued to Strandlund to try to salvage the company. The very fact that the Lustron house was so obviously factory-made also rendered its appearance the subject of widespread skepticism and in some cases outright derision. *Time* magazine, in particular, repeatedly railed against the house, eagerly reporting the company's financial woes and relaying descriptions of the house as a "bathtub" and a "hot dog stand" and asking if "people really want to live in steel homes?" In 1950 the company declared bankruptcy. Despite the conceptual strength of the project, the government was unwilling to salvage Strandlund yet again and the corporation closed its doors, having produced just under 2,500 houses.

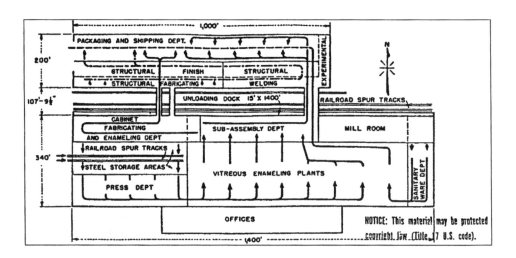

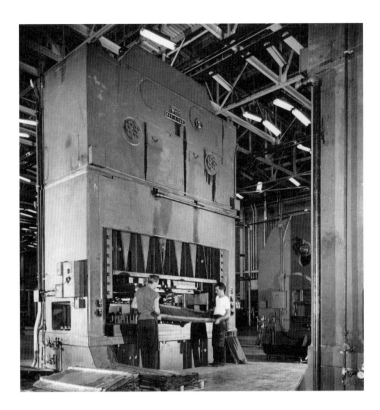

BELOW Assembly of roof and wall panels in New York City.
OPPOSITE, TOP Exterior view.
OPPOSITE, BOTTOM LEFT Dining room.
OPPOSITE, BOTTOM RIGHT Living room.

MAISON TROPICALE
JEAN PROUVÉ

"We need factory-built houses."
—Jean Prouvé, *Il Faut des Maisons Usinées*

Jean Prouvé's Maison Tropicale is not necessarily a house. The three structures realized were prototypes of an ambitious lightweight metal building system never placed in production though adaptable to any number of sites and functions. Fabricated in France to interest private- and public-sector decision makers in their potential mass production, they were sent to Africa for marketing purposes: the first as lodging for a secondary school headmaster in Niamey, Niger (1949); the other two as the office and residence of the commercial director of the regional information bureau of an aluminum company in Brazzaville, Congo (1951). They were meant to show the possibility of building entire colonial outposts out of a limited range of standardized metal components. When no orders materialized, they were abandoned to local use and passed into architectural oblivion for half a century. Fifty years after their implantation in the French colonies, two of the three have been resurrected, in very different contexts: one currently resides on the fifth-floor terrace of the Pompidou Center in Paris; the other was acquired at a Christie's auction in New York in summer 2007 by the hotelier André Balazs, who intends to use it as a lounge in a resort being developed in Costa Rica.

Prouvé was above all engaged by the possibilities of the industrial production of architecture, primarily low-cost or emergency housing. Prior to World War II, he had already participated in a number of prefabrication projects. From 1937 to 1939, with architects Eugène Beaudoin

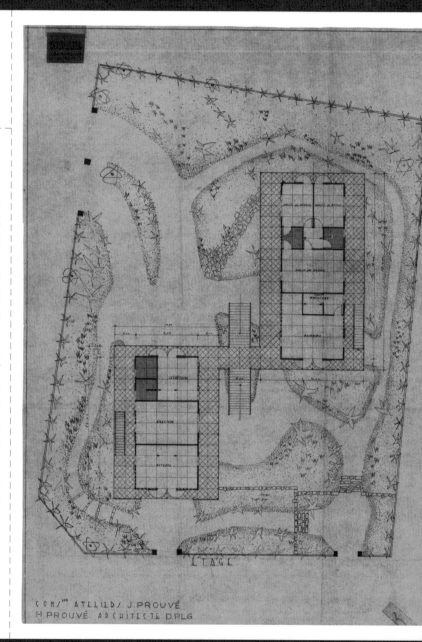

MAISON `T, A USAGE DE BUREAUX

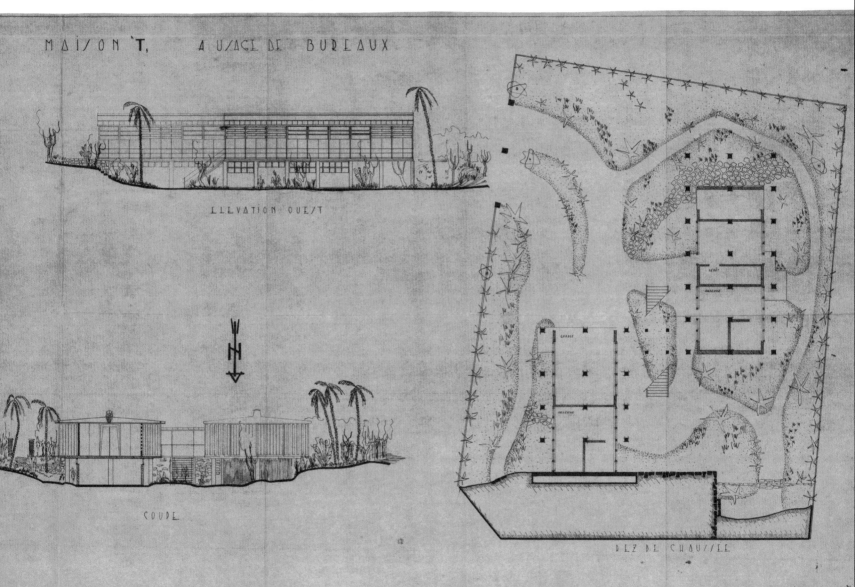

ELEVATION OUEST

COUPE

DEZ DE CHAUSSEE

PLAN N° T 600 071ᵇⁱˢ

and Marcel Lods, and in economic partnership with the Strasbourg steelworks, Prouvé developed the BLPS, a prefabricated vacation house capable of being dismantled. The idea for the project had been sparked by the initiation, in 1937, of paid vacations for workers by France's Popular Front government. The 3-meter-square structure could be assembled or dismantled by five workers in four to five hours. The whole house, including a kitchen nook, two folding beds, and a disappearing table, weighed less than two tons despite being made entirely of steel. In collabora-

tion with Pierre Jeanneret, Prouvé also made at least one mobile home (1938–39). With war imminent, he applied his know-how to army barracks and then, in 1945, at the war's conclusion, to emergency housing for displaced citizens of his native Lorraine. A year later, in partnership with a German steelworks, he produced a more elaborate steel prefabricated house prototype, Stahlhaus, with such elegant details as sliding, disappearing windows.

In 1949 Prouvé obtained a commission from the French Ministry for Reconstruction and Urbanism to build a fourteen-lot subdivi-

sion at Meudon, near Paris. At the same time, with Paul Herbe and Jean Le Couteur, he submitted designs for various public buildings in competitions for Niamey and Ouagadougou, the capital of Burkina Faso, including a hall of justice for Niamey that looks like the Maison Tropicale on steroids. The Coloniale (eventually Tropicale) system shared the basic features and elements of the system used at Meudon. Everything was designed to a 1-meter grid (approximately 3 feet). No element was more than 4 meters (13 feet) long or weighed more than 100 kilograms (220 pounds). Axial "fork"-

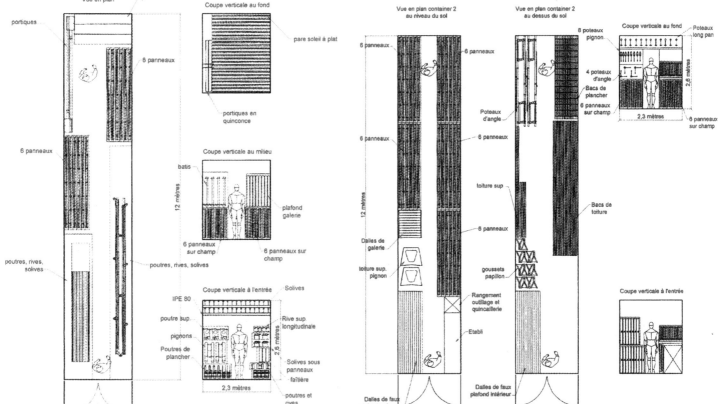

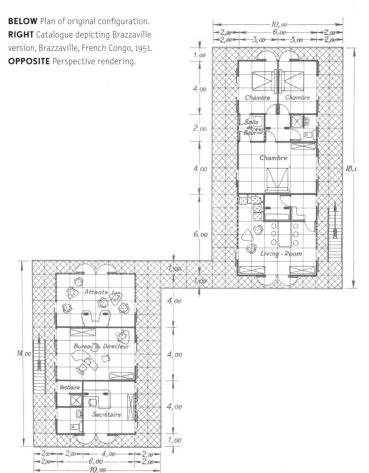

LE BUREAU D'INFORMATION DE BRAZZAVILLE

Le Bureau d'Information de Brazzaville a été officiellement inauguré le 3 décembre 1951 par M. Jean Dupin, président du Conseil d'Administration de L'Aluminium Français, entouré de MM. Marcel Pabellier, directeur de la Cégédur, Roger Voisard, directeur de Studal, et Jacques Piget, directeur de ce bureau africain. A cette manifestation assistaient les personnalités les plus marquantes de l'A. E. F. On notait la présence de MM. Bordier, chef de cabinet de M. Chauvet, Haut-Commissaire de la République; Mestre, représentant le Gouverneur Cédile; Cabou, directeur général des Affaires Économiques; Puech, directeur général des Douanes, ainsi que la plupart des autorités militaires et des dirigeants des affaires industrielles, commerciales, bancaires, etc.
Cette réception ayant eu lieu à la tombée de la nuit, il a été impossible de recevoir les personnalités du Congo belge par suite des horaires des vedettes traversant le fleuve. A leur intention, une deuxième réception a été organisée le mercredi 5 décembre à laquelle une quarantaine de personnes de tous les milieux assistaient.
La présentation du nouveau Bureau d'Information de L'Aluminium Fran-

58

style portico supports of folded and welded sheet steel were connected at the gable ends by a central roof beam, which was supported at its ends by aluminum wall panels, which also held up the roof. As everything was connected, the house gained stability. Thus the sequence of assembly was key.

For the Tropicale version, an extra degree of complexity addressed the issues raised by the climatic extremes of the tropics. Indeed, the idea for a tropical variant of the Meudon system had been suggested to Prouvé by Le Couteur who, during his posting to Africa as a government urbanist, found the nocturnal thermal inertia of the typical concrete building so intolerable he moved his bed out at night. Though hardly cool by today's hyper-air-conditioned standards, the Tropicale houses were habitable. Someone who lived in the Niamey structure

claimed the temperatures never exceeded the mid-eighties.

The engineer Peter Rice perhaps best summarized, in his *An Engineer Imagines* (1998), the "balance between constructability, materials and function" of Prouvé's building system:

The outer light reflecting skin of the Tropical House is separated from the inner insulated skin. Natural cooling and ventilation are used. There is moveable shading to control sunlight and direct ventilation where it is required. All the elements are flat for easy packing and transport and to give the minimum of fuss in assembly. This small . . . building would be a perfect answer in today's energy-conscious world, with its low consumption of energy in use, and perhaps more important, minimum use of energy consuming materials in manu-

facturing and construction . . . The use of a separate suspended floor above the locally made base provides insulation and helps control damp. The shape and geometry of the ventilation chimney in the center benefit from the stack effect (the tendency of hot air to rise), and, as with a fireplace, this can be used to control the amount of ventilation or natural cooling needed.

Unfortunately, the Tropicale houses were too strange looking for their intended buyers: the French colonial bureaucracy and business community. Moreover, they proved to be more expensive than local construction. During his tenure as the head of his Maxéville workshop, which he founded in 1947, Prouvé worked on a number of such innovative but ultimately unprofitable projects. By

1953, his incessant experimentation cost him his studio and factory, which by then employed more than two hundred people. The French aluminum monopoly, his major shareholder, foreclosed and dismissed him. Prouvé worked as a curtain-wall consultant for the rest of his career until his death in 1984. Deprived of control over the means of production, his ability to advance his vision of industrial architecture was subordinated to the more mundane goals of the developers of the now reviled housing projects of France's postwar boom years.

Two post-Maxéville projects warrant a mention in context of *Home Delivery*: Prouvé's own residence at Nancy (1954) was constructed entirely from materials he and his friends removed from Maxéville after his termination, on a steeply pitched plot of land previously deemed unbuildable by the bourgeoisie of Nancy. It is a masterful recycling operation, illustrative of Prouvé's ability to work with an astounding economy of materials and means. But it is not a prototype; rather it signals the end of an era. Prouvé's uncertain position in the building industry reflected the growing bureaucratization of architecture and engineering as professions within the industry during his lifetime. There was simply no comfortable place in the system for an artisan entrepreneur. Likewise his prototype House for Better Days (1956) for France's beloved advocate of the poor, Abbé Pierre, was erected on the banks of the Seine with great enthusiasm but never found a sponsor.

The Tropicale houses are at once iconic, inspirational, and cautionary. Ingenious "green" designs before the concept existed, they have become paradigms of minimalist architecture. As examples of a portable modular building system, they speak to a resurgent interest in prefabrication, and the engagement of architects in the design of emergency housing. Non–site specific, they are nonetheless inextricably bound up in cultural memories of colonial Africa. As the two restored houses circulate, these layers of meaning continue to expand.

—Robert Rubin

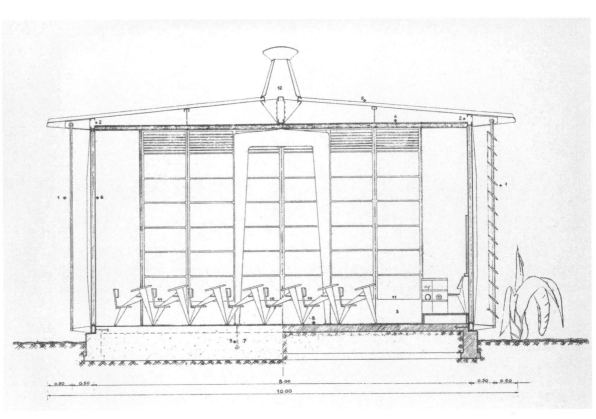

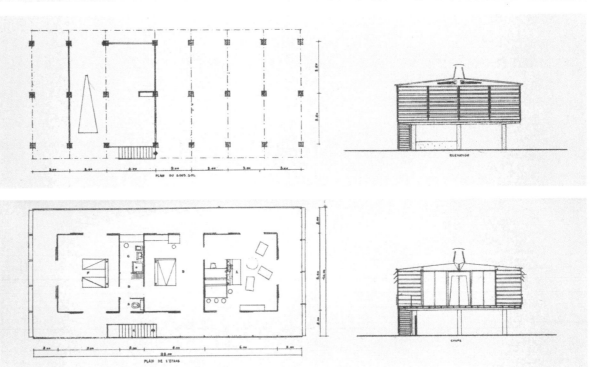

ELEVATION

PLAN DU SOUS SOL

PLAN DE L'ETAGE

COUPE

OPPOSITE, TOP Transverse section.
OPPOSITE, MIDDLE Rear elevation and ground-level plan.
OPPOSITE, BOTTOM Front elevation and upper-level plan.
BELOW LEFT Panel detail.
BELOW RIGHT Perspective, Maison Coloniale.
BOTTOM House as assembled in Long Island City for Christie's, New York, 2007.

MEUDON HOUSES
JEAN PROUVÉ

At the personal request of the French Minister for Urban Development and Reconstruction, Eugène Claudius-Petit, Jean Prouvé was awarded a commission for fourteen single-family homes in the Parisian suburb of Meudon. The houses continued Prouvé's rigorous study of aluminum as a primary building material, research that had begun in earnest following his completion of a large metalworking and furniture workshop in Maxéville in 1947 and first realized with the Tropical House (Maison Tropicale). The Meudon houses continued that investigation with a decidedly urban agenda. Rather than sitting in a relatively undeveloped and unfamiliar locale far away, the Meudon houses were to be embedded in an already built-up suburban context. And while the Maison Tropicale afforded Prouvé the design of a singular prefabricated structure of stature, the Meudon houses were explicitly made in bulk for low-income transitory residents who, in a forlorn postwar economy, simply needed modest housing. Prouvé welcomed the opportunity, stating, "I am ready to fabricate machine-made houses assembly-line style, as Citroën did as early as 1919 for the automobile industry ... With metal, one can build quickly and solidly," a clear echo of Le Corbusier twenty years earlier. Since his earliest housing prototypes in 1937, Prouvé had always held the idea of an affordable metal house as a personal design goal but had not yet been able to deploy a serial system.

Raised above the ground on a site-built masonry basement for cooling purposes, each of the fourteen houses is composed of a central aluminum *portique*, a tuning-fork-shaped central post Prouvé had first developed for the Maison Tropicale. Two prefabricated trusses latched into the *portique* resting on perimeter spandrels that, in turn, provided the exterior envelope on which cladding was placed. A series of nine modular panels, which included door units, perforated screens, opaque walls, canted window bays, and various combinations of such forms, could be selected as enclosures by the client, offering the houses a fairly high level of customizability, primarily with respect to the level of transparency of the structure. The panels, which were insulated and surfaced on both sides, simply slipped into place. The entire perimeter frame supported a minimally pitched roof. The open floor plan was amenable to a host of variable arrangements. Altogether construction took, in most cases, just three days.

Of the Maison Tropicale and Meudon houses, the latter are certainly the less familiar, despite their remarkably similar material palette and construction process. The Meudon houses elegantly manifest the architect's stalwart passion for industrialized housing and perhaps remain his most successful experiment in the field, if only because they were built in series and have stood up strong for almost half a century even though they were intended as temporary housing. Today they are protected historic monuments although many have been significantly modified.

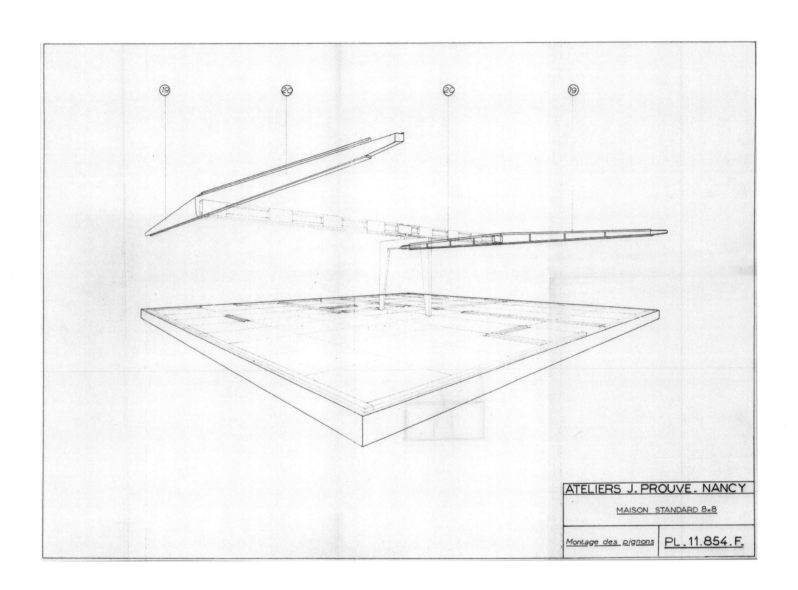

ALL PLASTIC HOUSE
IONEL SCHEIN

BELOW Watercolor rendering of exhibition site at Salon des Arts Ménagers, 1956.
BOTTOM Plan with perspective sketch.
OPPOSITE, TOP Model.
OPPOSITE, BOTTOM LEFT Sketch and sections in transit.
OPPOSITE, BOTTOM RIGHT View of house at Salon des Arts Ménagers, 1956.

Romanian-born French architect Ionel Schein is most widely recognized for his pioneering use of plastics in architecture. The earliest and most influential of these projects was his All Plastic House of 1956, consisting of a single level of eight discrete segments joining at a central point. The segments remain equal in radius until the final four sections, at which point the radii become increasingly large, forming a plan which recalls a Fibonaccian form (a sorted array which narrows or expands in non-linear intervals). The center point formed by the union of the segments constitutes the general area of a service core for a bathroom, kitchen, and other utilities. The living and sleeping spaces hug the entire circumference of the shell-shaped form, allowing for a great deal of natural light and a 360-degree panorama of the surroundings. A shallow porch provides additional outdoor space. For the realization of a built prototype, each slice was fabricated autonomously and hauled in on eight separate trucks to be connected on site. The structure, which organizes itself from the perimeter inward, is a fresh reinterpretation of the round house typology in contrast to Fuller's Dymaxion models, for example, where the structure is organized from the central point outward.

Perhaps even more relevant than its formal innovation is the remarkably advanced use of plastics, a material until then used almost exclusively in industrial situations. Massive single molds of remarkable durability, pliability, and strength were fabricated to create the floor, roof, and face, providing slots for glass or secondary inserts where necessary for each individual segment. Connections to neighboring segments consist of simple screw-and-bolt systems. Although plastic was already proving to be a cheaper alternative to traditional building materials, few architects considered it for house construction. Schein's project marks the beginning of a fascination for the application of plastic in housing design in late-1950s and 1960s France. His work would influence countless other architects interested in the novel form-making possibilities of affordable, replicable structures and design objects, such as Jean Maneval and Eric Clements in France and Gaetano Pesce in Italy.

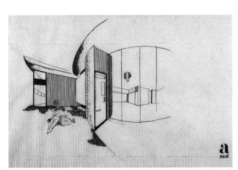

PLATTENBAU
UNATTRIBUTED

Plattenbau is the German word for buildings or structures constructed of large, prefabricated concrete panels in both the horizontal and vertical axes. The system is particularly associated with postwar housing construction in the former German Democratic Republic, though in considerably different form it was quite common in former West Germany as well. It remains one of the most ubiquitous prefabricated building systems throughout Europe. The earliest identified use of a plattenbau system is the Splanemann-Siedlung in Berlin's Lichtenberg district, completed in 1930. That project was inspired by another successful concrete system built in the Netherlands known as Betondorp, first developed in the Amsterdam suburb of Watergraafsmeer following World War I.

In East Germany, the most prolific period of plattenbau apartment buildings came in the 1960s. The system has subsequently become somewhat unfairly associated with its dismal counterparts in the former Soviet Bloc. In Europe the system actually enjoyed a high level of popularity for its relative value and spacious and clean interior accommodations. The concrete panels were articulated in different ways, often by a relief, which, along with color, allowed for a certain degree of identity for a particular apartment complex. By the 1980s the system even included precast, historically inspired decorations, an East German response to Postmodernism, notably in the units at the edge of the reconstructed medieval Nikolaiviertel in Berlin.

RIGHT Various cast reliefs of plattenbau exterior panel system.

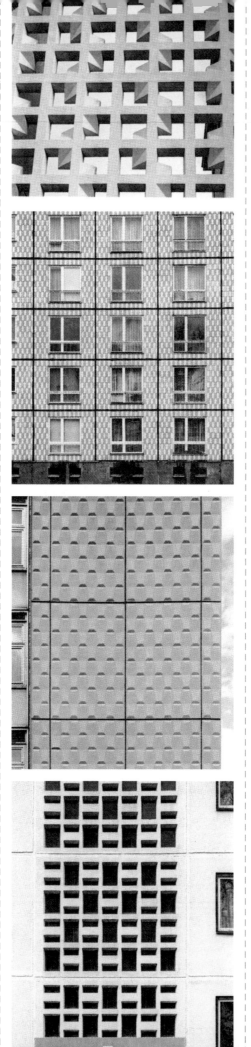

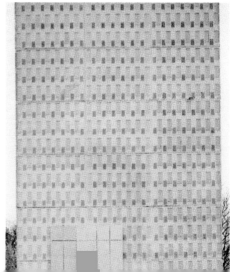

PLUG-IN CITY

PETER COOK/ARCHIGRAM

BELOW LEFT Longitudinal section.
BELOW TOP Axonometric view.
BELOW BOTTOM Section through "University Node"
showing structural tube system.

With the publication of their *Archigram I* pamphlet in 1961, the British architectural collective Archigram manifested a skepticism of Brutalism and other heroic architecture that held sway in Britain. Rather than considering the architect as an omnipotent author, Archigram believed that architecture had the untapped capacity to be contemporaneously monumental and open-source. Architects could create organisms to adapt to and facilitate the desires of inhabitants by exploiting the most up-to-date forms of technology. This credo simultaneously drew upon two major architectural movements with particular ramifications within the realm of prefabrication: Japanese Metabolism and the nascent British High-Tech movement. Taking cues from the seminal architectural projects of Futurists such as Antonio Sant'Elia, Archigram architects (Peter Cook, Warren Chalk, Dennis Crompton, David Greene, Ron Herron, and Michael Webb) were particularly fascinated with the notion of architecture as a type of scaffolding which could house ephemeral vessels, further aestheticizing and formalizing the architectural term *megastructure*.

Archigram's numerous megastructure proposals considered both the individual unit as well as the urbanistic whole, encompassing a comprehensive micro-to-macro set of design concerns that were simultaneously Utopian and decidedly unrealistic, lending them a certain phantasmagorical and whimsical playfulness. The most memorable of these proposals is Plug-In City, designed by Peter Cook. Consisting of an improvisational outcropping of clustered enclaves of prefabricated structural scaffolding, individual prefabricated house units were to be hoisted into place by means of a "craneway," which was not expected to last longer than forty years. The units would be temporarily clipped onto the structure as necessary. In addition to provisional space for residences, the structure would accommodate access routes, hotels, garages, offices, rail lines, galleries, universities, theaters, plazas, and concert halls among other functions. Changes, as dictated by growth or obsolescence, could be accommodated by the emigration, migration, or production of new nodes, in sum reflecting the collective will of the inhabitants. Cook produced among his drawings several mammoth sections that depict an arbitrary example of an infinite number of forms the Plug-In City could assume.

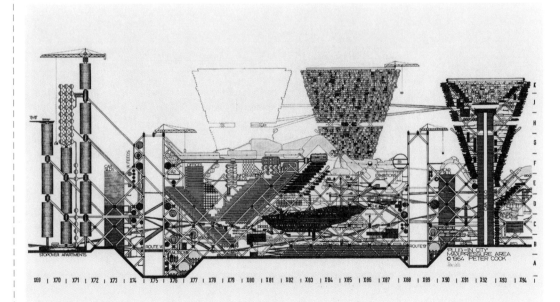

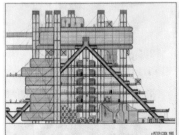

HABITAT '67
MOSHE SAFDIE

As a student at McGill University in the mid-1960s, Moshe Safdie closely watched the Japanese Metabolist movement as well as the work of Archigram in Britain. The Israeli-born Safdie felt an affinity to the Metabolist movement, despite the fact that it had no real foothold in North America, and applied many Metabolist principles to his master's thesis (1961), a proposal for a large-scale precast concrete housing unit. At the age of twenty-four his proposal was chosen to be built for Expo '67, which proved to be the best attended world's fair of the twentieth century. The housing complex remains one of the most familiar landmarks of Montreal.

The exposition, the formal title of which was *Man and His World* (based on Antoine de Saint-Exupéry's *Terre des Hommes*), focused on progressive architecture including works by Shoji Sadao, Frei Otto, and R. Buckminster Fuller. Safdie was selected as Canada's representative, deploying his thesis design as a thematic pavilion to be inspected by thousands of international admirers while also functioning as temporary housing for numerous dignitaries. Built on a man-made island in the Saint Lawrence River using soil excavated from the city's new metro system, the complex was dubbed "Habitat '67" and was one of the few constructions that would remain after the event, becoming middle-income housing for the growing city.

The project was constructed entirely of interlocking modules, and each unit, clad in precast concrete panels, had small yet comfortable private quarters with access to a spacious private garden and harbor and city view exposure on at least three sides. Unlike the work of the Metabolists, Safdie proposed a very different system in which

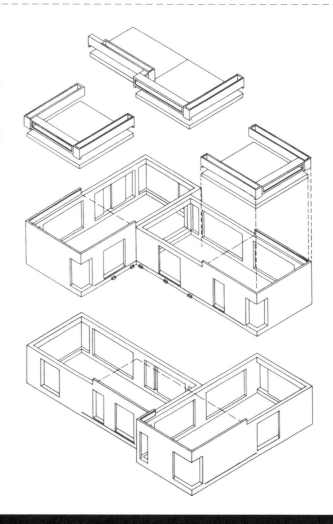

no megastructure was necessary. Rather than "plugged-in" prefabricated units, modules were interlocked and woven primarily in a horizontal direction. With the exception of necessary vertical circulation cores, the project's focus was entirely upon the unit rather than the global structure. Serpentine vehicular and pedestrian avenues weave their way between the structures, rendering an amoeba-like circulation system far different from that of the megastructures proposed by the Metabolists. The units, which torque and cascade around one another, create an infinite number of orientations to both the structure itself as well as the city. Each modular unit is always legible, but is also clearly understood as an absolutely irreplaceable part of a greater whole. A fascinating series of intact models allows one to track the formal development of the project beginning with Safdie's original thesis model, which is rigidly Metabolist in its structure, followed by a model produced for Expo planning purposes, which begins to suppress the megastructure and hint at a new typology, and culminating in a model of what was built; this ultimately breaks free of the megastrcture that had so vividly served as the project's inspiration.

While the complex took several years to build, Safdie believed the potential for replicability and ease of construction anywhere was vast. Safdie hoped the Montreal complex would be the first of many and he developed proposals for sites in Baltimore and Puerto Rico. No other Habitat was built despite the predominantly positive response to the project's incarnation in Montreal.

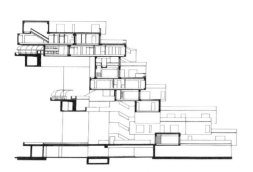

ASBESTOS CEMENT HOUSING MODULE

HUGO D'ACOSTA
AND MERCEDES ÁLVAREZ

BELOW Sketch showing large-scale configuration and inlaid beds.
OPPOSITE, TOP LEFT Constructed module.
OPPOSITE, MIDDLE LEFT Aerial view into module.
OPPOSITE, BOTTOM LEFT Constructed module in Havana.
OPPOSITE, RIGHT Interior view.

Although architectural production may have become increasingly efficient under communist regimes in the Soviet Union and Eastern Europe, they were only rarely amenable to architectural experimentation. Such was not the case with Fidel Castro's Cuba. After the 1959 revolution, Castro instigated an ambitious building program that not only encapsulated a palpable political optimism and desire for social reform but also gave rise to design creativity and experimentation. This was spearheaded by a generation of young architects committed to the revolution's social and aesthetic goals.

Hugo D'Acosta and Mercedes Álvarez, a husband-and-wife team, offered up their own take on prefabrication with the Módulo Experimental de Vivienda de Asbesto-Cemento or Asbestos Cement Housing Module, which they began designing in 1964. Conceived for a housing competition, the project received only a mention. It called for a construction system of basic 6-millimeter-thick sheets, double bowed for rigidity, formed by a single mold that could produce versions over and over again. The material of the house was variable; cement, asbestos, and plastics were possibilities envisioned by the architects. The sheets were subsequently screwed to neighboring pieces using a mechanical joint, the ultimate length and quantity of which remained at the discretion of the client, to form a single longitudinal volume. The module itself contains a sleeping area, bathroom, and living/dining area all within the compact envelope of a single, streamlined pod, the interior surfaces of which gently curve to form inlaid furniture, storage, and fittings. On its exterior the module takes on an otherworldly appearance with a series of tufted, closely-spaced volumes. A single set of molds was to be used over and over again. Easily transportable, the modules could accommodate urban and rural dwellers alike. Ten iterations were produced, only one of which remains standing today, in Havana.

The project is just one of many experimental projects completed in the first decade of Castro's regime, unearthed by architect and historian Eduardo Luis Rodríguez and displayed in an exhibition organized with Belmont Freeman in 2004 at the Storefront for Art and

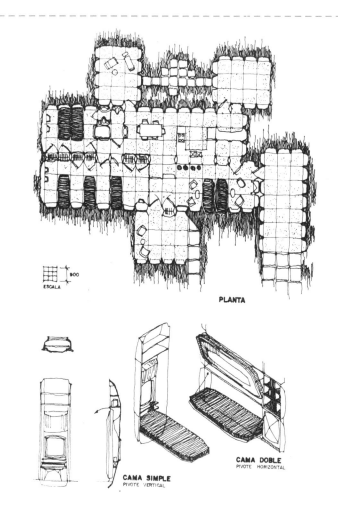

ESCALA

PLANTA

CAMA SIMPLE
PIVOTE VERTICAL

CAMA DOBLE
PIVOTE HORIZONTAL

Architecture (New York) entitled *Architecture and Revolution in Cuba, 1959–1969*. The project is particularly astounding when considered in a formal and conceptual comparison to better known projects designed simultaneously and subsequently, such as Archigram's Living Pod in Britain and Kisho Kurokawa's Nakagin Capsule Tower in Japan, and it presents a striking contrast to more common derivatives of the Soviet panel system that were being built throughout Cuba at the same time.

LIVING POD
DAVID GREENE/ARCHIGRAM

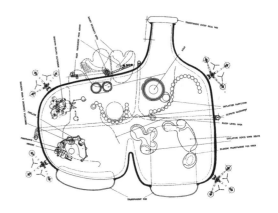

Archigram developed their interest in ephemeral and transportable living capsules begun in their megastructure proposals with David Greene's 1965 Living Pod. The project stands as the first investigation by a member of Archigram conducted into a housing unit that could function independent of a megastructure. The proposal consists of two parts, a "pod" and its "machinery," and draws a clear distinction between the physical envelope of the housing unit and the apparatus that rendered that envelope livable for a human being. Inspired by American "prefabs," i.e., trailer homes and mobile homes, the project was designed to accommodate what Greene thought of as the "Second Machine Age," when the necessity of the house as a permanent static container would disappear. In his view, human settlements would actually become akin to the nomadic settlements of earlier societies. And while the capsule could be plugged into a megastructure if the tenant so desired, the structure had the ability to sit in a barren landscape functioning equally well. The Living Pod was made up of twelve support nodes, six held in tension and six held in compression. Four apertures covered one quarter of the pod's surface area. Inflatable flooring and interior furnishing would allow the structure's largest members to deflate and be packed flat for ease of transport. Four automatic self-leveling compression legs would allow the structure to hover above up to five feet of water or a slope of forty degrees. Two "wash capsules" and two "rotating silos" with electrostatic disposal would afford commodes for laundry, dishwashing, handwashing, toilet facilities, and "corporal cleaning." Specially designed HVAC equipment, a self-cooking food dispenser, and a "teach and work" machine rounded out the machinistic amenities. Although the entire unit was considered an "appliance for carrying with you," Greene conceded that the Living Pod held the potential to usurp the control of its owner and ran the risk of becoming the "master" rather than being a subordinate organ, a danger implicit in the house's heartlike formal expression.

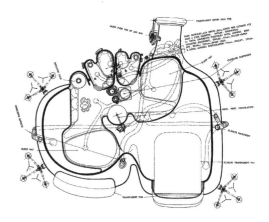

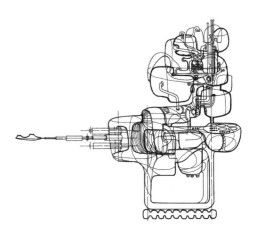

RIGHT (top to bottom) Plan 1; plan 2; Pod Eating Machine view 1; Pod Eating Machine view 2.
OPPOSITE Model and section.

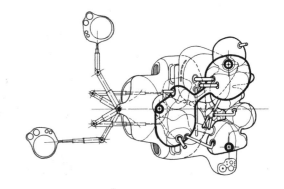

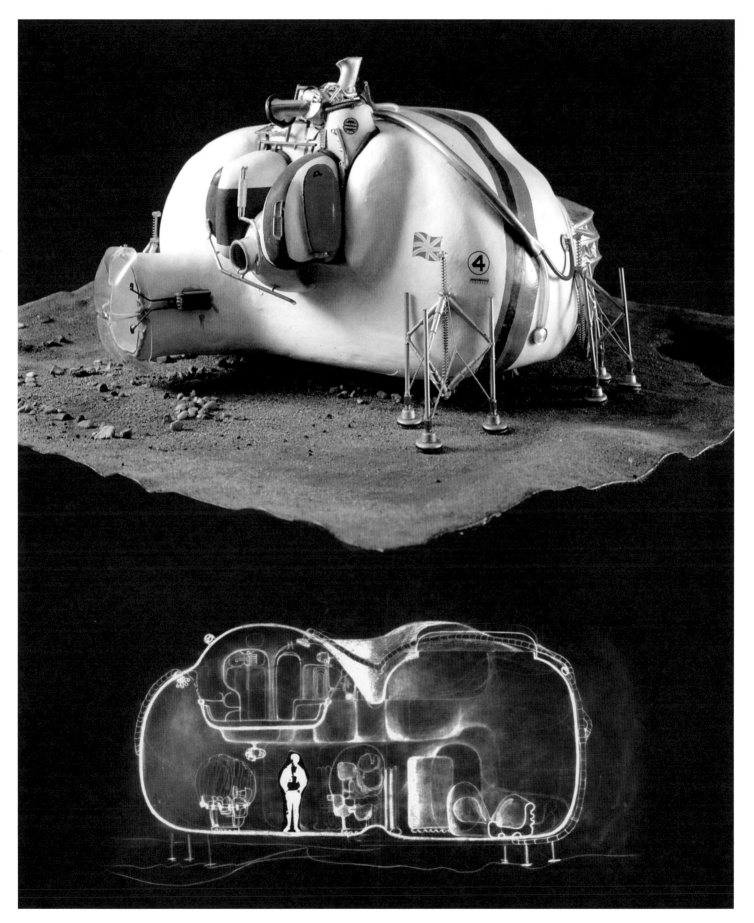

MACIUNAS PREFABRICATED BUILDING SYSTEM

GEORGE MACIUNAS

Lithuanian-born American artist George Maciunas, founder of the artist collective Fluxus, turned his attention to prefabricated housing in 1965, authoring a series of pamphlets with his proposal for a prefabricated building system. One pamphlet, entitled "Communists Must Give Revolutionary Leadership in Culture," consists of two double-sided pages. The first, smaller page is composed exclusively of a detailed text outlining how communists could surpass the United States and Western Europe as cultural leaders in five categories: "The Applied Arts," "Film," "The Visual Arts," "Fiction," and "Theory of Culture." The second page has seven appendices, the first five of which are illustrated. The first appendix provides an analysis of the design and cost-effectiveness of Soviet prefabricated building systems including a comparative analysis of preexisting building systems: a simple tent, a Levitt house, R. Buckminster Fuller's Wichita House, and Fuller's geodesic dome, each assessed for its "workability," "economy," "adaptability," and "durability." Appendix 2 introduces Maciunas's own system, which would, he claimed, prove even more efficient than the Soviet system, and would be both technically superior and rendered in a less brutal aesthetic. In addition, Maciunas draws several diagrams outlining the erection procedure, including a densely detailed exploded isometric cross section of the alumnium components. He even provides images of a model he had made. Appendices 3 to 5 function as homages to design items Maciunas reveres: Fuller's Geodesic Dome, the Citroën automobile, and the electric guitar and organ. In appendices 6 to 7 Maciunas turns his attention to film. The pamphlet is not only a fascinating and curious manifesto but also a rigorous architectural analysis by an artist, surprisingly convincing and entirely unexpected.

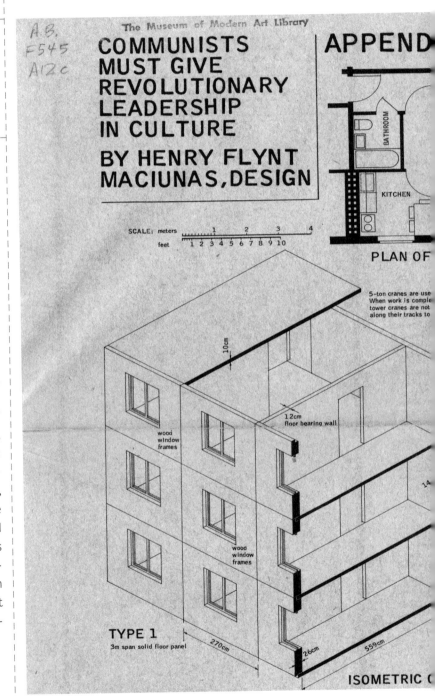

1. SOVIET PREFABRICATED BUILDING SYSTEM

CLOSET

NG ROOM

BEDROOM

CAL APARTMENT

The present Soviet housing program, using automated production of prefabricated concrete components in 440 plants, was started on a large scale in 1953, and by 1960 was producing about 3,000,000 dwelling units yearly, more per capita than any other country. The program is thus proven in practice. It is the most efficient mass housing program in production in the world today.

The Soviet program's efficiency is not a matter of having the least absolute cost, or requiring the least initial investment. A program which used tents would be much cheaper, but tents give very little performance for their low cost, as the following table details.

Efficiency is giving the most performance for the least cost. The Soviet system builds a 300 sq. ft. apartment, which performs as the table details, for $1,500, the cost in the U.S. of an average garage. This unit cost is proven reasonable in practice.

Maciunas' system (not in production) requires a developed chemical industry and a unit cost 10 to 15 per cent higher than that of the Soviet system, but it is even more efficient, as the table details. A 300 sq. ft. unit can be transported on a one-ton truck, while the Soviet system would require seven 5-ton truck-trailers to transport each dwelling unit.

s in place.
ock of flats,
t run over

15cm thick prestressed cellular concrete floor panels. One method of prestressing panel is to expand steel reinforcement by heating it to 400°C, to cast and cure concrete around steel, then to cool steel, contracting it and thereby developing compressive stresses in concrete.

15 cm

15cm floor bearing wall

26cm sandwich type cellular concrete external wall

wood window frames

15cm floor bearing wall

wood window frames

600cm

562cm

TYPE 2
6m span cellular floor panel

SECTIONS
Panels are connected structurally by welding the steel reinforcement together

COMPARATIVE ANALYSIS OF PREFABRICATED BUILDING SYSTEMS

OBJECTIVES		tent	Levitt house	Fuller's Wichita house*	Fuller's geodesic dome	Soviet housing system	Maciunas system
WORKABILITY							
Enclosure and protection from:	rain	yes	yes	yes	yes	yes	yes
	vapor	no	no	no	no	yes	yes
	dust	no	no	no	no	no	yes (filtering system)
	heat & cold	no	yes	yes	yes	yes	yes
	sunlight	yes	yes	yes	yes	yes	yes
	sound	no	no	no	no	yes	yes
Servicing:	traffic & communication	yes	yes	yes	yes	yes	yes
	temperature control	no	yes	yes	yes	yes	yes
	light & air control	no	no	no	no	no	yes
	storage facilities	no	yes	no	no	yes	yes
	hygiene	no	no	yes	yes	no (not washable)	yes
ECONOMY							
In material:	minimum use of material	yes	no	yes	yes	no	yes
	use of abundantly available material	yes	yes	no	yes	yes	yes (except alum.)
In manufacture:	minimum number of components	yes	no	no	yes	yes	yes
	simple method of fabrication	yes	no	no	yes	yes	yes
	simple tooling requirements	yes	yes	no	yes	yes	yes
	adaptability to automated fabrication	yes	yes	yes	yes	yes	yes
In labor use:	minimum use of labor on site	yes	no	yes	yes	yes	yes
	more productive use of labor in plants	yes	no	no	yes	yes	yes
	use of unskilled labor on site	yes	no	no	yes	no	yes
In transport:	light and well packaged	yes	no	yes	yes	no	yes
	building weight per m² of floor area	.5 kg			8 kg	1,150 kg	30 kg
In erection:	speedy and simple erection	yes	no	yes	yes	yes	yes
	no heavy equipment required	yes	yes	yes	yes	no	yes
In maintainance:	permanency of materials	no	no	yes	yes	yes (except wood)	yes
	efficiency of insulation	no	no	no	no	no	yes
	washability of all surfaces	yes	no	yes	yes	no	yes
estimated cost	per square foot	$.50	$10	$30**		$6 to 7	$7.50
ADAPTABILITY							
To function:	residential	yes	yes	yes	no	yes	yes
	institutional	no	no	no	yes	yes	yes
	industrial	no	no	no	yes	yes	yes
	agricultural	yes	no	no	yes	no (heavy transport)	yes
To plan:	flexibility in shape & size of building	no	no	no	no	no	yes
To climate:	climatic changes	no	no	no	no	no (fixed widows)	yes
To dwellers:	their special needs and habits	no	no	no	no	no (fixed plan)	yes
To site:	topography and soil conditions	yes	no	no	no	no (flat ground)	yes
DURABILITY							
Resist aging:	due to rot	no	no	yes	yes	yes (except wood)	yes
	termites	no	no	yes	yes	no	yes
	discoloration	no	no	yes	yes	no (concrete)	yes
	corrosion	no	no	no	no	yes	yes
Resist disasters:	hurricanes	no	no	yes	yes	yes	yes
	earthquakes	yes	no	yes	yes	no (concrete)	yes
	floods	no	no	yes	yes	yes	yes
	vandalism	no	no	no	no	no (concrete)	yes

*also Monsanto house and Nelson-Chadwick house
**estimate only - exact figures not available

COMPARATIVE DATA ON HOUSING IN VARIOUS COUNTRIES

Country	number of flats per 1000 persons built in 1960	total number of flats built in 1960	total floor area built in 1960	average area of each flat built in 1960	average rent in % of occupants budget	multistorey building weight per sq. meter of each floor area
U.S.S.R.	14	2,978,000	85,100,000 m²	29 m²	4%	1,150 kg.
U.S.A.	7.2	1,300,000	60,000,000 m²*	45 m²*	25%	3,500 kg
U.K.	5.9					
France	7.1					
W.Germany	10.7					
Italy	6					

* exact figures not available

REFERENCES:
Maxwell, Robert, (editor), "Countries of the world. Informations series." Vol.1, U.S.S.R., Oxford, 1962.
Tutuchenko, Semyon, "Housing in the U.S.S.R.," Moscow, 1960.
Woytinsky, W.S. and Woytinsky, E.S. "World Population and Production - Trends and Outlook," New York, 1953.

STADT RAGNITZ
EILFRIED HUTH AND GÜNTHER DOMENIG

Eilfried Huth and Günther Domenig's Stadt Ragnitz multi-use rede-velopment proposal for the Austrian city of Graz won the Grand Prix d'Urbanisme et d'Architecture in February 1969. Jury members Louis Kahn and Jean Prouvé celebrated the project for its highly inventive structural system, consisting of alternating layers of prefabricated paired deep trusses sandwiching open-faced cubic volumes, all sep-arated by layer upon layer of diagonal struts which independently provided support for cubic dwelling volumes. Vertical "multiplex clus-ters" for circulation of people and supplies, horizontal ducts, and roads were all woven through the rigid megastructure. Habitable and commercial capsules were to be clipped on and off of the structure as desired. The project reflected a growing fascination with the mega-structure as an architectural paradigm and was a testament to the immediate influence of Archigram and their seminal experiments with plug-in and clip-on megastructures. Stadt Ragnitz, however, stands out among the post-Archigram megastructures that proliferated in European architecture schools for its high level of elaboration and intricacy. Designed as a massive kit of parts that could be infinitely expanded, the beauty of the project lay in its highly articulated join-ery. The architects challenged some of the conceptual and stylistic tenets of their Austrian contemporaries such as Hans Hollein and Walter Pichler insofar as the proposal emphasized system-making over form-making. Nonetheless, the scaleless presentation model built for the competition became something of a commodity in and of itself, traveling to exhibitions across Europe for many years; eventually it fell apart beyond repair. In 2001 the FRAC Centre in Orléans reconstructed a model using fragments of the original as well as documentary photo-graphs and drawings. Although never built, Stadt Ragnitz remains the work for which Huth and Domenig are most noted.

RIGHT Detail, mechanical column.
OPPOSITE, TOP Model.
OPPOSITE, BOTTOM LEFT Diagram of sections through housing unit.
OPPOSITE, BOTTOM RIGHT Site section and unit section.

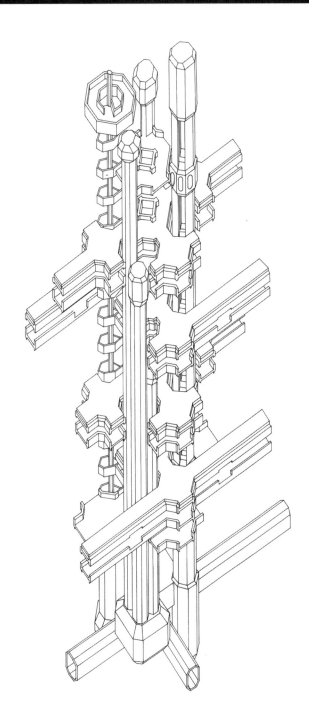

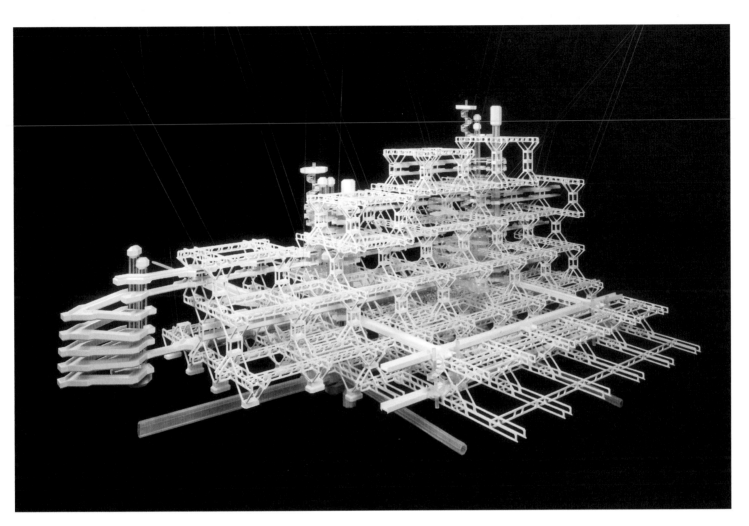

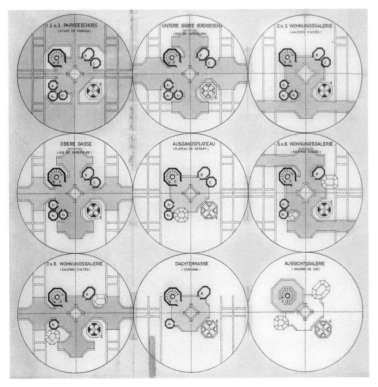

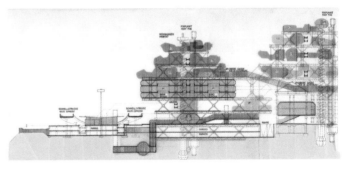

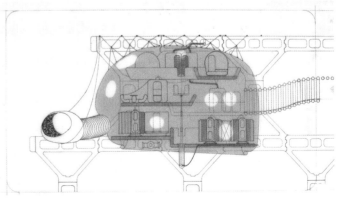

METASTADT-BAUSYSTEM

RICHARD J. DIETRICH

BELOW LEFT Cartoon of project.
BELOW MIDDLE Details, axonometric and joint assembly.
BELOW RIGHT Construction photo.
OPPOSITE Model, module in repetition.

In 1965 Richard J. Dietrich, an architecture student at Munich's Technische Hochschule (known today as the Technische Universität), initiated a series of lectures and exhibitions dealing with the application of industrial fabrication methods to building construction, inviting Konrad Wachsmann, Jean Prouvé, Eckhardt Schulze-Fielitz, and Yona Friedmann to speak. Inspired by the lectures, Dietrich began working on the concept of a prefabricated urban building system while continuing his studies. Dietrich's approach called for the gradual redensification of city centers within an overall structural system, integrating a mix of urban uses: residential as well as working, commercial, cultural, and entertainment spaces.

The structural system developed for the project was an orthogonal steel framework with flex-resistant joints. The small dimensions of the structural elements meant that the structure could be precisely adapted to specific spatial needs. The space-defining elements and technical infrastructure were inserted into the frame, suspended from steel pylons. The absence of diagonal bracing created the maximum of space and permitted the greatest possible flexibility in how it was used. The execution of the structural details meant that the building and ground-floor plan could be altered or enlarged at any time, or that the structure could be completely dismantled. With specially developed software it was possible to calculate automatically the variable load in the overall system to guarantee its constant adaptability.

In 1969 Dietrich started the implementation of his Metastadt-Bausystem (Metacity building system), together with Bernd Steigerwald and others, financed by OKAL, the most important manufacturer of prefabricated housing in Germany at that time. In 1971 an experimental structure was erected on the grounds of the Technische Hochschule, and in 1972 OKAL erected a demonstration building to be used as its headquarters. In that same year the Metastadt-Bausystem was presented at the Hannover Fair, and a Metastadt project was commissioned for Wulfen, near Duisburg. The Metastadt-Bausystem is unusal in the history of construction in that it combines city planning, architecture, and structural engineering. In its program, organization, and methodology, and in the means employed in its conception, development, planning, and execution, it was far ahead of its time.

—Florian Breiphol

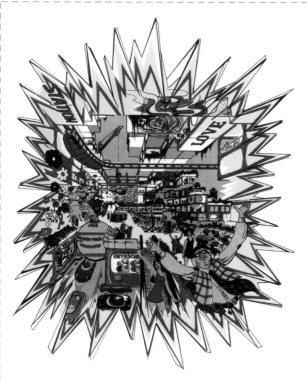

STELCO CATALOGUE HOUSING
BARTON MYERS ASSOCIATES

The Canadian firm Barton Myers Associates, led by its American-born principal, after whom the firm is named, made a particularly noteworthy contribution to the discourse on prefabrication in the late 1960s. At a time when plastics engaged most architects' creativity, the Canadian steel company Stelco announced an unlikely competition, organized in conjunction with *Canadian Home* magazine, to develop a steel housing prototype. Steel had dominated research in the 1930s, but had not regained favor since. Myers's entry, the most arresting, but not the winner, consisted of a system of steel column sections, hollow tube beams, and a number of different sandwich panels of prefinished steel with a urethane core for horizontal and vertical surfaces, all on a 3-foot-square module, making up autonomous sections of 12 feet square. These sections were framed in a host of combinations with the potential to be stacked as high as three stories. The individual panels fit into the frame with industrial Velcro. Joints between the panels were sealed with neoprene tongues. The use of technologically advanced and unusual materials within a regular steel grid system is a unique translation of some of the contemporary High-Tech experiments in Britain, notably those of Richard Rogers, Michael Hopkins, and Richard Horden. The most astounding aspect of the proposal was that the system of discrete, catalogue-ordered parts could be assembled by two unskilled persons in just one hour per square frame, with later additions and modifications being infinitely possible. Because all of the parts remained individual and unaltered by means of their fastening, they were also reusable. The system promised to be the simplest and most rapid of its time, but as it was never built the project remains relatively unsung in the annals of prefabrication.

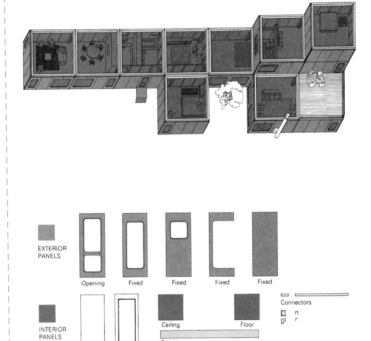

EXTERIOR PANELS

Opening | Fixed | Fixed | Fixed | Fixed

Connectors

INTERIOR PANELS

Ceiling | Floor

Fascia

Fixed | Opening

FRAMING MEMBERS

Joist

Column

Edge beam

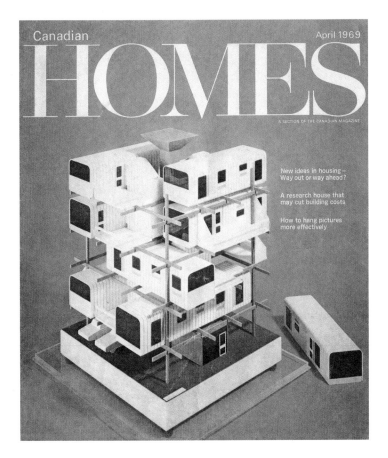

LEFT Cover, *Canadian Homes*, April 1969; published in conjunction with Stelco Steel Competition.
BELOW Final model.
BOTTOM LEFT Study model, assembly phase 1.
BOTTOM MIDDLE Study model, assembly phase 2.
BOTTOM RIGHT Study model, assembly phase 3.

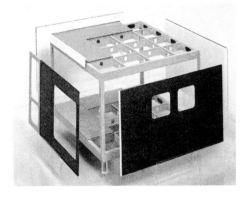

FUTURO HOUSE
MATTI SUURONEN

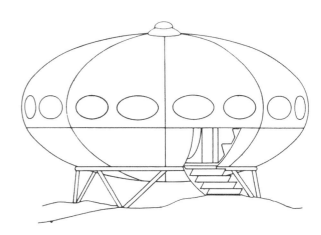

If the space-age craze of the 1960s and 1970s had an architectural icon it would undoubtedly be Matti Suuronen's Futuro House, a work as famous for its otherworldly appearance as for its cult following. Some one hundred Futuros were manufactured between 1968 and 1978, and while the house has come to typify a short-lived architectural movement linked largely with the aesthetics of science fiction, its form belies its significance as an early investigation of the role plastics could play in prefabricated housing.

The Futuro is a single saucer-shaped volume, 11 feet high at its center and 26 feet in diameter, which in turn rests on a steel support structure. A hatch door in the lower half unfurls to reveal steps, similar to the hatch of an airplane. Inside, a single room is outfitted with six plastic bed-chair units and a central fireplace core as well as a kitchenette and a bathroom. Made entirely of fiberglass reinforced polyester plastic, a fairly inexpensive but durable material, the Futuro sold in the United States for between $12,000 and $14,000 (approximately $80,000 in 2008). It was manufactured by the Finnish plastic company Polykem and came in sixteen radial pieces that were easily transported by truck or helicopter and could be assembled in just a few days. Suuronen's foray into domestic plastics was largely unrehearsed, as his first project in plastic was for an industrial purpose: a dome for a grain silo in the Finnish town of Seinäjoki. The manufacture of the silo domes easily lent itself to the design of the Futuro, which is essentially two of the domes placed end on end, retaining the original twenty-six foot diameter, a form of reappropriation with echoes of Edison and Fuller.

Some critics have characterized the Futuro as an exception in an otherwise golden era of elegant and understated Finnish architecture. But to others the house is a canonical manifesto à la Stanley Kubrick or

TOP RIGHT Elevation and section.
RIGHT Early blueprint, planar sections A and B.
OPPOSITE Futuro being lifted onto ship for transport from Helsinki, 1969.

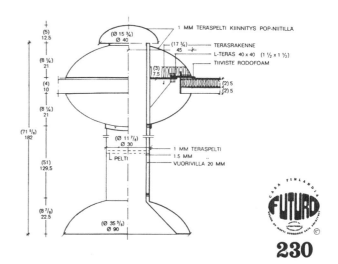

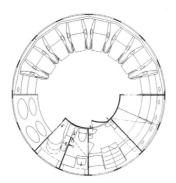

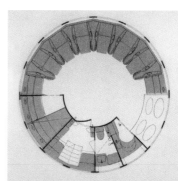

Kurt Vonnegut that pushes the aesthetic and material envelope, a recurring theme in the major utopian visions of prefabricated housing in the twentieth century. The house also aligns with a movement in industrial design in which manufacturers such as Kartell and designers such as Verner Panton ardently sought to usher plastics into the domestic realm.

In 1998 Finnish filmmaker Mika Taanila rekindled interest in the house with his film *Futuro: A New Stance for Tomorrow*. According to Taanila, the Futuro reflected the era's "economic boom and optimism about the future. Suuronen could not have come up with the idea fifteen years earlier or ten years later." The majority of Futuros still standing are in Finland, New Zealand, and the United States.

OPPOSITE, TOP TWO ROWS Assembly in Polykem plant, 1968.
OPPOSITE, BOTTOM LEFT Futuro installed on mountain as ski chalet.
OPPOSITE, BOTTOM RIGHT Model depicting the never-realized Hotel Futuro.
BELOW Interior view.

NAKAGIN CAPSULE TOWER
KISHO KUROKAWA

BELOW Typical plan.
BOTTOM LEFT Longitudinal section.
BOTTOM RIGHT Transverse section.
OPPOSITE Construction photo.

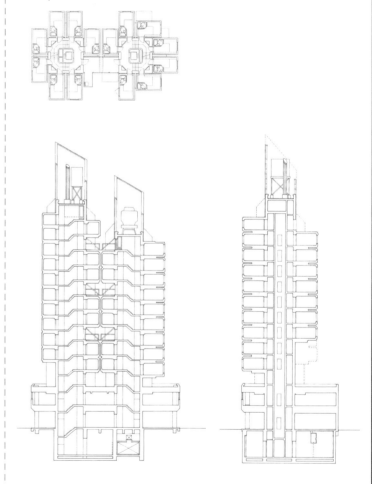

Completed after the unofficial demise of the Japanese Metabolist movement, the Nakagin Capsule Tower by Kisho Kurokawa nonetheless remains the movement's most emblematic built work. As with other Metabolist proposals, the Capsule Tower is nothing more than a superstructure with numerous prefabricated units "plugged in." The structure was conceived as an infinitely alterable helicoidal infrastructure that could afford the building, or organism, qualities of adaptability and flexibility unfamiliar to the conventional tall building or even to the megastructure typology. Built in Tokyo's Ginza district, the tower was initially designed as a hotel to provide affordable accommodations for single businessmen unable to take the time to commute home.

Each "capsule" is actually a steel-trussed box measuring some 8 by 13 feet, clad in galvanized reinforced steel and coated with a glossy rust-proof paint spray. Each contains a built-in bed and drop-in bathroom unit. The capsules were outfitted off site and hoisted into place by crane, latching onto the fourteen-story superstructure and its concrete core shaft of vertical circulation. Capsules could be combined to create larger spaces, although this was done infrequently. None of the original capsules has been replaced. The core, built on site, also employs numerous prefabricated elements. The precast concrete floor slabs that were part of the core's structure were erected at a rate of one every two days, alternating with the construction of the steel frame, affording a fully operational core to facilitate the periodic construction of the framework without an external scaffold. The building has evolved into a multi-use complex, alternating between varying combinations of hotel, residential, and office uses for the past thirty-five years. In recent years the building has sadly fallen into disrepair and is, at the time of publication, scheduled for demolition.

The clip-on capsule structure is decidedly compact, leaving little room for customization of any sort. Even alarm clocks, task lights, soap dispensers, and flip-down desk surfaces were predetermined. In a sense, they presage much of the minimal urban living that has gained prominence in more recent years. In that vein, the Capsule Tower is a seminal work in that it is not only emblematic of Japanese metabolism but also reinvents the apartment and hotel building types. Hyperdense, prefurnished, and in a sense antifamily, Kurokawa's capsules celebrated the flexibility and freedom of bachelorhood by minimizing the domestic choices the inhabitant had to make and maximizing the flexibility of the larger organism to accommodate future versions of itself.

BELOW LEFT Axonometric view.
BELOW MIDDLE Composite of elevations and ground-level plan.
BELOW RIGHT Axonometric cut-away view of capsule.
OPPOSITE Interior view of capsule.

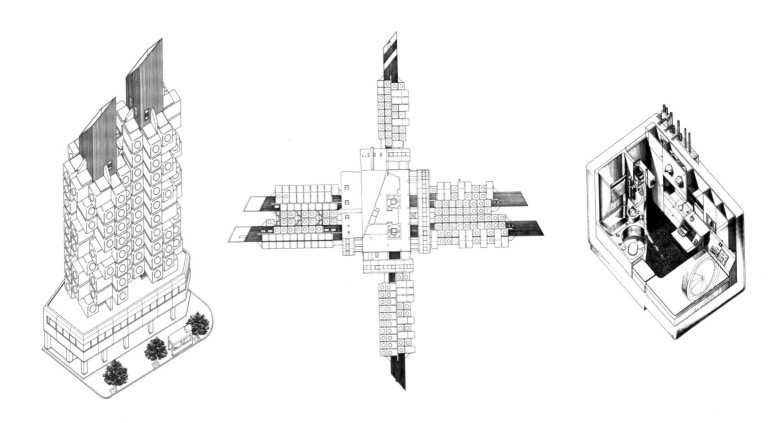

ZIP-UP ENCLOSURES NOS. 1 AND 2

RICHARD AND SU ROGERS

BELOW Plan.
BOTTOM Sketch.
OPPOSITE Model.

Convinced that the future of housing in the United Kingdom lay with mass production, Richard and Su Rogers set out to design a housing "resource" that would be expandable and portable. They were particularly inspired by the monocoque construction of the transportation industry, in which airplanes, boats, and cars are constructed so that the body is combined with the chassis as a single unit and the vehicular "skin" provides its own structural support. During his student days in America in the 1960s, Richard Rogers was particularly interested in the Airstream trailer and other American modes of economical and flexible living. The two versions of the never-realized Zip-Up Enclosure were created for competitions sponsored by DuPont for the 1969 and 1971 Ideal Home exhibitions. The project employed DuPont products to demonstrate how a house could be built out of the newest high-tech materials, including hybrid plastics, rubber, and PVC. While neither project was granted first prize, the designs set a line of research for the Rogerses and were very influential on others.

The floor, walls, and roof components were to be fabricated off site in separate pieces and then attached on site to create a structural ring some 3 feet in width and 30 feet in length. Each of the ring's four sides could be customized in a variety of ways, including color, fenestration, and texture. Furthering the enclosure's customizability would be its ability to "zip up" with other rings in a potentially infinite tube adapted to the spatial needs of the customer. The customer could go to a local home store to purchase as many rings as needed to begin or add to their home. Of primary concern was the ability to control the climatic environment through the choices of customization (i.e., which facades

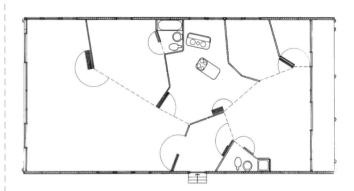

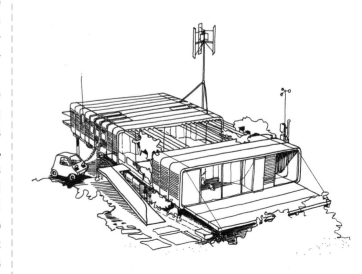

were glazed versus those left solid), while the insulation installed on the structural panels had seven times the capacity of traditional options, substantially lowering HVAC costs. To be produced on a massive scale, the Zip-Up was intended to compete on the market with traditional prefabricated options in 1960s and 1970's Britain. For site adaptability, the house could be adapted to any topographic contours using its adjustable steel jack stilts. The elim-

ination of a concrete foundation would free the structure from both expensive foundation preparations and a permanent marriage to a particular locale. Movable partitions and specially designed mobile furniture further opened up options in the interior of the house, while an outlet for an electric car was provided on the outside. In the second proposal (1971) the architects further elaborated the scheme to adapt to tighter, multistory urban situations.

Conceived in the nascent stages of the British High-Tech movement the Zip-Up Enclosures are remarkable examples of proto-sustainable architecture. And although technology and industrialization were at the core of the High-Tech movement, Richard and Su Rogers devised a project eminently realizable and with little of the Pop irony of contemporary proposals by Archigram and others.

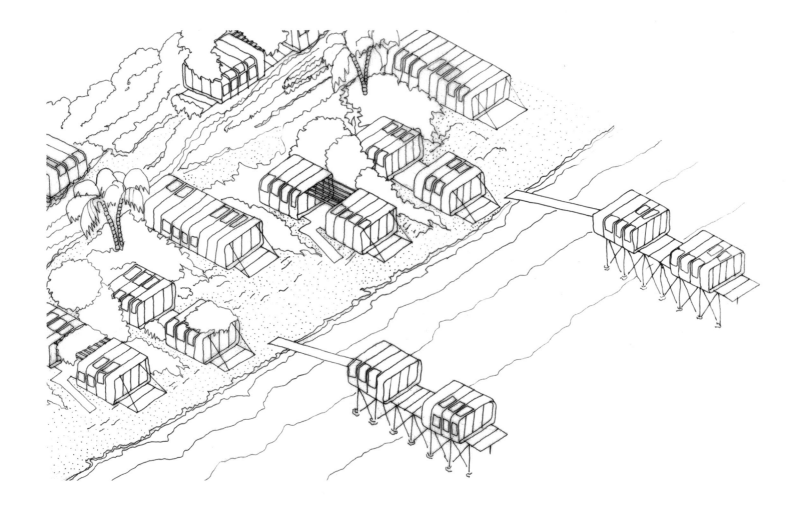

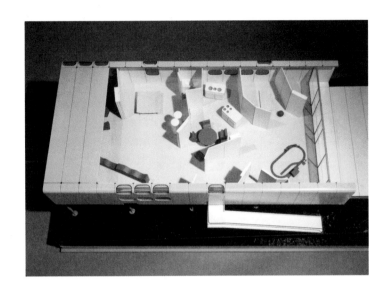

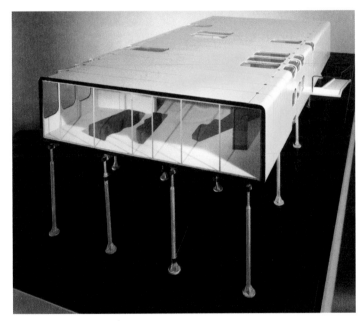

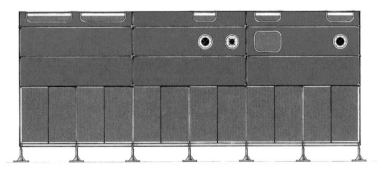

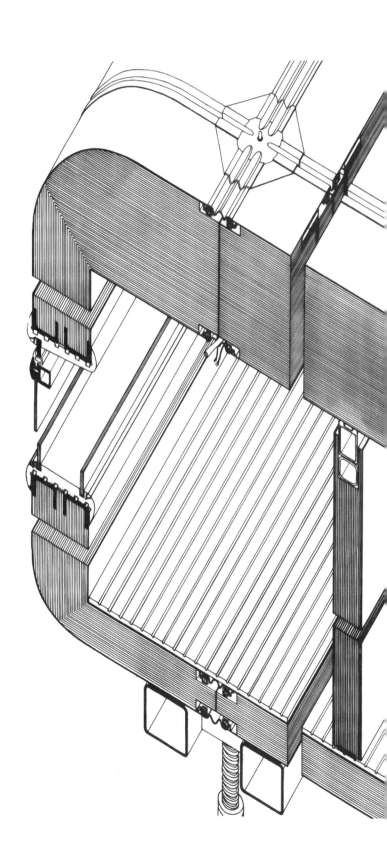

MODULI 225
KRISTIAN GULLICHSEN AND
JUHANI PALLASMAA

The Moduli 225 by Finnish architects Kristian Gullichsen and Juhani Pallasmaa (also widely known as a historian and critic), built throughout Finland between 1969 and 1971, continued a tradition of prefabricated housing in the Nordic countries. However, Gullichsen and Pallasmaa updated that tradition with the formal sensibilities of modern and modular housing models and reembraced traditional timber, which was increasingly being supplanted by steel.

Taking its name from the use of a single module measuring 225 centimeters in each of its cubic dimensions (approximately 7.5 feet cubed), the house could be configured in an almost infinite number of combinations. Each space frame module has three vertical or horizontal slots measuring 75 centimeters (approximately 2.5 feet), which allow panels to be inserted on any given side—fully glazed panels, opaque panels, slotted panels, door panels, or the absence of infill altogether. The space frames adjoin neighboring frames with a simple, elegant screw system. The foundation consists of joinery where the vertical wooden post meets a stout metal pylon, eliminating the need for an on-site, poured foundation, a system that affords the house the ability to hover slightly above the ground plane, accommodating a range of topographic shifts of up to a 5-foot differential. Assembly could be as rapid as two days for simple configurations, and the price was markedly more affordable than existing housing systems. While intended primarily as a summer cottage, the house came to be widely used as a primary residence. Several dozen iterations stand throughout Finland.

In form, the house recalls Mies van der Rohe's Farnsworth House in its horizontal expansiveness and relationship to the ground plane. In genesis, however, the Moduli 225 is completely different, offering an alternative to the material palette and constructive process of the most celebrated modernist houses.

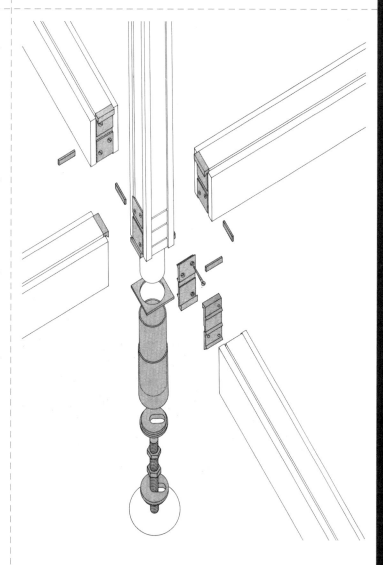

   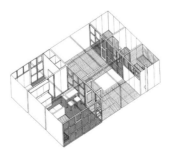 

ORIENTAL MASONIC GARDENS

PAUL RUDOLPH

BELOW Plan, level 1.
BOTTOM Plan, level 2.
OPPOSITE Perspective rendering.

In 1970 Paul Rudolph labeled the mobile home the "Brick of the Twentieth Century." This statement remains provocative on two levels, the first being the notion that the building module, aka "the brick," is something that could be inhabitable and not merely constructive (volumetric and structural); the second is the suggestion that architects must scale up building density to meet housing needs. The Oriental Masonic Gardens in New Haven, Connecticut, is the fifth and only realized attempt Rudolph made to use the mobile home as a building unit. On a 15-acre inner-city site, the project was engineered as quality housing for middle- and low-income tenants. Rudolph celebrated the fact that the project, unlike some of his other works, contained virtually no technological innovation. Rudolph's accomplishment, as he described it himself, was "political innovation."

Clusters of four prefabricated mobile units pivoted in pinwheel formation, each unit with its own private entrance and outdoor space, features unusual in contemporaneous low-income housing projects. The gently rolling site allowed the collection of pinwheels to offer differentiated orientations, collectively recalling a large village that is simultaneously substantial yet manageable in scale. Apartments consisted of either two or three connected units that were delivered via the interstate highway, and hence did not exceed the maximum allowed width of 12 feet, with lengths being either 36 or 60 feet. Modules were made entirely of wood with a concrete firewall set in situ between apartment units. A two-bedroom unit sold for $16,000 ($90,000 in 2008). Because of the modularity and mobility of the units, the entire arrangement had the potential to be disbanded and reconstituted.

The project recalls an important moment when leading American architects turned their attention to the period's housing crisis, seeking innovative, attractive, and affordable solutions. The mobile unit had long been disdained by most prominent architects; Rudolph's bold embrace of the vernacular remains one of the first and stands as an early example of the mobile unit as a greater architectural building block.

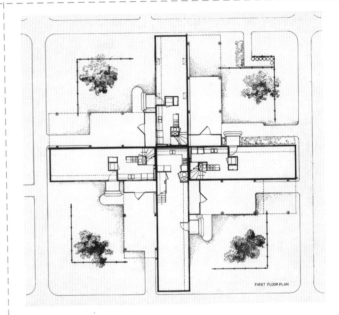

FIRST FLOOR PLAN

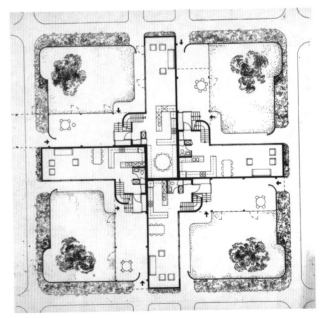

BELOW LEFT Model.
BELOW RIGHT Assembly of cluster.
BOTTOM Exterior view.
OPPOSITE Aerial view.

RAMOT HOUSING
ZVI HECKER

OPPOSITE Facade detail.

The establishment of the Israeli state in 1948 led an unprecedented number of Jews to settle in Israel seeking a new life. A large portion of the settlers were housed in *ma'abarot*, or camps, largely improvised communities consisting of tents and temporary tin dwellings. Eventually many of the improvised *ma'abarot* evolved into formal, permanent settlements. As the Israeli economy prospered into the 1970s, Israeli architects were increasingly charged with designing permanent housing for settlers moving out of the *ma'abarot*. Polish-born architect Zvi Hecker emerged as one of the leading figures in Israeli architecture in the 1960s and was thus the prime candidate for a major commission from the Ministry of Housing to design one of the largest of the new residential complexes being built in the area of Ramot on the outskirts of Jerusalem. The complex, designed for a strict Orthodox community, was eventually completed in 1985, built in five separate stages. It was composed of five separate "fingers" of star-shaped buildings enclosing a string of interconnected courtyards and pedestrian walkways, with each "finger" developed in distinct phases as financing became available; eventually it comprised 726 apartments. The first stage, completed in 1975, used prefabricated building technology for its economic efficiency. But this method was phased out by the third stage, when the Housing Ministry substituted the general contractor with a builder who preferred the local practice of building with small slabs of stone instead of concrete. Although construction techniques were altered, the design was not, and thus the building remains a curious mélange of genuinely prefabricated construction juxtaposed with handcrafted construction done on site mimicking a certain prefabricated formalism.

The system that Hecker prescribed in his original design consisted of hundreds of dodecahedrons sitting tightly one on top of the other, resembling a natural honeycomb. Each face of the dodecahedron was cast from a single pentagonal slab of precast concrete that was lifted into place by a crane, each unit having one face with a window. A concrete skeletal frame formed interstitial voids that functioned as vertical and horizontal circulation between units. Exterior terraces provided by the roof of the unit below functioned as vital design elements, serving the residents during Succoth—the Feast of Tabernacles—as living, eating, and even sleeping spaces in accordance with Jewish religious law. The central courtyards recalled the traditional court arrangement of housing in the Old City of Jerusalem. Hecker had followed the work of the Metabolists, particularly Kisho Kurokawa and Arata Isozaki, and their influence is certainly evident, despite the fundamental difference that the Ramot Housing project was not designed as a structure in which individual units could be plugged in, removed, and interchanged. The emphasis was rather on permanence and solidity, a felicitous reinterpretation considering the context of the settler residents.

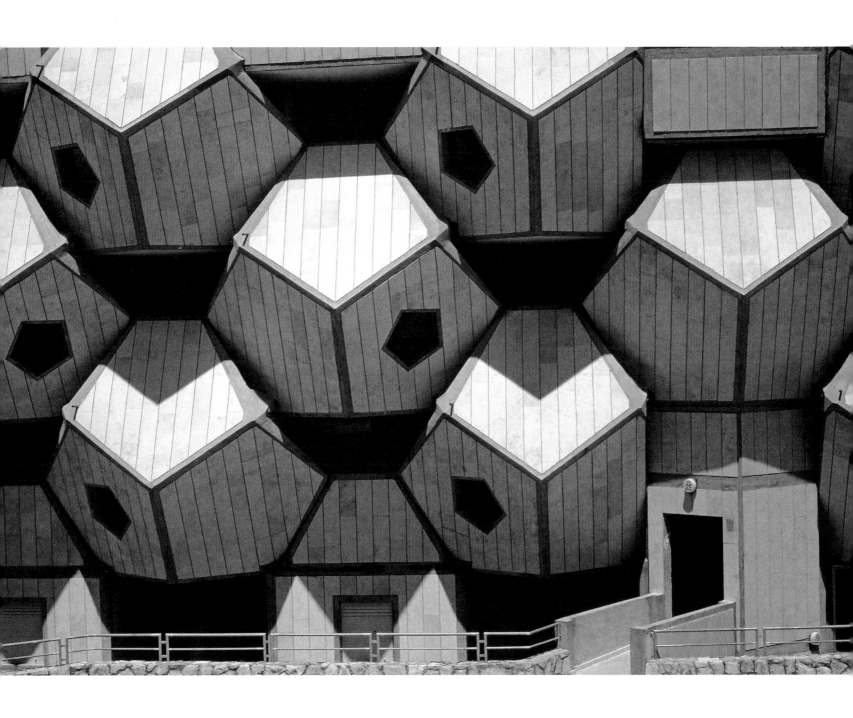

RIGHT Axonometric view of site proposal.
BELOW LEFT Assembly system for prefabricated elements.
BELOW RIGHT Plan diagrams.
BOTTOM Site elevations.
OPPOSITE, TOP LEFT AND RIGHT Construction photos.
OPPOSITE, MIDDLE LEFT Aerial view of site.
OPPOSITE, BOTTOM LEFT Courtyard view.
OPPOSITE, BOTTOM RIGHT Courtyard view.

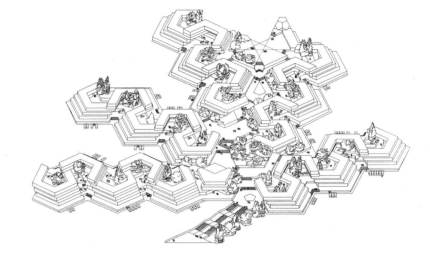

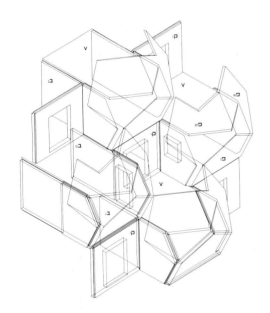

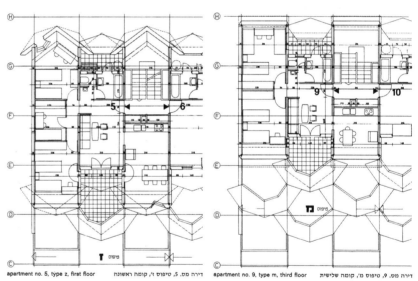

apartment no. 5, type z, first floor   דירה מס. 5, טיפוס ז', קומה ראשונה

apartment no. 9, type m, third floor   דירה מס. 9, טיפוס מ', קומה שלישית

GEN-AN (FANTASY VILLA)

OSAMU ISHIYAMA

Osamu Ishiyama's Gen-An (Fantasy Villa), a project he describes as a "hut in the age of industrialization," appears to be anything but the product of Japanese manufacturing. Employing the inexpensive vernacular building materials of rural Japan, including corrugated steel and cheap wood, the Gen-An house is simultaneously steeped in tradition and entirely novel.

The Gen-An, built as a prototype in Aichi Prefecture, is a semicylindrical volume with a generously proportioned poured concrete foundation, corrugated steel sheathing, and a playfully decorated wooden and glass front and back. A lofted sleeping space distinguishes the simple living quarters from the more private area above. The house could be built with a low standard of construction skills in no more than two weeks.

The Gen-An encapsulates Ishiyama's role as the spokesperson of the Japanese New Wave, a group of architects who turned their backs on both the Metabolist and Postmodern movements in Japan, seeking to re-create a generic approach to site. An admirer of R. Buckminster Fuller, Ishiyama believed indeterminate, siteless, and modest architecture could provide general solutions to social woes as well as offering inhabitants an opportunity for a less scripted lifestyle. Ishiyama was also an early pioneer of sustainable housing systems in Japan, with the Gen-An having the potential to function off grid, and Ishiyama having coined the term "direct dealing," in which consumers could bypass conventional commercial networks that made housing and architects more expensive. In Ishiyama's view this affords the consumer the opportunity to educate themselves about design. Ishiyama was particularly enthusiastic about the Japanese publication of *The Whole Earth Catalog*, which presented a series of primers on tools and ideas that would allow consumers to build their homes themselves.

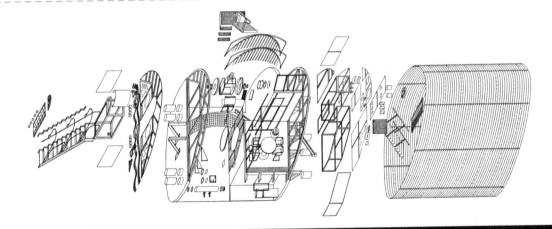

ALMERE HOUSE
BENTHEM CROUWEL ARCHITECTS

BELOW Sketches of structural system.
BOTTOM Rear elevation.
OPPOSITE, TOP Interior view.
OPPOSITE, BOTTOM LEFT Exterior views.
OPPOSITE, BOTTOM MIDDLE Construction photo.
OPPOSITE, BOTTOM RIGHT Foundation detail.

Benthem Crouwel Architects' Almere House is a rare example of innovative prefabricated housing built in the 1980s. Completed in 1984, it was designed for the "Unusual Homes" competition held by De Fantasie in Almere, the Netherlands. Participants were presented with a brief to design a house unrestricted by any building regulations. Prizewinners were awarded a plot of land on loan for five years. This meant that the house and its foundations had to be easily demountable. In Benthem Crouwel's compact house, the living room is bounded on three sides by glass sheets to gather the surrounding landscape into the house. Sandwich panel walls enclose the private zone comprising the two bedrooms, kitchen, and bathroom. The extraordinary construction of the house combats wind pressure in three ways: the space-frame floor structure is attached to a foundation of concrete slabs, stabilizing fins are placed strategically at the seams of the toughened glass sheets, and finally two steel tension cables secure the lightweight profiled steel roof borne aloft by the glazing. The house embodies a structural forthrightness and machinelike aesthetic reminiscent of Dutch modernism, in particular the work of Mart Stam. The firm, which had no prior interest in prefabrication, nonetheless created one of the most subtle examples of prefabricated housing at odds with the postmodernism then prevalent in Europe and the United States. While the architects recognized the immense potential for the house's replication, no others were built. Despite the unencumbered, fantastical nature of the competition brief, the house is rational and subdued, belying the fantastical nature in which it was conceived.

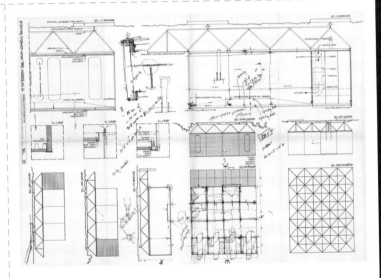

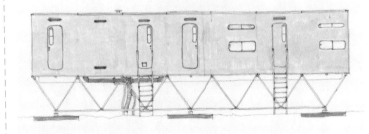

YACHT HOUSE

RICHARD HORDEN/HORDEN CHERRY LEE ARCHITECTS

BELOW LEFT Plan.
BELOW RIGHT Concept sketches illustrating technology transfer.
OPPOSITE, TOP LEFT (bottom to top) Assembly process, phases 1, 2, and 3.
OPPOSITE, TOP RIGHT Exterior view.
OPPOSITE, BOTTOM LEFT Assembly detail.
OPPOSITE, BOTTOM RIGHT View of mast joint.

One of the last great examples of residences within the High-Tech movement in Britain, Richard Horden's Yacht House, was built for a family of modest means who wanted the potential to expand their property from 1,320 to 2,250 square feet. The original house was single-story, with a specially engineered alloy space-frame grid of perfect cubic units. Concrete footings on the short ends held the structural lattice taut and level over a slight slope while aluminum compression and steel tension members held the space frame together. The family assembled the house themselves in just a few weeks. A notable characteristic of the project was its "technology transfer," or appropriation, of a tubular aluminum yacht mast designed by Rodney Marsh into the series of horizontal tubes that enclosed the white polyester, powder-coated aluminum space frame. This skin acts as a strong "wind frame,"

increases the structure's rigidity, and functions as the armature into which the floors, roof, and interior wall modules lock. "Technology transfer" was a particularly popular concept of the High-Tech movement in general, where other fields of design proved to be rich sources for new thinking in form-making and architectural production. Horden would eventually split his time between practice and research into manufactured housing as a professor at the Technische Unversität in Munich, where he began research on the micro compact home, exhibited for the first time in the United States in this exhibition.

The Yacht House illustrates some of the initial questions into housing and technology to which Horden has committed his research and practice. Several variations on the Yacht House have been built for both domestic and trade purposes.

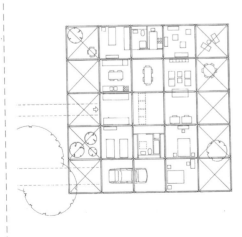

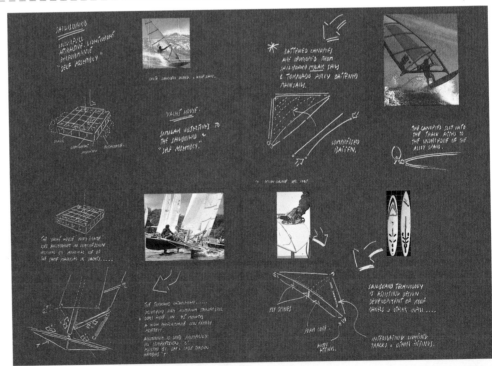

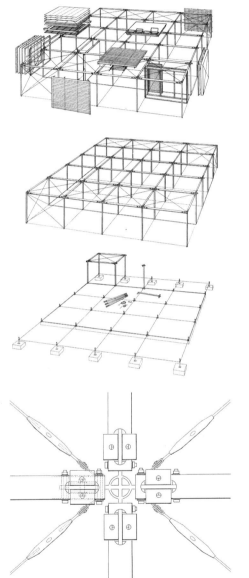

KIM HOUSE
WARO KISHI

Waro Kishi's Kim House is characteristic of the dilemma many Japanese architects have faced with industrialized housing: understanding the economic benefits while decrying the aesthetics of the ubiquitous model homes built by manufacturers like Toyota and Sekisui. One of Kishi's earliest projects, the Kim House, is a stunning example of the architect's ability to assemble off-the-shelf materials under numerous limitations to create a completely singular house, ripe for replication, although never intended to be explicitly replicable.

Situated in a gritty industrial neighborhood of central Osaka, the Kim House is set within the confines of a typical prewar row house plot. After eliminating part of a preexisting row house, the site's footprint was limited to a mere 8.5 feet in width and 18 feet in depth.

Four wide-flange prefabricated steel frames were erected in equal intervals along the depth of the plot, followed by the placement of a standardized steel deck for a second level and another for roofing. Within the house's diminutive plan the architect carves out an intimate courtyard that recalls the traditional Japanese courtyard house typology. White tiles line both inside and outside spaces to maintain an even flow throughout. Using techniques similar to hanging a curtain wall, the construction was completed by hanging a series of modularly proportioned cladding elements including molded cement panels, windows, and doors. Totaling a mere 743 square feet for a family of six, the house was remarkably inexpensive and remains a modest masterpiece within the architect's evolving oeuvre.

CONTAINER HOUSE AND PRIMITIVE HUTS

WES JONES/JONES PARTNERS: ARCHITECTURE

Architect Wes Jones's fascination with the ubiquitous shipping container goes back to the early 1990s; he inspired a number of architects similarly to commit their practices to refurbishing these inherently readymade, durable building blocks. Responding to the proliferation of unused shipping containers cluttering ports around the globe, Jones saw immense potential to use them as elemental units for refurbished homes. In his designs the standard container would be dissected, articulated, added onto, and otherwise modified depending on the needs of the client. With additional off-the-shelf ramps, shades, photovoltaic panels, HVAC systems, furniture, porches, pools, and struts, the house is part readymade, part collage, and, at the time it was introduced, entirely novel. One of the earliest such proposals was for the Hesselink Guest Hut (also known as the Container House), for which Jones developed a distinct drawing style with annotations and exploded axonometrics conveying, quite lucidly, the house as a kit, or perhaps assemblage, of parts. A model he created for the project was equally dynamic, appearing as though it had been paused during a moment in the construction phase.

Four years later, Jones articulated these ideas with a series of proposals, built as models, called Primitive Huts, a reference to the seminal concept of Marc-Antoine Laugier's 1753 *Essay on Architecture*. Laugier argued that architecture must derive all its forms from the most basic requirements of structural solidity, an ideal embodied in the primitive hut. Consisting of a standard cube-shaped shipping container wrapped, flanked, ramped, and hovered upon by a series of

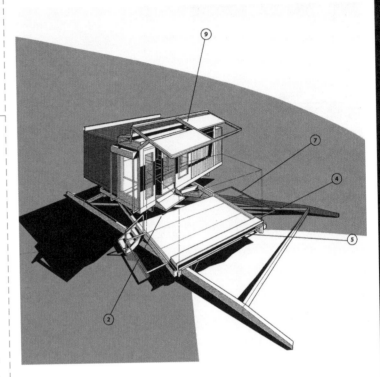

materials forming ancillary architectural functions—logs, twigs, I-beams, trusses, glass, and aluminum—Jones's proposal is architecture for the hunter-gatherer, for persons who seek to scavenge materials, or recycle them, without depending upon market infrastructure for their livelihood. The proposal, while radical in its polemic, is perhaps even more significant in its anticipation of the "green" phenomenon of more recent years, in which consumers have become increasingly interested in sustainable structures that have no adverse impact on the environment and do not depend on utility infrastructure. Jones continues his practice today, developing a line of container homes called PRO/Con (Program/Container).

OPPOSITE Rendering, Hesselink Guest Hut/Container House.
BELOW Model, Primitive Hut, Variation 1.
BOTTOM LEFT AND RIGHT Model, Primitive Hut, Variations 2 and 3.

GREAT HANSHIN EARTHQUAKE COMMUNITY SHELTER

ANDERSON ANDERSON ARCHITECTURE

The Great Hanshin Earthquake of January 1995, in Kobe, Japan, was, at the time, the costliest natural disaster to befall any single country, resulting in $200 billion worth of damage and taking more than 6,000 lives. A multinational task force was set up to provide assistance to the local government, ranging from food and clothes to shelter. The Hyogo prefectural government, which includes the city of Kobe, was remarkably well equipped to house the millions of displaced people, primarily in schools, community shelters, and offices. The relocation of displaced persons to public spaces at nearly maximum capacity created an urgent need for rapidly deployable, multiuse community shelters that could function as schools, clinics, offices, and housing all at the same time. Anderson Anderson Architecture, based in Seattle and San Francisco, had been developing sophisticated prefabricated housing systems since the early 1990s, and conceived a

shelter in just a matter of days using readily available building materials donated in kind by construction product companies in Washington state, along with a small palette of standardized, off-the-shelf components. Construction methods were exceptionally simple and could be executed by unskilled local labor with no special equipment.

The shelter was designed as a replicable prototype that could be customized to meet the needs of each particular community and the programs it required. Entire kitchens, storage units, bookshelves, and other furnishings all sat on wheels and could be reconfigured quickly. A rooftop garden would provide respite above the ad hoc community. Although never built, the project is an early and refined example of the growing interest of architects in disaster housing during recent years. Additionally, the house marks a moment in the firm's history that crystallized

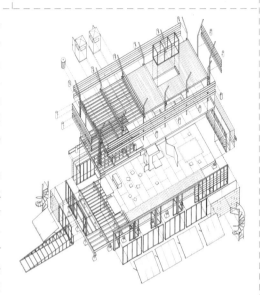

a host of design tenets relating to open-source architecture, which the architects have pursued in noteworthy prototypical prefabricated homes, detailed in their 2006 book, *Prefab Prototypes: Site-Specific Design for Offsite Construction*.

TOUCH HOUSE

HEIKKINEN-KOMONEN ARCHITECTS

Even within a firmly established prefabricated Nordic housing industry, Finland stands out as a hotbed of state-sponsored research into prefabrication. Every few years the state mounts a housing fair with the aim of improving the quality of housing and living conditions by promoting high industry standards and skills as well as research into new modes of living. Many of the country's leading architects use the fair as an opportunity to experiment with replicable housing models. Heikkinen-Komonen Architects participated in the 2000 fair in Tuusula, creating one of the country's most memorable works to date, known in English as the Touch House.

The single-family Touch House prototype, as well as a handful of rep-licas created subsequently, comprise 1,500 square feet arranged on two floors, with a quintessentially Finnish material palette: slotted wood of various species, glass, and a sculptural fabric awning. The reading of these materials from the exterior hints at the fact that the volumes are fabricated individually in the factory and later joined in a single composition on-site. Prefabricated volumes include the kitchen, the living space, bedrooms, bathroom, and the requisite sauna unit. Although the building's modules are constructed individually, a remarkably open plan on the ground level is maintained, and the high level of Finnish craftsmanship allows the joints between units to virtually disappear. Assembly takes just three weeks.

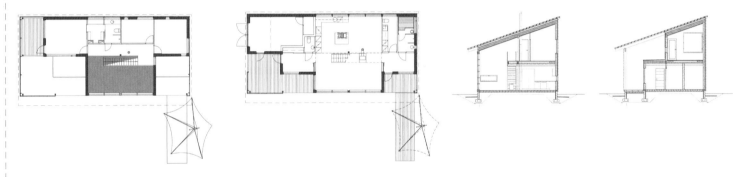

EMBRYOLOGICAL HOUSE
GREG LYNN FORM

Greg Lynn has been pursuing nonstandard computer-generated architectural form since the mid-1990s. The most significant such investigation to date in the residential realm is his Embryological House, an interactive system through which a user would be able to invent a domestic space using an architect-engineered software program. The program addressed many issues relevant to contemporary prefabrication, including brand identity and variation, customization and continuity, parametric modeling, flexible manufacturing and assembly, and, as the architect states, "an unapologetic investment in the contemporary beauty and voluptuous aesthetics of undulating surfaces rendered vividly in iridescent and opalescent colors." The geometrical limits and generic sensibility of the program's code are the only controls in a system that can unleash infinite variations. No two houses are ever identical.

In the architect's eyes, this technique "engages the need for any globally marketed product to have brand identity and variation within the same graphic and spatial system, allowing both the possibility for novelty and recognition." Adaptations to lifestyle, site, climate, construction methods, materials, functional needs, and "special aesthetic effects" all further articulate the specificity of each dwelling. The house, in effect, has no ideal or original form, image, or personality. Its form is shaped from the rich and intricate variations that arise from client and site demands, all the while maintaining formal continuity with other houses born of the same program. This paradigmatic project signaled a sea change in the conception of kit homes, embodying a more fluid, biological approach to scripting, designing, and constructing a home. An Embryological House has yet to be built.

TOP RIGHT Constructive diagram.
RIGHT Structural variants.
OPPOSITE, TOP Detail showing study model.
OPPOSITE, BOTTOM LEFT Views of study models.
OPPOSITE, BOTTOM RIGHT Installation of ½-scale prototype.

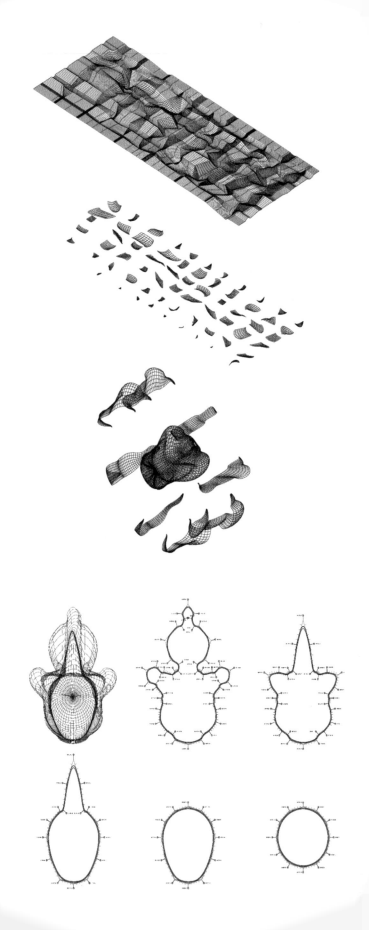

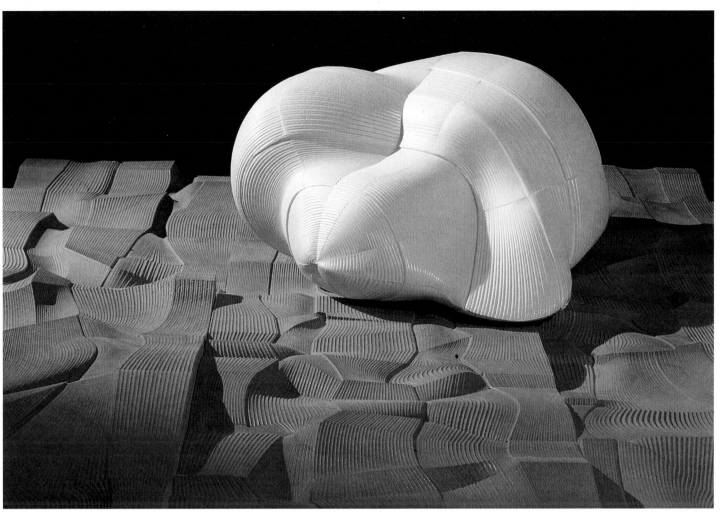

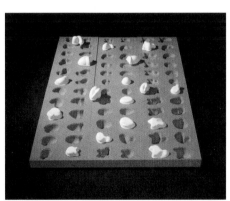

QUIK HOUSE VARIATIONS

ADAM KALKIN

BOTTOM LEFT Brochure cover.
BELOW LEFT Interior view showing containers.
BELOW RIGHT Bedroom.
BOTTOM RIGHT Push Button House.
OPPOSITE Bunny Lane House, interior view.

Artist/architect Adam Kalkin's unique practice is largely centered on his fascination with everything prefabricated. Since 1998 Kalkin has been a leading figure in the appropriation of shipping containers and prefabricated sheds. Kalkin's Quik House is less an actual product than it is a system. In this vein, Kalkin has set up, by means of a catalogue, diagrammatic models and games, ways in which potential clients can visualize the layout of their house based on the ingredients they choose to include, salvaged shipping containers and Butler prefabricated sheds being the main components. Based on the volume of the desired house, a price is derived and a few options are offered including color, configuration, and specifications for the surgical-like incisions made on the existing containers to function as doors and windows.

Kalkin works with each client to determine the specific composition for their Quik House and conducts all the fabrication on the premises of his own workshop near his studio in New Jersey. Kalkin has built a handful of iterations of the Quik House, the least expensive costing just $99,000. A particularly elaborate variant is Kalkin's own home, the Bunny Lane House, in Bernardsville, New Jersey. In this project, Kalkin, working with interior designer Albert Hadley, enclosed a nineteenth-century farmhouse in a Butler shed, and carved out a series of pentagonal incisions on the shed that recall the silhouette of the original house. The front lawn became the living room, the farmhouse sitting as the focal point of the entire composition.

Kalkin's Quik House iterations have a striking formal simplicity and a cunning wit, the result of fabricating traditional notions of home with industrial apparatus. Kalkin's role as architect is admittedly minimal as he allows his clients to arrange their homes as they see fit, using his system as their guide. He has, however, facilitated a compelling and witty system that is poised between architecture and ironic artistic commentary on housing conventions.

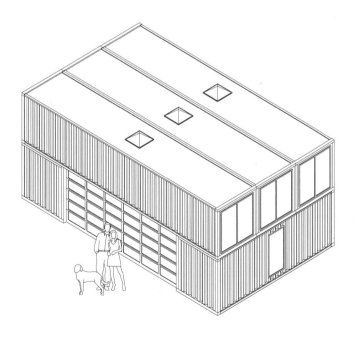

Kalkin
QUIK HOUSE®

Quik Satisfaction.

M-VIRONMENTS/M-HOUSE

MICHAEL JANTZEN

BELOW View of front vestibule.
BOTTOM Assembly phases 1, 2, and 3.
OPPOSITE, TOP Exterior view.
OPPOSITE, BOTTOM LEFT Interior view, kitchen.
OPPOSITE, BOTTOM RIGHT Interior view, bedroom.

Artist-architect Michael Jantzen's infinitely manipulable M-Vironments housing system is a significant example of the emphasis on advanced customizability and flexibility that has emerged in recent years. Fully relocatable, the M-House is made of a wide variety of components that can be connected in many different ways within a modular grid of seven interlocking space frames.

A palette of slotted and opaque panels are hinged to the frame in either a horizontal or a vertical orientation. The hinging allows the panels to fold into or out of the cubic space frame. This operability allows each panel to take on distinct architectural characteristics, with various planes functioning as walls, furniture, roofs, floors, doors, windows, eaves, or porches. Select panels are insulated and placed strategically to enclose spaces that are cooled or heated. Noninsulated panels operate as passive shading devices or rain and wind deflectors.

The panels are assembled with a structural steel frame that supports thin sheets for an optional concrete composite veneer. All of the exposed surfaces of the structure are painted on-site. The platforms and the cubic frames are supported by adjustable legs that are attached to load-bearing footpads. In many cases the support frames do not require a foundation, and they can be adjusted to accommodate terrain variations, eliminating the need for any on-site foundation work.

Functioning as a single private vacation retreat, the house can be tailored to be powered by solar and wind energy. Jantzen, who built the 968-square-foot M-House entirely himself, envisions the M-Vironments system accommodating a wide range of markets through different space-frame sizes, shapes, and panel types. Assembly by a crew of four takes approximately one week.

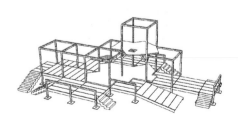 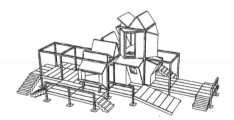 

MUJI HOUSE

MUJI/NET MUJI HOUSING DIVISION

BELOW Interior view.
BOTTOM Exterior view.
OPPOSITE Axonometric view of variations.

Kazuhiko Namba's MUJI House is the first of two prefabricated homes developed by architects working in tandem with Tokyo-based retailer MUJI, which expanded its product range from housewares to housing with Namba's design in 2004. More recently it was joined by a design of far fewer components by Kengo Kuma. Namba's design is a simple rectangular volume particularly well suited to urban and semi-urban contexts in Japan. It offers a private side, which would typically face a neighboring residence, and a more public side for frontage to a small courtyard or a driveway. On one of its long sides the house is largely opaque while on its other the house is opened up with extensive glazing. Inside, a U-shaped second-floor balcony flanks a double-height living space. The house's various storage compartments as well as areas specially designated for furniture are perfectly suited for additional MUJI products, making the house a seamless integration of architecture, industrial design, and retail marketing from top to bottom. The house sells for approximately $185,000 exclusively in Japan.

The house is distinguished among a number of prefabricated homes being developed by companies who have turned their drawing boards over to architecture. Its cool simplicity, subtle modularity, and high quality make it an excellent addition to the affordable housing market.

MUJI+INFILL 木の家は、
土地の環境によって選べる
16サイズ、35パターンの品揃えでデビューします。

無印良品では、今後MUJI+INFILLのコンセプトに基づいて、これからの住まい方をいくつか提案していきます。
今回はまず、「MUJI+INFILL 木の家」をご紹介します。
「MUJI+INFILL 木の家」はすべて、内部は開放的な吹き抜けをもった箱形の「一室空間」です。

タイプバリエーション

N-1 北側玄関 1階リビングタイプ
S-1 南側玄関 1階リビングタイプ
N-2 北側玄関 2階リビングタイプ
S-2 南側玄関 2階リビングタイプ

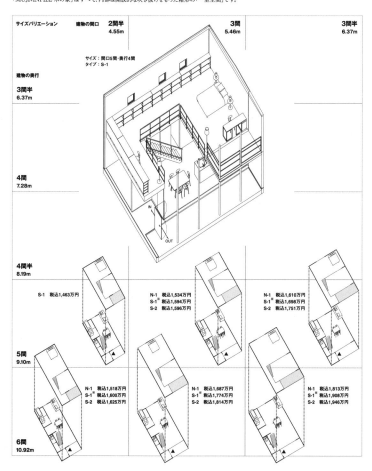

サイズバリエーション　建物の間口
2間半 4.55m　3間 5.46m　3間半 6.37m

建物の奥行
3間半 6.37m
4間 7.28m
4間半 8.19m
5間 9.10m
6間 10.92m

サイズ：間口5間・奥行4間
タイプ：S-1
IN / OUT

S-1 税込1,463万円
N-1 税込1,534万円　S-1 税込1,594万円　S-2 税込1,596万円
N-1 税込1,610万円　S-1 税込1,698万円　S-2 税込1,751万円

N-1 税込1,518万円　S-1 税込1,600万円　S-2 税込1,625万円
N-1 税込1,687万円　S-1 税込1,774万円　S-2 税込1,814万円
N-1 税込1,813万円　S-1 税込1,908万円　S-2 税込1,946万円

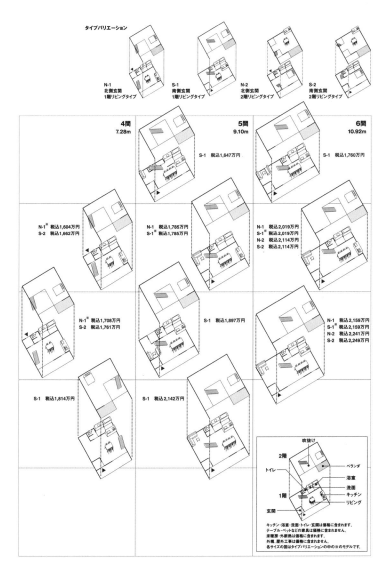

4間 7.28m　5間 9.10m　6間 10.92m

S-1 税込1,647万円　S-1 税込1,760万円

N-1 税込1,604万円　S-2 税込1,662万円
N-1 税込1,785万円　S-1 税込1,785万円
N-1 税込2,019万円　S-1 税込2,019万円　N-2 税込2,114万円　S-2 税込2,114万円

N-1 税込1,708万円　S-2 税込1,761万円　S-1 税込1,897万円
N-1 税込2,159万円　S-1 税込2,159万円　N-2 税込2,241万円　S-2 税込2,249万円

S-1 税込1,814万円　S-1 税込2,142万円

吹抜け
2階　トイレ　ベランダ　浴室　洗面　キッチン
1階　リビング　玄関

キッチン・浴室・洗面・トイレ・玄関は価格に含まれます。
テーブル・ベッドなどの家具は価格に含まれません。
床暖房・外断熱は価格に含まれます。
外構、屋外工事は価格に含まれません。
各サイズの図はタイプバリエーションの中の※のモデルです。

MAQUILADORA
ESTUDIO TEDDY CRUZ

The Maquiladora is one of the more recent infrastructural systems designed by Guatemalan-born architect Teddy Cruz and his studio, Estudio Teddy Cruz, the result of a decade-long practice of research into the border conditions between the wealthy sprawl of suburban San Diego, California, and the ad hoc, scrappy shantytowns of Tijuana, Mexico. Cruz's primary focus has been investigating the way in which Tijuana's residents have reconstituted material waste, often that of the residents of San Diego, in improvisational and unexpected ways to form patchwork neighborhoods. His various design works and proposals have been infrastructural rather than compositional in that he finds ways in which to support the extemporaneous building already at play with greater elemental order through prefabricated building apparatuses such as scaffolding, jacks, pedestals, ladders, and awnings.

The Maquiladora is a scaffolding system that will allow Tijuana's quarters to achieve a greater level of density, a quality Cruz sees as essential to maintaining a modicum of order in an urban setting already approaching entropy. The scaffolding functions as the space frame upon which milk crates, tires, sheets of corrugated metal, rammed earth, and cinder blocks can be arranged, with a particular emphasis on vertical development. Beyond the simple modular and rapidly deployable scaffolding system itself, there is very little work that Cruz can or even wants to control.

Despite his keen interest in the built environment, Cruz's practice is highly unusual in that he is loath to generate new buildings. His interest is more in infrastructure and policy, from the micro to the macro level. As outlined in an unpublished proposal produced for this exhibi-tion, Cruz is particularly critical of what he sees as the New Urbanism movement's fixation on aesthetics, which "creates a fake facade of difference without considering the lifestyle of the community." In a sense, the formlessness and malleability of Tijuana's architecture is much more representative of actual lifestyles and community function than is the landscape of Southern California. Although the Maquiladora was conceived specifically for Tijuana, it is deeply informed by its border condition. Cruz believes that the Maquiladora and similar systems have immense potential around the world where prefabricated infrastructures have the power to solve individual and urban planning problems alike at the edges of privilege and need.

OPPOSITE Study photo collage.
BELOW Collage showing Maquiladora in Tijuana.
BOTTOM Photo documentation of existing building conditions and infrastructure in Tijuana.

MIGRATING FORMATIONS

ALI RAHIM AND HINA JAMELLE/CONTEMPORARY ARCHITECTURE PRACTICE

One of four small-scale commissions produced specifically for this exhibition, this wall fragment by Contemporary Architecture Practice's Ali Rahim and Hina Jamelle employs the most recent computer-aided design and manufacturing techniques of parametric modeling to explore the extremes to which a scripted computer program could generate variation within the relatively regular volumetric envelope of a standard vertical wall. As such, the project has great potential to increase the focus of digital design's ability not only to produce building elements en masse, particularly for housing, but to imbue such systems with ample opportunity for individual client customization without significantly affecting cost. A series of wall cavities vary in terms of their aperture size, depth, articulation, and subsequently their ability to transmit light from one side to another and express the system's own nonrepetitive, morphing patterning.

RIGHT Rendering of fragment.

FLATFORM

SCOTT MARBLE AND KAREN FAIRBANKS/MARBLE FAIRBANKS

This wall fragment by Scott Marble and Karen Fairbanks and their office outlines a modular building system exploring the potential of prefabrication through digital means. For the architects, the most exciting innovation provided by computer-aided manufacturing is the ability to engage and control manufacturing processes. The design, consisting of a series of triangulated envelopes, offers a reconsideration of the standard vertical wall. The shape allows each module to sit completely flush with a neighboring module, all the while accommodating customizability by varying the size, angles, and depth of the triangular pieces. The architects simply set a given material on a cutter and/or CNC router to cut the predetermined perforations, making it possible for the system to work with steel, glass, plastic, wood, and other materials. For them the perforations achieve programmatic requirements such as light distribution, air distribution, acoustics, etc., while the gradient of perforation size and the greater triangulated composition produce the qualitative effects of a potentially rapid and affordable building system.

BELOW Renderings of fragments.

VECTOR WALL

JESSE REISER AND NANAKO UMEMOTO/REISER + UMEMOTO

With the Vector Wall Jesse Reiser and Nanako Umemoto imagined ways in which a simple laser cutter could perforate a flexible or semiflexible material with multidirectional patterning. Once cut, the material emerges from a flat sheet to form a volumetric, scalable, diaphanous scrim that reinterprets the common wall module. For this exhibition the architects have used a standardized 4-by-4-foot aluminum sheet which, once cut, renders a flexibly dimensionable wall module that can extend from its original 4-by-4-foot envelope all the way to a 5-by-10-foot panel—and potentially beyond, to the yield point of whatever material is chosen for future production using such a system. This particular approach to laser cutting enables a standardized system to transcend its own standard dimensions not only in the X and Y axes but also in the Z axis, exponentially increasing the variety of articulation for a standardized material.

BELOW Detail of study model.

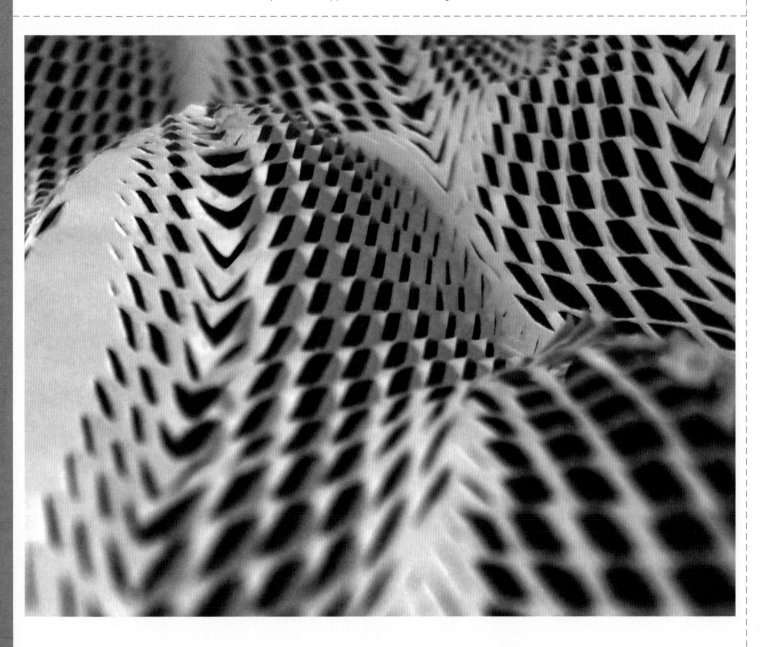

WATER BLOCK HOUSE FRAGMENTS
KENGO KUMA AND ASSOCIATES

Specially commissioned for this exhibition, Kengo Kuma's Water Block House Fragments are an imaginative take on the traditional building block. Taking inspiration from LEGO, the water blocks are rectangular units with grooves on their tops and niches on their undersides. The blocks only take on their full form when they are filled with water on the site of their installation. Left unfilled, the blocks are hollow plastic shells that can be vacuum packed flat for economic shipping. The water provides natural insulation to the interior. The system has the potential to be outfitted with an impregnated electrical system that remains protected from the water, allowing the blocks to be illuminated. Because of their modularity, the blocks have the potential to compose dwellings of infinite configurations.

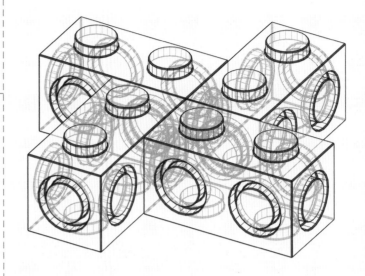

ABOVE Rendering of water block.
BELOW Exterior perspective of Water Block House.

COMMISSIONED PROJECTS

The following section contains documentation of the five architectural projects erected specifically for this exhibition. Each of these five projects is accompanied by a short descriptive text and a selection of key imagery. The projects are sequenced chronologically by their initial design date, beginning with the micro compact home, which, at the time of publication, was the one commercially available project of the five. Both BURST*008 and the Digitally Fabricated Housing for New Orleans had been developed as prototypes at the time of publication. The SYSTEM3 and Cellophane House projects were constructed solely as part of this exhibition. Principal architects or architectural firms are listed in the heading. An online journal documents this portion of the exhibition: www.moma.org/homedelivery.

MICRO COMPACT HOME
HORDEN CHERRY LEE ARCHITECTS/
HAACK + HÖPFNER ARCHITECTS

BELOW Plan.
OPPOSITE Exterior view.

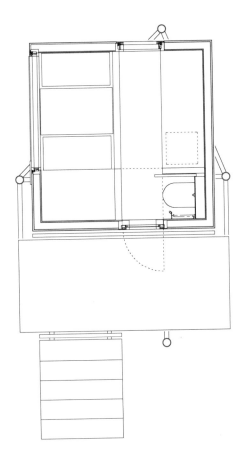

"Smart living for a short stay." So goes the slogan for this petite house-machine designed by British architect Richard Horden of Horden Cherry Lee Architects with Haack + Höpfner Architects of Germany. Horden began designing the micro compact home (mch) in 2001 as part of his design studio at the Technische Universität of Munich, where he is professor of architectural design. Along with Haack + Höpfner, Horden partnered with the Tokyo Institute of Technology to create the ultimate prototype for compact, efficient, and sustainable housing, a goal they have achieved with both compositional and commercial acumen.

At a mere 76 square feet (and weighing 2.2 tons), this perfect cubic form packs a remarkable amount of muscle into its tiny envelope. At its very core, the project is intended as a modern "machine for living," "modern" specifically referring to the absolute extraction of domestic vestiges of a predigital age such as books and personal papers as well as to the rejection of the collection of clothing, appliances, and other personal belongings beyond the absolutely essential. While such possessions have typically been measures of prosperity, the architects argue that prosperity now is something entirely different: mobility instead of permanence, streamlining instead of acquisitiveness. Taking inspiration, as so often in the history of prefabrication, from the aerospace and automobile industries, the architects fashion a "high performance" cocoon specifically geared toward single persons with a mobile work or leisure-oriented lifestyle. The mch has served as temporary housing for traveling athletes and students, notably at the Technische Universität of Munich. Interior fittings, built in monocoque fashion, include two compact double beds, a sitting area, a sliding table for work and meetings, dining space

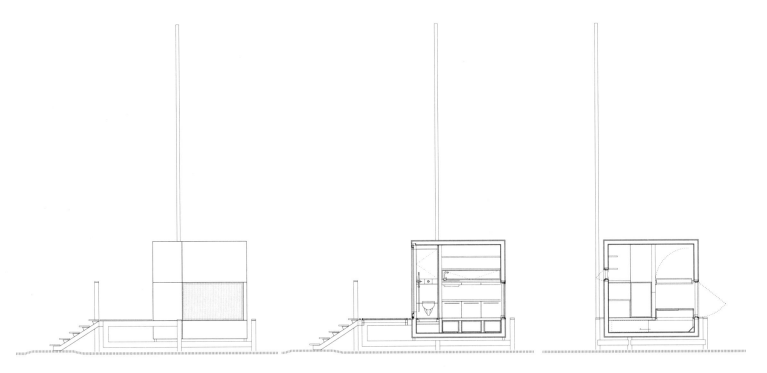

for up to five, full HVAC capabilities, a shower, toilet, kitchen, two flat-screen televisions, LED lighting, broadband Internet and telephone connection, clothing storage, and two mirrors. Optional amenities include a terrace, ski storage, and solar cell and turbine energy sources. With a modicum of passive energy equipment, the mch has the potential to be completely off-grid. The aluminum exterior can be sprayed or anodized in a range of colors. Graphic adhesive films can also be applied to the exterior for decoration or advertising purposes.

Constructed with a timber frame and clad in a panelized system of durable, flat anodized aluminum sheets, the house is insulated with polyurethane and fitted with aluminum-frame double-glazed windows. Vacuum insulation is used for the construction of the roof not only for its thermal efficiency but to minimize weight. Following the installation of the support frame at the chosen site, the mch is normally hauled by truck or trailer and

installed with a crane in a matter of minutes. It can also be jacked into place or installed by a helicopter in challenging or remote locations. Because of its minuscule footprint, the house can be installed strategically around trees and other vegetation to avoid their removal. The mch is produced by micro compact home GmbH, an Austrian construction company with over sixty years experience in manufacturing and marketing prefabricated conservatories in glass, timber, and aluminum. Horden holds patents in both the European Union and the United States for the design. In 2008 the mch is available exclusively in Europe for between €25,000 and €35,000. The mch is delivered in eight to ten weeks upon receipt of a 33 percent deposit. Consultation, delivery, and installation costs are not included. The house comes with a five-year warranty on all parts, with micro compact home GmbH available to conduct repairs or issue replacement parts. All cladding and fittings are completely recyclable.

The cubic units can also be part of a greater "village," recalling some of the plug-in or clip-on techniques of the Metabolists and Archigram. There is, however, no established structural framework in which the mch's would be configured. The system is, instead, an improvisational one, morphing to the objectives of each particular clustering scheme. Certain other schemes—some built and many others unbuilt—consist of mchs arranged in configurations ranging from simple pairs to massive highrises. For example, two mch units could be modified with a second door at the kitchen end to create a larger mch environment. A proposal for a "tree village" lies at the other end of the spectrum and takes the form of a taut stacking of cubes within a 1,500-square-foot urban site. A cluster of structural steel columns can be given brackets to support individual units in infinite configurations and orientations. An elevator core, flanked by a stairwell, lies at the center of the massing.

OPPOSITE, LEFT Elevation.
OPPOSITE, MIDDLE Longitudinal section.
OPPOSITE, RIGHT Transverse section.
RIGHT Model.
FAR RIGHT Model, "tree village."
BELOW RIGHT Model, ski chalets.

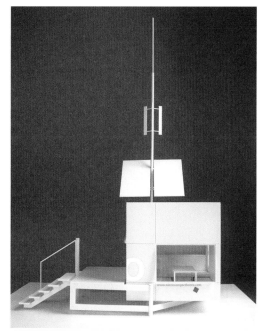

An individual unit could be removed, whether for maintenance or replacement, without disturbing the structure at large, similar to Kurokawa's Nakagin Capsule Tower. The fully passively energized version typically creates a surplus of energy, particularly in summer months, that could be diverted back into the grid, generating income for its owner.

The mch is a most outstanding commercially available example of a contemporary prefabricated house. It marries elegant form with high technology and viable sustainable practices. In delimiting the boundaries of the house to such a small envelope, the architects make a bold statement regarding what is essential to life in the twenty-first century without sacrificing a meticulous aesthetic and brilliantly organized composition in a confident, compact package.

RIGHT Interior view, dining area.
BELOW RIGHT Interior view, kitchen area.
OPPOSITE Construction photo.

DIGITALLY FABRICATED HOUSING FOR NEW ORLEANS

MASSACHUSETTS INSTITUTE OF TECHNOLOGY SCHOOL OF ARCHITECTURE AND PLANNING/ASSOCIATE PROFESSOR LAWRENCE SASS

In 2004 Massachusetts Institute of Technology Associate Professor Larry Sass began research on an architectural project that he dubbed the "Instant House." The goal of the Instant House was to find a way to harness the speed and precision of laser cutters to fabricate simple shelters quickly and inexpensively. The very first models, and later full-scale mock-ups, were of simple pitched-roof, one-room dwellings. All of the schemes were cut entirely by the laser cutter using notches and special grooves as joinery instead of nails or screws. The first full-scale version was installed by five students in two days using only rubber mallets. The scheme was startlingly simple and simultaneously attention-grabbing. Sass's absolute emphasis on such simple tenets as low cost and ease of construction stands in stark contrast to some of the more formal preoccupations of architects' relationship with technology. As such, the Instant House is radical for its desire to distill technology's power solely to solve problems rather than invent a new formal language.

In an effort to deploy the Instant House as a replicable design, Sass envisions a structure that can morph its forms to suit its context. Sass and his students have deployed specifically for this exhibition a prototypical iteration of the Instant House called Digitally Fabricated Housing for New Orleans, a 196-square-foot one-room shotgun house intended as one proposal for the rapid reconstruction of New Orleans, a major topic of debate since Hurrican Katrina ravaged the Gulf Coast in 2005.

As part of his research on adapting the generic Instant House specifically for New Orleans, Sass and his students documented in situ the city's rich vernacular architecture. Focusing on major historic districts (the French Quarter, the Garden District) they analyzed a handful of individual houses that, in their view, are emblematic of New Orleans's architectural identity.

They then modeled their selections using two methods: digital fabrication and 3-D printing, the former dealing with architecture as a planar system, the latter as a volumetric one. Accepting that the house would eventually have to be constructed out of planar sheets of cut plywood, the group identified ways to take cues from the volumetric models to give the planar model relief, filigree, and contours, albeit orthogonal ones. The house was installed by five people in five days.

For Sass, a house at its most elemental level is shelter. Basic shelters, primarily vernacular and unextraordinary ones, are almost always relegated to the annals of anthropology or the study of building culture. It is uncommon for basic shelters to enter into the greater architectural discourse because they typically are not built for clients who have the financial capacity to aspire to formal or procedural experimentation. More importantly, and with a few notable exceptions, they are rarely built by trained designers equipped with such a clear concept. Sass sets out to harness the power of digital technologies to manufacture at breakneck speed (rapid prototyping) and to apply its potential toward solving basic housing needs at unprecedented scale and pace. Sass's system confronts a myriad of geographical contexts as well as the gerrymandered line between that which has been considered building and what has been granted the status of architecture.

More importantly, the house for New Orleans is just one example of the adaptive and chameleonesque qualities of its original incarnation as a simple unadorned shed. In a sense, Sass seems resolved to revisit

BELOW Laser-cut study components.
BOTTOM Example of assembled laser-cut column.
OPPOSITE Sectional axonometric of assembly.

Robert Venturi and Denise Scott Brown's concept of the "decorated shed" in their seminal *Learning from Las Vegas* (1972). They identified there two universal building types: "ducks" and "decorated sheds," the former being structures which explicitly articulate their programmatic content in sculptural form, the latter being mundane structures dressed up in decoration that articulates their programmatic content. While the house for New Orleans, or any future site-specific iteration of the Instant House for that matter, may literally be a shed that is decorated with a sort of pixilated historicism, the project is arguably more akin to the "duck" insofar as the house is unabashedly about a New Orleans shotgun house and makes no other claims. It might equally be said that in reinvigorating the precut houses of a century ago, Sass's design transcends that distinction altogether. Sass estimates the cost to be approximately $40,000 per house if set into large-scale production. With its high-technology production and low-technology assembly, its utlity could spread far beyond the Louisiana coast.

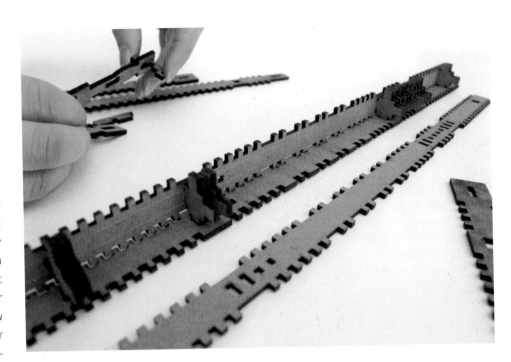

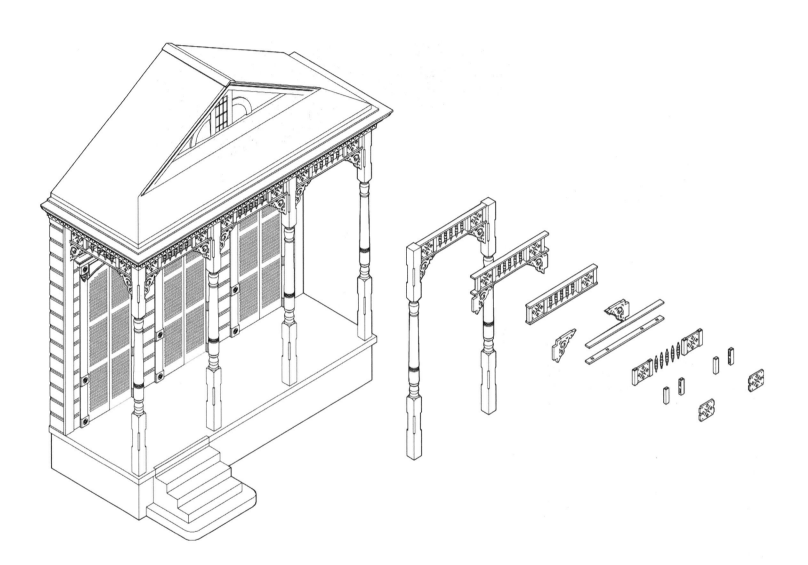

BELOW LEFT Photodocumentation of New Orleans house types.
BELOW RIGHT Facade variations 1, 2, 3, and 4.
BOTTOM RIGHT Detail, facade variation 2.
OPPOSITE Detail, facade variation 4.

BELOW Assembly rendering.
OPPOSITE, TOP Options for customization.
OPPOSITE, MIDDLE (left to right) Plan, front elevation,
side elevation.
OPPOSITE, BOTTOM Map showing type locations.

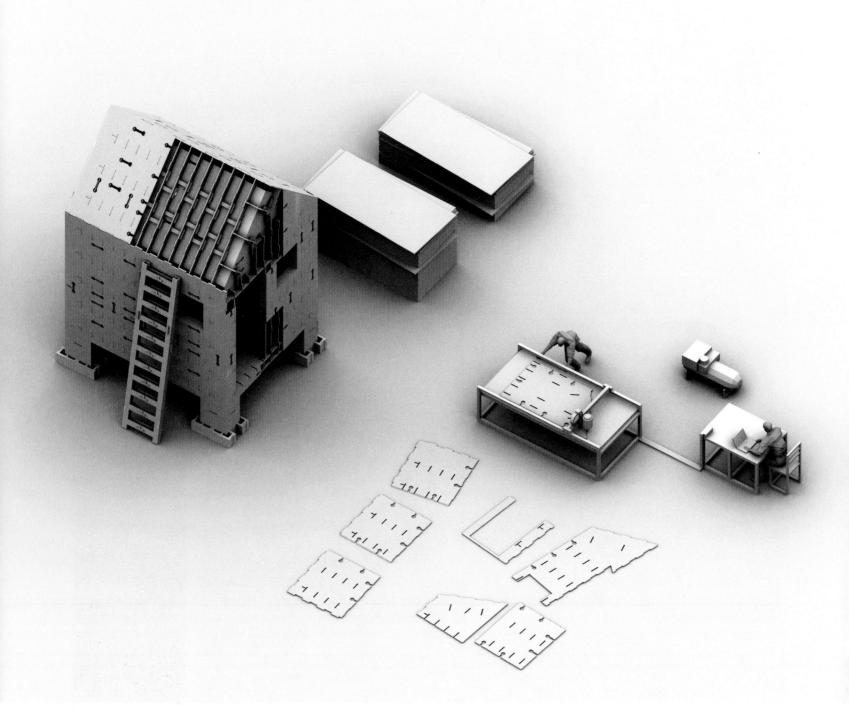

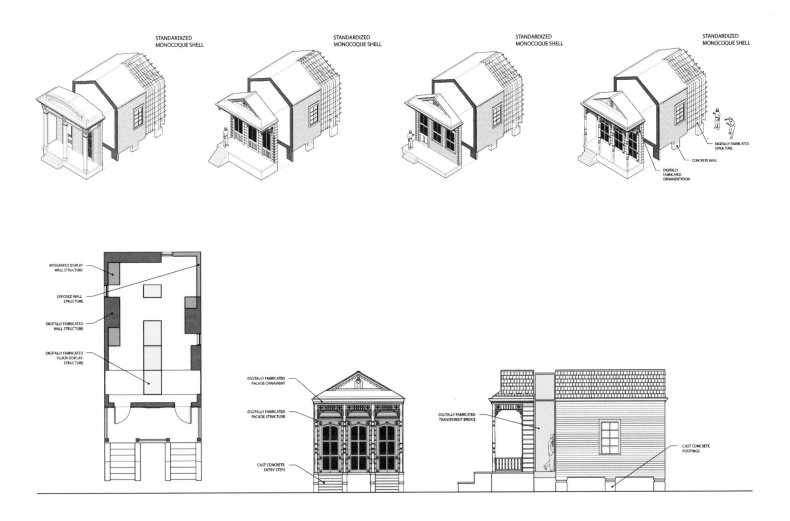

STANDARDIZED
MONOCOQUE SHELL

STANDARDIZED
MONOCOQUE SHELL

STANDARDIZED
MONOCOQUE SHELL

STANDARDIZED
MONOCOQUE SHELL

DIGITALLY FABRICATED
STRUCTURE

CONCRETE BASE

DIGITALLY
FABRICATED
ORNAMENTATION

INTEGRATED DISPLAY
WALL STRUCTURE

EXPOSED WALL
STRUCTURE

DIGITALLY FABRICATED
WALL STRUCTURE

DIGITALLY FABRICATED
FLOOR DISPLAY
STRUCTURE

DIGITALLY FABRICATED
FACADE ORNAMENT

DIGITALLY FABRICATED
FACADE STRUCTURE

CAST CONCRETE
ENTRY STEPS

DIGITALLY FABRICATED
TRANSPARENT BRIDGE

CAST CONCRETE
FOOTINGS

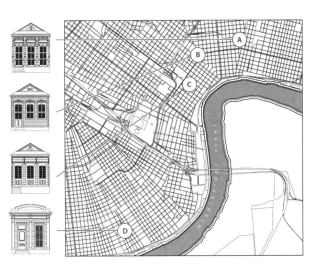

BURST*008

JEREMY EDMISTON AND DOUGLAS GAUTHIER

BELOW Plan, upper level.
BOTTOM Constructive drawing of sectional pieces.
OPPOSITE Study model views.

Jeremy Edmiston and Douglas Gauthier's BURST*008 house, built for a second time for this exhibition, is intended less as a statement about prefabrication than it is as a demonstration of what fabricated housing can achieve by mining the possibilities of the computer. The architects are more interested in creating a system of production than in creating forms. They use the computer and collateral technologies as tools to draw and fabricate architecture in a way that is not merely a digitization of hand drawing and traditional production. Emphasis is on systematizing architectural design, channeling the free will and conceptual bias of the architect into the script of a formula or design algorithm. According to their vision a client essentially could sit down with the architects in front of a computer and discuss specific needs (number of bedrooms, distribution of private and public realms, etc.) and site conditions (sun angle, natural disaster potential, etc.). The architects would then open up a series of template drawings—three sections and one plan—and shift and toggle the standard configurations to respond to these needs. Once the drawings are done, the computer reconstitutes the 3-D model of the house, and, in a matter of seconds, the house is fully designed. Beyond a few tweaks for the specific client, the architects have happily surrendered the design decisions to the computer. Where their hand is most evident is in the formula itself, the coding that tells the computer how to make these infinitely changeable decisions—a method the architects dub "analogue parametrics."

Their first house built within this framework—BURST*003—was conceived as a summerhouse for a young family in a coastal hamlet four hours north of Sydney, Australia, and built in 2005. The house is proudly at odds with its neighbors, appearing as a rumpled version of the quotidian box that has been hoisted on *pilotis*, blunt not only in appearance but in tectonic candor as well. Upon closer inspection, however, it is evident that the house is constructed entirely of planar pieces of plywood, with an astonishing absence of even moderately volumetric elements.

After Gauthier and Edmiston had plugged the client's configuration into the program Form Z (they also use Rhino), the formula exploded all 1,100 non-identical pieces apart. The pieces were then assigned placement on more than three hundred sheets of standard 4 x 8 plywood, using the program String IT, traditionally deployed in industrial design, to guarantee that the sheet's pieces had been distributed with minimum waste. The pieces were then laser cut en masse (including an

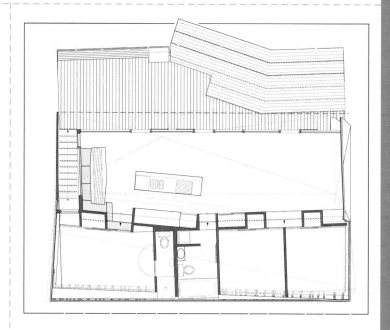

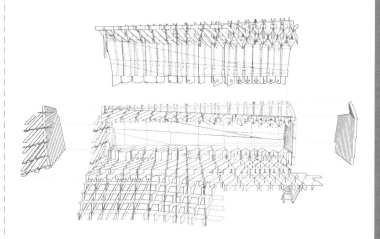

TOP RIGHT Study model, aerial view.
MIDDLE RIGHT Rendering of skin and ribs assembly system.
BOTTOM RIGHT Diagram of unfolded skin.
OPPOSITE, LEFT Exploded axonometric view of assembly sequence.
OPPOSITE, TOP RIGHT Diagram, sustainable heating and cooling.
OPPOSITE, MIDDLE RIGHT Programmatic section.
OPPOSITE, BOTTOM RIGHT Numbered cutting plates for ribs.

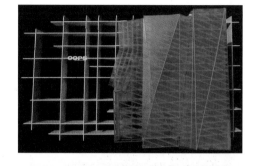

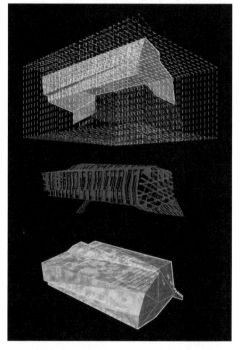

embossment of every piece's number for identification purposes), packed flat, and delivered to the site by truck. Laser cutting this amount of material in this fashion was so unfamiliar to traditional architectural fabricators that Gauthier and Edmiston had to look to a fabricator who typically created signage in order to produce this modern-day kit home.

Gauthier and Edmiston's best builders would be familiar with the generative software and the process in which the house is fabricated, hence they enlisted local architecture students to help with the construction, an event the architects liken to a barn raising. Indeed, this process of form-making is so standard in architecture schools today that the fabrication and assembly process was virtually indistinguishable from the ways in which students construct presentation models. Although the project generally "resists linear logic," according to Edmiston, the transposition from model scale to full scale is so effortless that there is something remarkably linear, if not downright simple, about the production.

The first elements to be constructed are the pylons, followed by the columns, and then the structural cage, an irregular three-dimensional diamond-shaped latticework that consists of ribs attached by collapsible steel X clips welded off-site, depending on which is more economical. If the cage is assembled off-site, the house has the ability to arrive in a concertina configuration, whose full tensile capabilities are realized only once fully unfolded and secured into the columnar field. The latticework has more structural elements on its perimeter, reflecting the need for greater tension where wind forces are higher. The structure is subsequently clad with "skin" (walls) and "gashes" (windows), and a generous bleacher-style staircase unfolds from the glazed side of the house to connect the raised living level with the ground. The plywood is coated with a paint-resin mixture. The undercroft of the structure contains several apertures which follow the direction of the house's air vents, doubling as cubbies for surfboards, in its Australian iteration, or other large objects. The only structural element not made of plywood is a steel C-channel that affords a column-free span making space available to park an automobile underneath. On the interior, lightbulb fixtures are mounted at rib joints, creating a staccato rhythm of light that celebrates the structure's irregularity.

"Prefab isn't about saving money; it is about controlling risk," says Edmiston. Indeed, the project was, at U.S. $250,000, by no means inexpensive in its incarnation in Australia and nearly double what the architects had originally estimated. That said, in focusing their energy on the system rather than the price point, the architects' achievement is double. First, they have explicitly chosen not to rely on standard fabrication practices to inform their architectural form-making for the purposes of saving money—money that would be saved eventually the more frequently the house would be fabricated. Moreover, they have authored an ever adaptable, quasi-mathematical formula that can be replicated over and over—accepting, if not beckoning, variables of all sorts, a primary tenet of the most polemical prefabricated houses throughout history, made all the more astounding here by the capacity of computer technology.

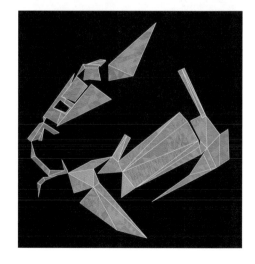

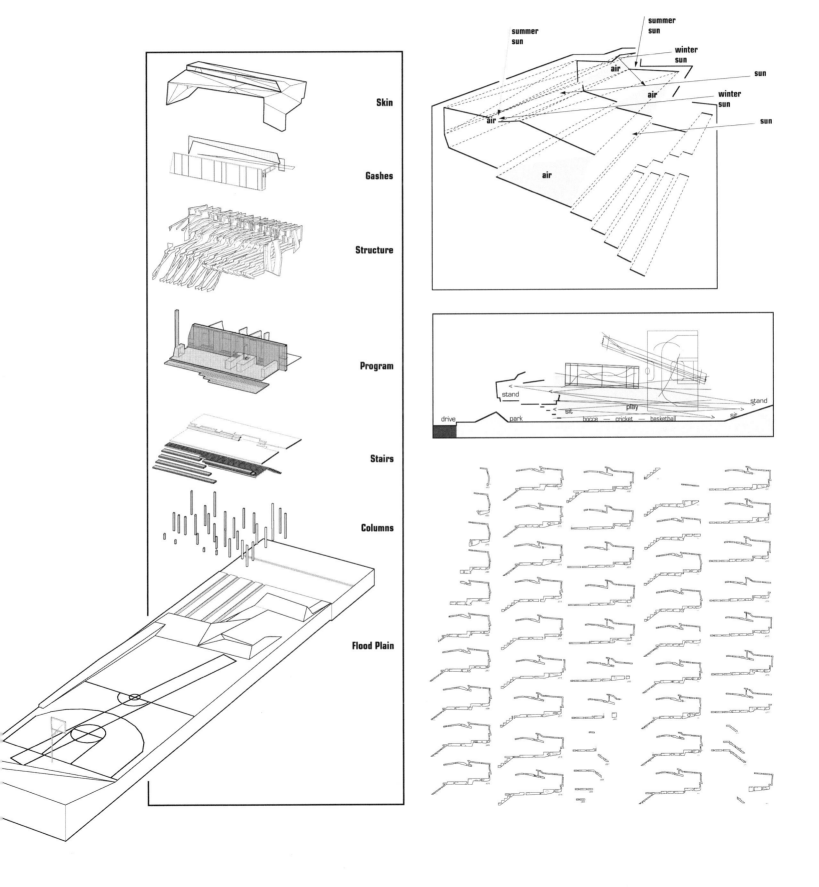

Skin

Gashes

Structure

Program

Stairs

Columns

Flood Plain

summer sun

summer sun

winter sun

air

sun

air

winter sun

air

sun

air

stand

stand

drive

park

sit

play

sit

bocce — cricket — basketball

RIGHT AND OPPOSITE Numbered cutting plates for skins.

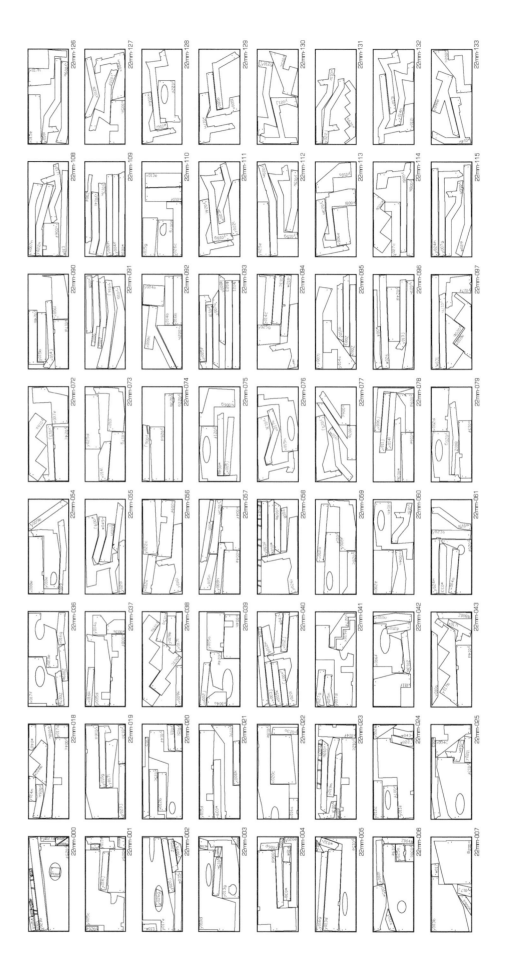

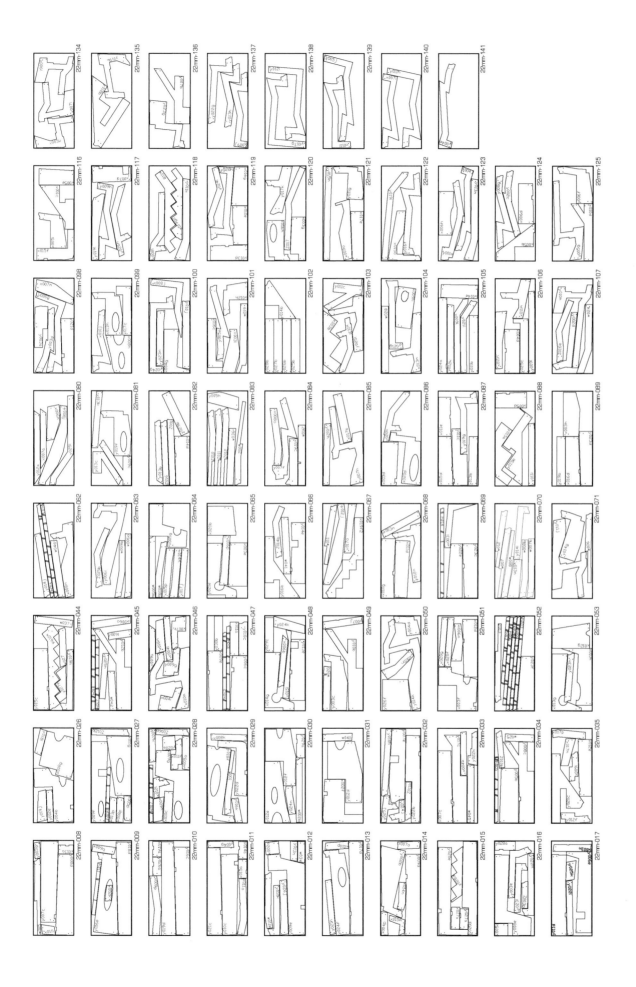

BELOW Construction photos.
OPPOSITE Detail of undercroft.

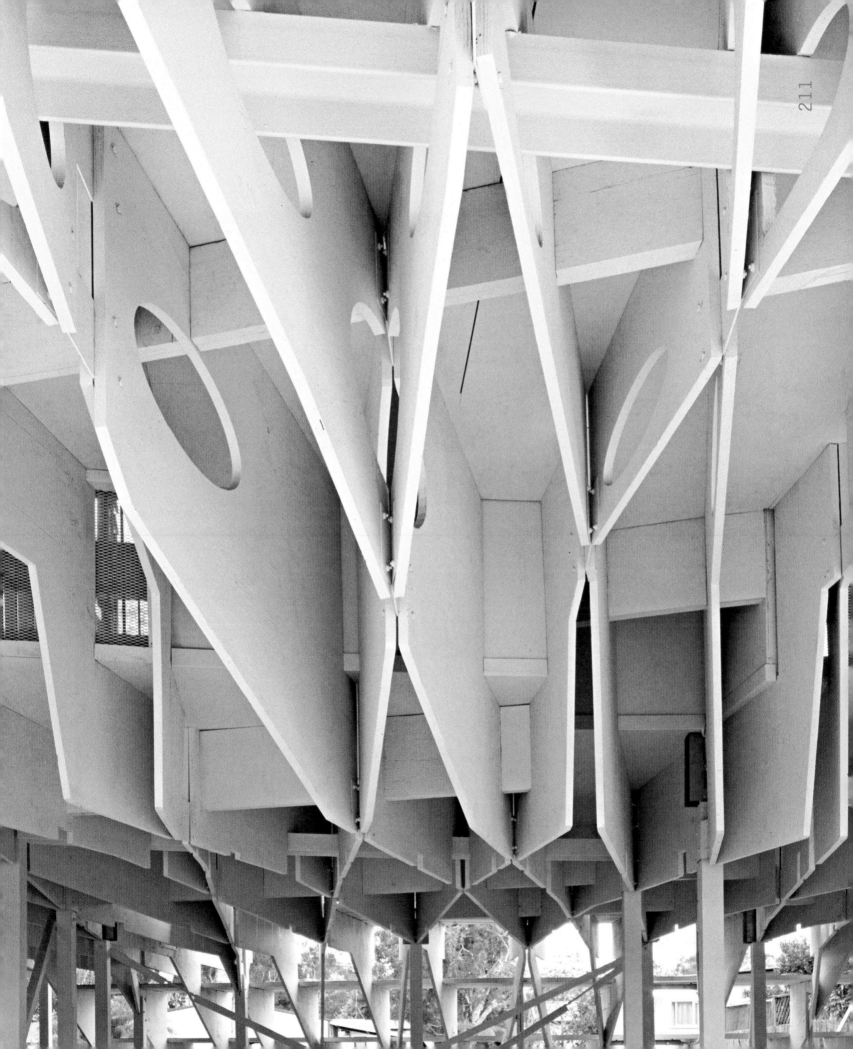

SYSTEM3

OSKAR LEO KAUFMANN AND
ALBERT RÜF/KFN SYSTEMS

Austrian architects Oskar Leo Kaufmann and Albert Rüf's SYSTEM3 debuts at The Museum of Modern Art but continues their firm's seven-year pursuit of low-cost, high-quality design. In fact, SYSTEM3 is, from afar, virtually indistinguishable from its predecessors within the firm's impressive portfolio: single-unit dwellings that the architects conceive of as potential building blocks for greater "communities," primarily in the form of efficient wooden rectangular volumes. The system does, however, bring the architects' work to a higher level, proving itself to be the most sustainable, technologically advanced, flexible, and cost-effective model to date, all the while retaining the firm's signature sobriety and supreme level of craftsmanship.

Kaufmann and Rüf's house is a single unit consisting of two space types: a "serving" space and a "naked" space, in a twist on Louis Kahn's influential distinction between "servant" and "served" spaces. The serving space refers to a completely prefabricated unit that provides all requisite functions: kitchen, bath, electricity, Internet, laundry facilities, dishwashing, heating, cooling, ventilation, and vertical circulation in the event the units are stacked. The serving space comes delivered as a completely composed volume. Conversely, the naked space is formed by entirely planar elements: floor slab, walls, windows, optional "skins," and a roof. The only element that defines the interior of the naked space is the furniture chosen by the inhabitant. The naked space encloses a volume of equal size to the serving space, butting up against one of its sides and creating the juxtaposition of two equally proportioned rectangular volumes of completely different structural derivation measuring 19 by 38 feet together.

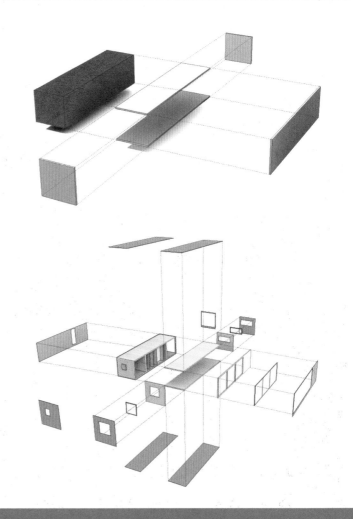

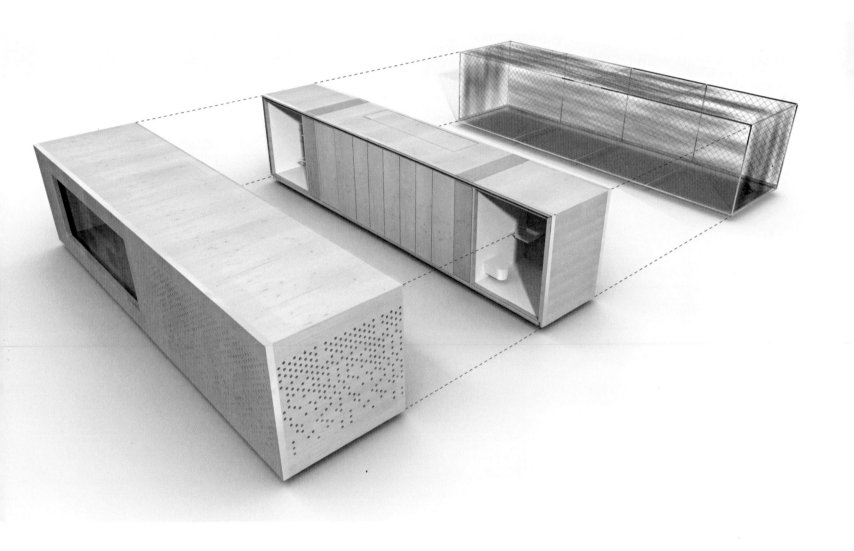

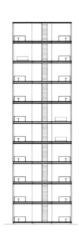

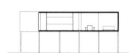

The architects envision that once they have streamlined the system, they would choose a "planner" who would then delegate all fabrication, delivery, and assembly duties as outlined in a scheme by the architects, allowing for rapid production and deployment. First, the serving unit is produced in one designated factory. Electricians, plumbers, and others conduct all work at the service-unit factory. The flat elements of the naked space are made of solid slabs of unpainted wood. The producer of these elements, who is separate from the producer of the serving unit, employs CNC technology to cut all of the openings out of the slab of wood, based on a simple CAD file provided by the planner. Those elements are then delivered directly to the service-unit factory, as are prefabricated window elements from a window producer and the building "skin"—including its thermal insulation, waterproofing, and vapor barrier—which is produced by yet another manufacturer. Together, all elements are bundled together, flanking the service module and perfectly fitting in the envelope of a standard shipping container to allow the entire house to be shipped by sea or by truck to be simply extracted and assembled upon arrival. The architects imagine that the total cost for a single unit with typical provisions and site work would be approximately $130,000 once the production system is fully operational.

For the opaque surfaces of the naked space, the architects intend to use whatever wood species is of sufficient building quality and readily available in a given region. Each element is 4¾ inches thick, guaranteeing good climatic and acoustic conditions. Depending on the amount of glazing acceptable for a given condition, the walls can be easily customized by the CNC mill to create a range of opacities within a given wall, also affording the opportunity for apertures with different shapes, from simple circular openings to perforations creating larger supergraphics. The skin system works essentially like a jacket as it is removable, changeable, and washable. Consisting of different membranes and foils and having the potential to integrate photovoltaic cells, the skin's composition mimics that of the wooden wall, providing an exterior sealant of all exposed wood. The windows can also be customized by single or double glazing; sun and mosquito screens can be integrated as required.

Within the serving unit, all elements are fabricated out of stainless steel with a regular pegboard-like pattern for the integration of hooks and screws for customization of shelving and storage organization. Lighting is integrated into the serving unit while extended cables can connect to freestanding light sources in the neighboring naked space. Further customizable options include the ability to hoist the entire unit on *pilotis* and the integration of an enclosed patio on the opposite side of the serving space. The MoMA version sits on very stout supports to level it on the asphalt and includes a semi-exterior patio space, which functions as the house's primary entrance.

The design of flat floor and roof plates are also conceived to accommodate vertical stacking, pivoting, and the vertical loads associated with larger structures, so long as vertical circulation is maintained through the core of stairs in each unit's service module. The project for MoMA represents the minimal configuration, but the architects also imagine a potential maximum configuration of thirty units stacked and arranged to create a ten-story, 11,000-square-foot office tower.

The house and its generative systems take the most rudimentary and traditional notion of what constitutes a prefabricated house today and imbue it with an austere elegance not typically associated with economy of means, materials, and time.

OPPOSITE (left to right) Plan, office alternative plan, office alternative section, hotel alternative plan, hotel alternative section.
BELOW Exterior rendering.

BELOW Basic unit assembly diagram.
OPPOSITE Programmatic unit.

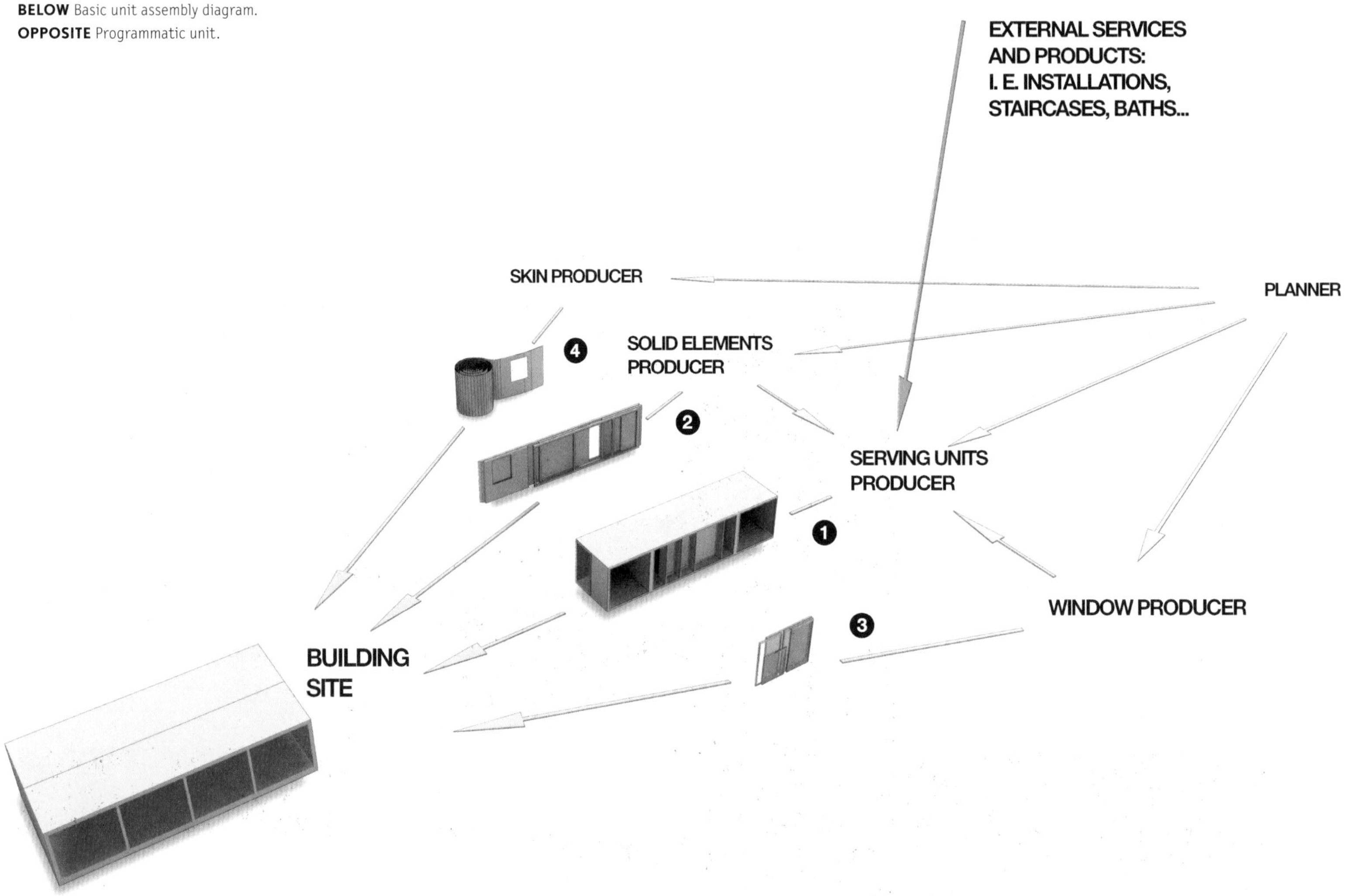

EXTERNAL SERVICES
AND PRODUCTS:
I. E. INSTALLATIONS,
STAIRCASES, BATHS...

SKIN PRODUCER

PLANNER

SOLID ELEMENTS
PRODUCER

❹

❷

SERVING UNITS
PRODUCER

❶

WINDOW PRODUCER

❸

BUILDING
SITE

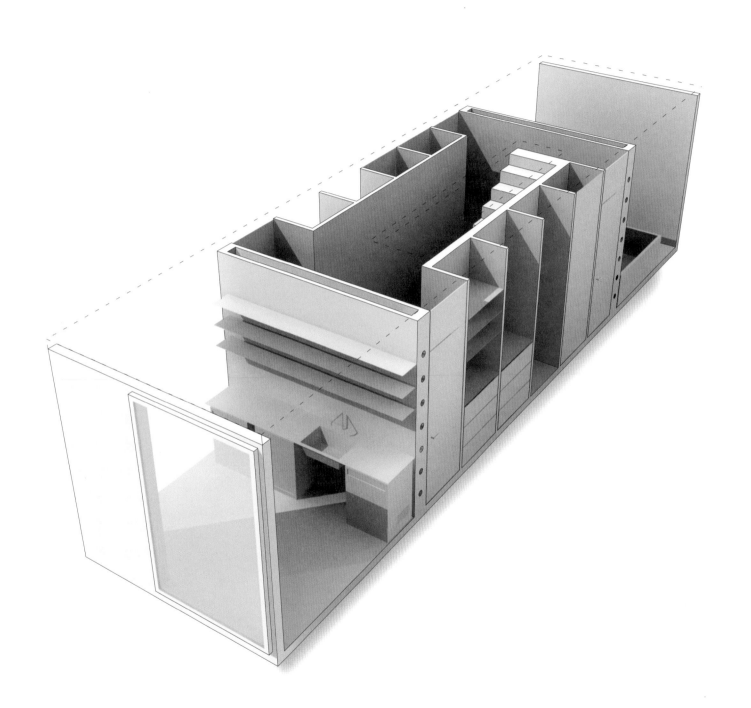

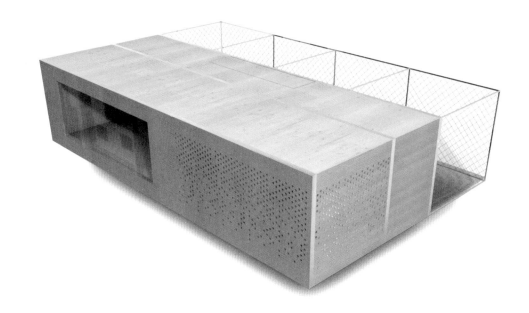

RIGHT Exterior rendering.
BELOW Interior rendering.
OPPOSITE, TOP Skin layers 1, 2, 3.
OPPOSITE, MIDDLE Kitchen components.
OPPOSITE, BOTTOM Views of large-scale, stacked assemblies.

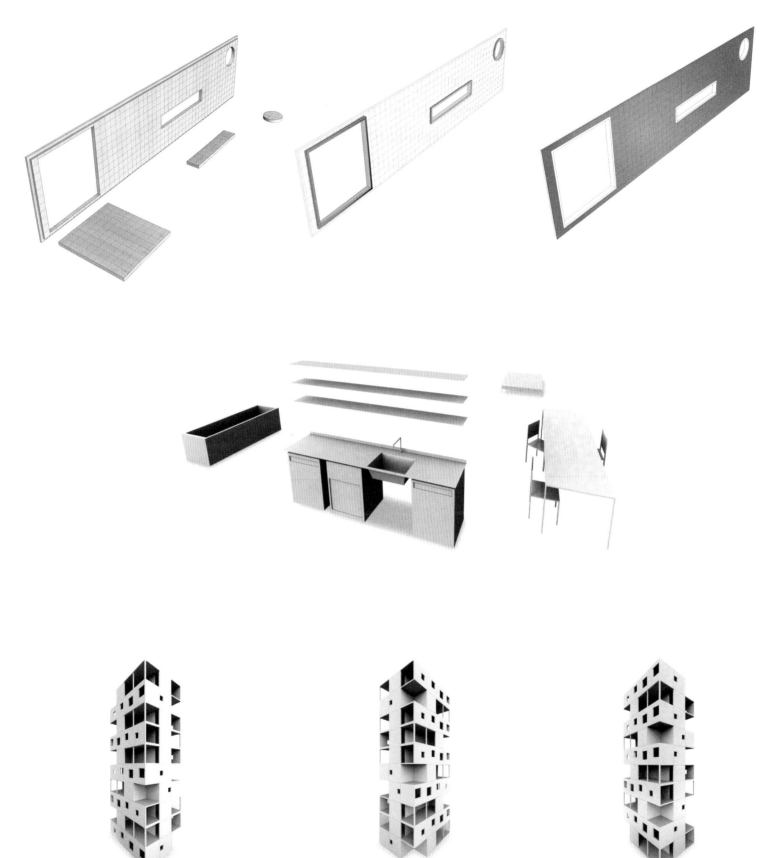

RIGHT Exterior rendering, minimal version.
BELOW Aerial rendering of large-scale linear alignment.
OPPOSITE Rendering of site corridor comprising several large-scale assemblies.

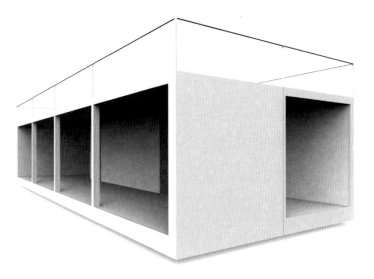

CELLOPHANE HOUSE
KIERAN TIMBERLAKE ASSOCIATES

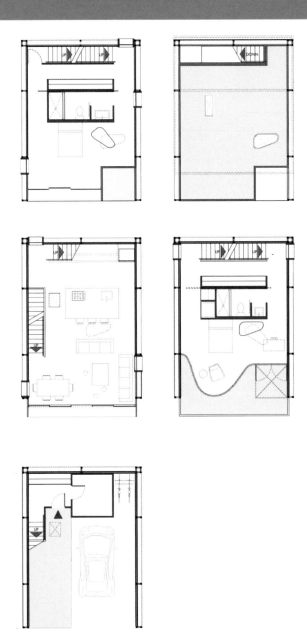

"Architecture should consider building holistically," write architects Stephen Kieran and James Timberlake, two of the most passionate and pioneering voices in the field of prefabricated architecture today. Their influential book *Refabricating Architecture* (2003) is an unequivocal critique of architecture as a top-down system where architects design a building and then devise a system to make it work. As they see things, architects are not masters of the universe; they are instead mere interlocutors who allow architecture to grow out of its opportunities as well as its constraints. According to them, "what emerges from such a process is a design that is holistic in its approach, irreducible in its makeup." Cellophane House is a towering manifesto expressing these beliefs, a material moment of equilibrium that surrenders itself to any and all entropic forces which may come its way.

Preferring the term "off-site fabrication" to "prefabrication," the architects speak of building using terms such as "chunks," "blocks," and "integrated component assemblies," this last term borrowed from the manufacturing revolution in airplane and car manufacturing. They believe in developing strategies instead of formulas and hybrid assembly methods that resist the perennial debate over flat pack or modular. Cellophane House, a four-story, single-family structure, makes no claims to permanence. The structural frame of the house is made entirely of off-the-shelf structural steel, which the architects conceive of as the matrix upon which materials are collected rather than fixed. This allows the materials not only to retain their identity as discrete elements, but also to be disassembled instead of demolished, and eventually to be recycled instead of wasted. A structure can appear as easily as it can

disappear. Consequently, the material palette is virtually irrelevant; what is important is a stratagem of joinery between any two raw materials within systems that allow every element to remain discrete and reusable. It is a large structure, whose essence lies in its smallest details, and every element within the structure is off-the-shelf and open-source: aluminum framing, steel connectors, PET film, aluminum frame IGU, polypropylene sheet walls, aluminum window frames, aluminum-grate and polyethylene-sheet flooring and stairs. Understanding how these elements affix to the steel frame is crucial; the point, as the architects put it, is "not to reinvent, but to revise … to capitalize upon and extend the capacities of existing technologies."

Horizontal and vertical joints bracketed to one another use steel connectors, instead of welding, and, as a result, they are debracketed

with ease. Flooring systems are dropped in and bolted into place. Interior walls snap in and out. The exterior skin is clamped and wrapped or unwrapped and declamped. Entire chunks of the larger volume are stacked and unstacked. The house is largely assembled off-site and arrives on a truck carrying its numerous components, some entire volumes, some individual pieces. The entire structure is modeled on the computer using a system called building information modeling (BIM) and Revit, a software program that automatically and simultaneously tracks needed materials based on a set of required tolerances, a process also known as parametric modeling. Consequently, the need both for two-dimensional construction and for shop drawings is completely eliminated. The process does rely on the designer to consider the ways in which the components will be shipped, lifted into place, and, most impor-

tantly, affixed. The consolidation of all project information into a single file obliterates boundaries between design and construction and minimizes the statistical odds of disconnect between the architect, the manufacturer, and the constructor/assembler.

The Cellophane House contains a myriad of seamless sustainable strategies that are remarkably integrated, inconspicuous, and unselfconscious. For one, the house takes advantage of the sun for more than just daylighting. Photovoltaic cells integrated into the thin film PET membrane and roof canopy gather energy during the day and channel it to a battery array in a dedicated mechanical room. Water is heated by a solar collector installed on the roof canopy and the rear of the house. Heated water flows through a convective loop to a holding tank. An active double wall system, open on three sides of the house and containing oper-

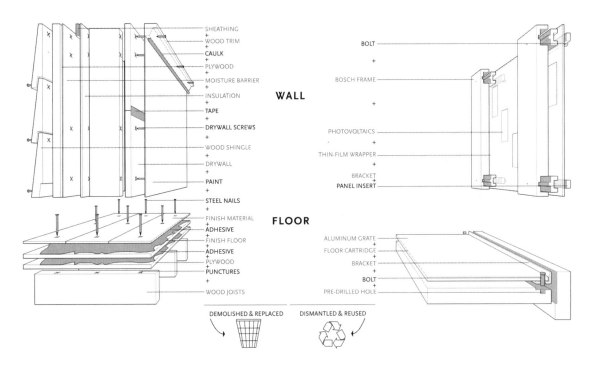

PERMANENTLY FIXED · TEMPORARILY HELD
CONSTRUCTION vs. **ASSEMBLY**

WALL

SHEATHING + WOOD TRIM + CAULK + PLYWOOD + MOISTURE BARRIER + INSULATION + TAPE + DRYWALL SCREWS + WOOD SHINGLE + DRYWALL + PAINT + STEEL NAILS

BOLT + BOSCH FRAME + PHOTOVOLTAICS + THIN-FILM WRAPPER + BRACKET + PANEL INSERT

FLOOR

FINISH MATERIAL + ADHESIVE + FINISH FLOOR + ADHESIVE + PLYWOOD + PUNCTURES + WOOD JOISTS

ALUMINUM GRATE + FLOOR CARTRIDGE + BRACKET + BOLT + PRE-DRILLED HOLE

DEMOLISHED & REPLACED   DISMANTLED & REUSED

OPPOSTE Comparative exploded structural sectional perspectives showing differences from typical constuction.
BELOW LEFT Assembly process diagram.
BELOW Facade assembly diagram.

227

able dampers and minuscule fans, anticipates internal climatic needs and eliminates the possibility for unwanted heat gains and losses. As designed for the exhibition *Home Delivery*, the house has the ability to operate entirely off-grid. Upon disassembly, the architects intend to donate the building materials to a non-profit agency.

At its core, the project is no more than a framework onto which a designer or client can transform it into an enclosure using a virtually infinite palette of off-the-shelf elements, a veritable model of mass customization. Through simple modifications, the house can adapt to a range of site conditions including climatic factors, solar orientations, slopes, and adjacencies, but also to material, textural, and color options as required by the budget and tastes of the client. Because all structural loads are carried exclusively by external frame elements, it is a simple task to rearrange interior floor plans, accessibility options, and opacity.

Rather then preoccupying themselves with building as an image, the architects have directed their energy and research to the close study and exploitation of transferable technologies and processes. The Cellophane House acknowledges, if not insists, that architects need not reinvent infrastructure. At the same time, architecture should not merely be an academic formal exercise. It is the architect's role to procure and edit the material options, acting as a bridge between the vast and seemingly endless universe of unconfigured building materials and the temporal, sustainable moment that happens when a house is assembled, if only for an exhibition. That the firm received the coveted AIA Firm Award in 2008 indicates that such research increasingly engages a larger sector of the architectural profession.

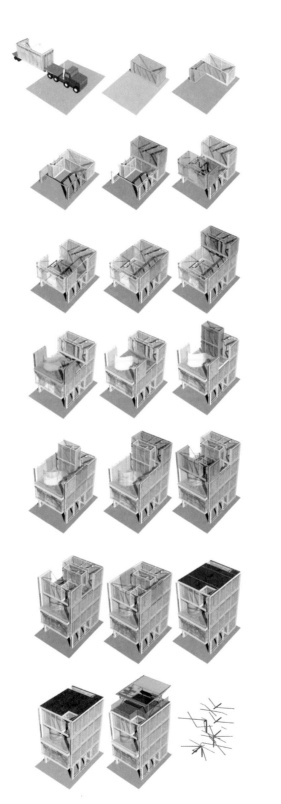

BOSCH FRAME SYSTEM

FLOOR CARTRIDGES

SERVICE CORES

WALL PANELS

WINDOWS

THIN-FILM WRAPPER

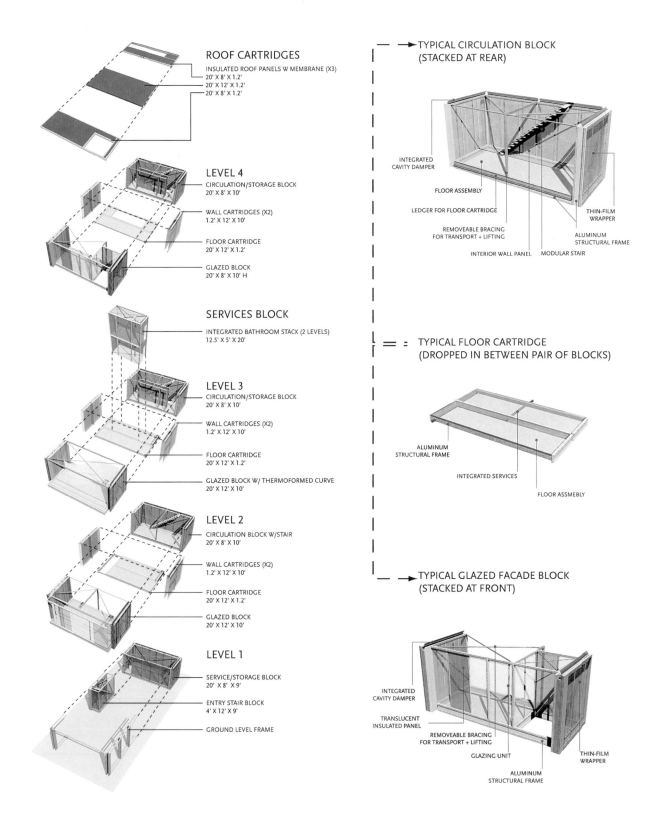

ROOF CARTRIDGES

INSULATED ROOF PANELS W MEMBRANE (X3)
20' X 8' X 1.2'
20' X 12' X 1.2'
20' X 8' X 1.2'

LEVEL 4

CIRCULATION/STORAGE BLOCK
20' X 8' X 10'

WALL CARTRIDGES (X2)
1.2' X 12' X 10'

FLOOR CARTRIDGE
20' X 12' X 1.2'

GLAZED BLOCK
20' X 8' X 10' H

SERVICES BLOCK

INTEGRATED BATHROOM STACK (2 LEVELS)
12.5' X 5' X 20'

LEVEL 3

CIRCULATION/STORAGE BLOCK
20' X 8' X 10'

WALL CARTRIDGES (X2)
1.2' X 12' X 10'

FLOOR CARTRIDGE
20' X 12' X 1.2'

GLAZED BLOCK W/ THERMOFORMED CURVE
20' X 12' X 10'

LEVEL 2

CIRCULATION BLOCK W/STAIR
20' X 8' X 10'

WALL CARTRIDGES (X2)
1.2' X 12' X 10'

FLOOR CARTRIDGE
20' X 12' X 1.2'

GLAZED BLOCK
20' X 12' X 10'

LEVEL 1

SERVICE/STORAGE BLOCK
20' X 8' X 9'

ENTRY STAIR BLOCK
4' X 12' X 9'

GROUND LEVEL FRAME

TYPICAL CIRCULATION BLOCK
(STACKED AT REAR)

INTEGRATED
CAVITY DAMPER

FLOOR ASSEMBLY

LEDGER FOR FLOOR CARTRIDGE

REMOVEABLE BRACING
FOR TRANSPORT + LIFTING

INTERIOR WALL PANEL

MODULAR STAIR

THIN-FILM
WRAPPER

ALUMINUM
STRUCTURAL FRAME

TYPICAL FLOOR CARTRIDGE
(DROPPED IN BETWEEN PAIR OF BLOCKS)

ALUMINUM
STRUCTURAL FRAME

INTEGRATED SERVICES

FLOOR ASSMEBLY

TYPICAL GLAZED FACADE BLOCK
(STACKED AT FRONT)

INTEGRATED
CAVITY DAMPER

TRANSLUCENT
INSULATED PANEL

REMOVEABLE BRACING
FOR TRANSPORT + LIFTING

GLAZING UNIT

THIN-FILM
WRAPPER

ALUMINUM
STRUCTURAL FRAME

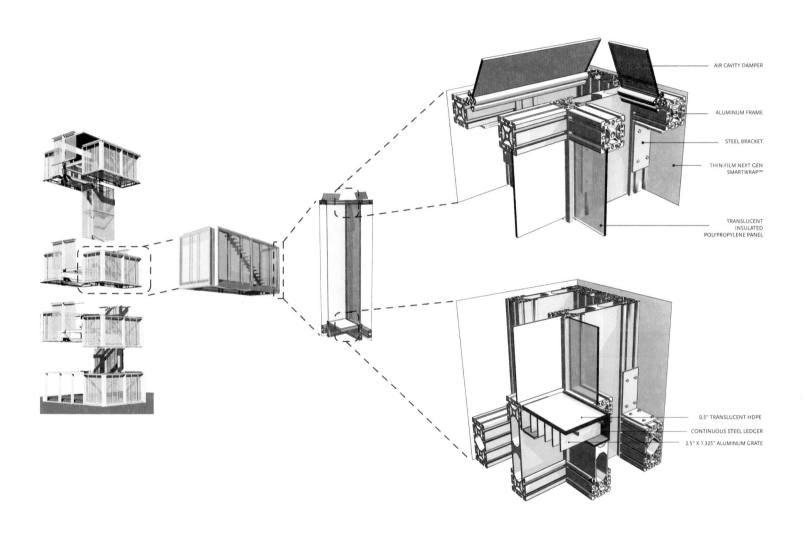

AIR CAVITY DAMPER

ALUMINUM FRAME

STEEL BRACKET

THIN-FILM NEXT GEN
SMARTWRAP™

TRANSLUCENT
INSULATED
POLYPROPYLENE PANEL

0.5" TRANSLUCENT HDPE

CONTINUOUS STEEL LEDGER

2.5" X 1.325" ALUMINUM GRATE

CHRONOLOGY

Compiled by Peter Christensen. Partially adapted from a chronology prepared by Andrew Blauvelt for the pamphlet produced in conjunction with the 2005 Exhibition Some Assembly Required *organized at the Walker Art Center.*

1772   Clarke and Hodgdon of Portsmouth, New Hampshire, build a 50-by-18-foot wood-framed house for shipment to the island of Grenada consisting of three rooms fronted by a continuous gallery 12 feet deep topped with a pavilion roof. The elements—doors, glazed windows, shutters, verandah posts, planed and beaded sheathing—are included in the inventory of components. The elements required less site work than normal and were sent with two carpenters and a foreman to assemble the house.

c. 1790   British shipbuilder John King builds and assembles a double-story house at his shipyard, disassembles it, and hauls it, in pieces, to its present site in Emsworth, England, reerecting it in only sixteen hours.

c. 1833   Augustine Taylor popularizes the use of the balloon frame in Chicago.

1833   London builder by the name of H. Manning develops the Manning Portable Colonial Cottage for Emigrants, the first recorded replicable prefabricated house model, made for British settlers to Australia and New Zealand.

1882   N. G. Rood secures the first U.S. patent related to architectural prefabrication, a design for a "Portable Summer House."

1895   Sears, Roebuck and Company begin selling building elements out of their catalogues.

1906   Thomas Edison designs, patents, and eventually realizes the Single Pour Concrete System.

        Aladdin Readi-Cut Houses produces a kit house of numbered, precut pieces.

1908   Sears, Roebuck and Company begins selling homes via catalogue, offering twenty-two different models to choose from.

1911   Frank Lloyd Wright begins designs for the American System-Built Houses.

1914   Le Corbusier designs and subsequently patents the Maison Dom-ino.

1919   Le Corbusier writes the article "Mass Production Houses."

1920   *One Week*, a film starring Buster Keaton, about a newlywed couple who builds a faulty prefabricated home, opens to audiences.

1922   Walter Gropius and Adolf Meyer work with Fred Forbat to study prefabricated houses for the Bauhaus in Weimar, generalized as a system called Baukasten (Building Blocks).

1927   R. Buckminster Fuller begins design of a factory-producable metal house, known as the Dymaxion House.

c. 1930   The German Copper House Company designs prefabricated houses made of copper, which prove popular with Jewish emigrants settling in Palestine.

1930   Albert Frey and A. Lawrence Kocher begin designs of the Aluminaire House, touted as the first lightweight steel house ever realized.

1932   Ole Kirk Christiansen designs LEGO in Bilund, Denmark.

1933   The Chicago Century of Progress exposition opens with a section dedicated to progressive housing prototypes meant for replication including the Good Housekeeping Stran-Steel House and George Fred Keck's Crystal House.

1936   Frank Lloyd Wright designs the first of his Usonian houses, the Jacobs House in Madison, Wisconsin.

1935   Wally Byam introduces his iconic aluminum-shell Airstream "Clipper," a trailer easily towed by an automobile.

1940   R. Buckminster Fuller patents a drop-in, prefabricated bathroom.

1940   Otto Brandenberger designs the T-Rib Quonset Hut to house naval personnel in Quonset Point, Rhode Island.

1941   Konrad Wachsmann and Walter Gropius begin designs for the Packaged House/General Panel System. Wachsmann receives a patent for the system a year later.

Sigfried Giedion publishes *Space, Time and Architecture*.

1942   Marcel Breuer designs prototypes for two prefabricated houses: the Yankee Portables and the Plas-2-Point House.

1944   John Entenza, editor of *Arts & Architecture* magazine, publishes "What Is a House?" introducing the Case Study House Program and espousing tenets for modern prefabricated housing.

1945   Developer and builder William Levitt begins Levittown construction. His traditional stick-built, high-volume house assembly method rivals projected prefabricated housing volumes. By 1948 he is producing 150 houses per week.

Charles and Ray Eames design Case Study House No. 8, initially with Eero Saarinen, in Pacific Palisades, California.

1946   R. Buckminster Fuller unveils the Wichita House, an update of the Dymaxion House.

1947   Le Corbusier designs the Unité d'Habitation, illustrating the notion of the apartment as a discrete slide-in unit.

Research begins in the U.S.S.R. for large-scale housing projects in Moscow and St. Petersburg employing precast concrete panel systems assembled rapidly.

Industrial designer Henry Dreyfus and architect Edward Larrabee Barnes collaborate on the design of a prefabricated house for Vultex Aircraft Company consisting of paper core panels outfitted in aluminum.

1948   Thomas Strandlund's Lustron Corporation, established three years earlier, begins designing and producing its first model, the Westchester Two-Bedroom Model House, which is assembled in a vacant lot on the corner of Fifty-second Street and Sixth Avenue, a block away from The Museum of Modern Art.

1949   Marcel Breuer's House in the Museum Garden is unveiled at The Museum of Modern Art.

Jean Prouvé designs the Maison Tropicale in his Maxéville workshop, eventually sending the house's principal units to Brazzaville in the French Congo to be the local headquarters for Air France's offices.

1950   Jean Prouvé further develops the system he began with the Maison Tropicale as the Meudon Houses, a series of varied houses in the Parisian suburb of Meudon.

1956   Ionel Schein pioneers the use of plastics in home design with his All Plastic House.

1957   American designer Norman Cherner publishes *Fabricating Houses from Component Parts*, a do-it-yourself guide.

c. 1960 The precast concrete panel system known as Plattenbau takes hold in the German Democratic Republic.

1964   Archigram designs Plug-In City.

1965   George Maciunas of the Fluxus collective publishes a pamphlet proposing an American prefabricated building system that could compete with those of the Soviet Union in terms of efficiency.

Hugo D'Acosta and Mercedes Álvarez design the Asbestos Cement Housing Module in Havana.

1966   Archigram designs the Living Pod, the first residential structure they envision being autonomous from a megastructure.

1967 Moshe Safdie builds Habitat '67, consisting of 158 concrete modules stacked atop each other in eighteen different versions, as a centerpiece attraction at Expo '67 in Montreal.

1968 Richard and Su Rogers propose their Zip-Up Enclosure No. 1, a series of standardized components that users could purchase to design a living structure.

Paul Rudolph begins designs for the Oriental Masonic Gardens in New Haven.

Canadian architect Barton Myers participates in a prefabricated housing competition sponsored by *Canadian Homes* magazine, winning second place with a project in steel and Velcro.

Finnish architect Matti Suuronen designs the Futuro House.

Kisho Kurokawa designs Nakagin Capsule Tower in Tokyo with living units that can be alternated over time.

1969 Kristian Gullichsen and Juhani Pallasmaa design the wood-based prefabricated housing system entitled Moduli 225.

1970 The geodesic dome becomes a do-it-yourself phenomenon, as reflected in the publication of Lloyd Kahn's *Domebook 1* and, one year later, *Domebook 2*, which sold more than 175,000 copies.

1972 Zvi Hecker begins designs for the Ramot Housing complex in Jerusalem containing 720 polyhedral modules arranged in a beehive configuration.

1975 Post-Metabolist Osamu Ishiyama ushers in a new era in Japanese architecture with his Gen-An (Fantasy Villa).

Professor Richard Dietrich of the University of Stuttgart designs a steel-frame modular building system called Metastadt-Bausystem.

1976 U.S. Congress passes the National Mobile Home Construction and Safety Act to ensure the use of approved construction standards.

Reyner Banham publishes *Megastructures: Urban Futures of the Recent Past*.

1980 The National Mobile Home Construction and Safety Act is renamed the National Manufactured Housing Construction and Safety Act, reflecting the difference between truly mobile recreational vehicles and more permanently sited manufactured homes.

1982 Dutch firm Benthem Crouwel Architects begins design of the Almere House.

1983 AutoCAD 1.4, the first computer drafting software program, is released for MS-DOS.

1984 Richard Horden, of Horden Cherry Lee Architects, designs his seminal technology-transferring Yacht House.

Gilbert Herbert publishes *The Dream of the Factory-Made House*.

1986 Waro Kishi designs the Kim House in Tokyo.

1993 Mark and Peter Anderson develop their first balloon-frame panel house on Fox Island, Washington.

1994 Wes Jones uses standard shipping containers as the basis for his Primitive Hut series.

1995 Shigeru Ban completes Furniture House in Japan, which uses factory-finished and site-installed floor-to-ceiling shelving as structural support for the roof.

Mark and Peter Anderson design the Great Hanshin Earthquake Community Shelter.

1996 Mass-market retailer IKEA introduces its traditional-style Bo Klok house in Sweden.

1997 Oskar Leo Kaufmann of Dornbirn, Austria, completes Two-Family House, a timber-framed house based on a modular system created with a group of traditional carpenters.

2000 Mikko Heikkinen and Markku Komonen present the Touch House at the Tuusula Housing Fair in Finland.

Adam Kalkin begins marketing the Quik House.

Artist-architect Michael Jantzen designs the M-House, based on his M-Vironments system.

Greg Lynn begins research on the Embryological House.

2001 Australian architect Sean Godsell creates Future Shack, an emergency housing prototype built from a discarded shipping container, which is later installed on the grounds of the Cooper-Hewitt National Design Museum in New York City.

Richard Horden, along with Lydia Haack and John Höpfner, begins research on the micro compact home.

R. Buckminster Fuller's Dymaxion House is restored and installed at the Henry Ford Museum in Dearborn, Michigan.

2002 Allison Arieff and Bryan Burkhart publish *Prefab*.

2003 The architectural firm LOT-EK completes its prototype for their Mobile Dwelling Unit, a shipping container converted into a home featuring extendable and retractable modules that increase usable interior square footage, exhibited at the Whitney Museum of American Art.

Dwell magazine launches its prefabricated house competition. A design by Resolution: 4 Architecture is selected for construction at a North Carolina site.

Teddy Cruz begins research on the Maquiladora, an improvisational building system for the city of Tijuana.

Stephen Kieran and James Timberlake publish *Refabricating Architecture*.

Alchemy Architects complete its first Wee House, a one-room prefabriated modular cabin in rural Wisconsin.

2004 The "no-brand" retailer of minimalist consumer goods MUJI offers a prefabricated, metal-clad house designed by Kazuhiko Namba in the Japanese market.

Charles Lazor completes his prototype FlatPak, a panelized prefabricated system, in Minneapolis. In 2005 the FlatPak is offered by Empyrean International LLC.

Michelle Kaufmann's Glidehouse, a modular prefabricated house, debuts in Menlo Park, California, and enters production.

2005 The Field Museum in Chicago mounts the exhibition *Design Innovations in Manufactured Housing*.

The National Building Museum in Washington, D.C., mounts the exhibition *The Green House*.

Colin Davies publishes *The Prefabricated Home*.

The Alaska Design Forum mounts the exhibition *Quonset Hut: Metal Living for a Modern Age*.

The Walker Art Center in Minneapolis mounts the exhibition *Some Assembly Required: Contemporary Prefabricated Houses*.

2008 The Museum of Modern Art in New York mounts the exhibition *Home Delivery: Fabricating the Modern Dwelling*.

SELECTED BIBLIOGRAPHY

Anderson, Mark, and Peter Anderson. *Prefab Prototypes: Site-Specific Design for Offsite Construction*. New York: Princeton Architectural Press, 2007.

Arieff, Allison, and Bryan Burkhart. *Prefab*. Layton, Utah: Gibbs Smith, 2002.

Baldwin, Neil. *Edison: Inventing the Century*. New York: Hyperion, 1995.

Banham, Reyner. *Megastructures: Urban Futures of the Recent Past*. New York: Thames and Hudson, 1976.

Beeren, W. A. L. *Jean Prouvé: Constructeur*. Rotterdam: Museum Boijmans Van Beuningen, 1981.

Bemis, Albert Farwell. *The Evolving House*. Cambridge, Mass.: The Technology Press MIT, 1936.

Blaser, Werner, ed. *Richard Horden: Light Tech*. Basel: Birkhäuser, 1995.

Carr, A. L. *A Practical Guide to Prefabricated Houses*. New York: Harper and Brothers, 1947.

Chiei, Chris, and Julie Decker. *Quonset Hut: Metal Living for a Modern Age*. New York: Princeton Architectural Press, 2005.

Cook, Peter, et al. *Archigram*. New York: Princeton Architectural Press, 1999.

Culvahouse, Tim, ed. *The Tennessee Valley Authority: Design and Persuasion*. New York: Princeton Architectural Press, 2007.

Davies, Colin. *The Prefabricated Home*. London: Reaktion Books, 2005.

Dean, Edward. "The New Foreign Import: Manufactured Housing Systems." *Journal of Architectural Education* 37 (1984): 12–19.

Ebong, Ima. *Kit Homes Modern*. New York: Harper Collins, 2005.

Enjolras, Christian. *Jean Prouvé, Les maisons de Meudon, 1949–1999*. Paris: Editions de la Villette, 2003.

Fetters, Thomas T. *The Lustron Home: The History of a Postwar Prefabricated Housing Experiment*. Jefferson, N.C.: MacFarland Company, 2002.

Fuller, R. Buckminster. *Critical Path*. New York: St. Martin's Griffin, 1982.

Furuyama, Masao. *Waro Kishi: Works and Projects*. Milan: Electa, 2005.

Gerchuk, Iurii. "The Aesthetics of Everyday Life in the Khrushchev Thaw in the USSR (1954–64)." In *Style and Socialism, Modernity and Material Culture in Post–War Eastern Europe*, ed. Susan E. Reid and David Crowley, 81–100. Oxford and New York: Berg, 2000.

Giedion, Sigfried. *Space, Time and Architecture: The Growth of a New Tradition*. Cambridge, Mass.: Harvard University Press, 1941.

Giedion, Sigfried. *Walter Gropius: Work and Teamwork*. London: The Architectural Press, 1954.

Gloag, John, and Grey Wornum. *House Out of Factory*. London: Bradford and Dickens, 1946.

Goldstein, Barbara. *Arts & Architecture: The Entenza Years*. Cambridge, Mass.: MIT Press, 1990.

Graff, Raymond, Rudolph A. Matern, and Henry Lionel Williams. *The Prefabricated House: A Practical Guide for the Prospective Buyer*. Garden City, N.Y.: Doubleday & Company, 1947.

Grüning, Michael. *Der Wachsmann-Report, Auskünfe eines Architekten*. Baden: Birkhäuser, 2001.

Guidot, Raymond. *Jean Prouvé*. Paris and New York: Galerie Patrick Seguin/Sonnabend Gallery, 2005.

Hannemann, Christine. *Die Platte: Industrialisierter Wohnungsbau in der DDR*. Wiesbaden: Vieweg, 1996.

Herbers, Jill. *Prefab Modern*. New York: Harper Collins International, 2004.

Herbert, Gilbert. *The Dream of the Factory-Made House: Walter Gropius and Konrad Wachsmann*. Cambridge, Mass.: MIT Press, 1984.

Herbert, Gilbert. "The Portable Colonial Cottage." *Journal of the Society of Architectural Historians* 31, no. 4 (December 1972): 26–75.

Herbert, Gilbert. *Synthetic Vision of Walter Gropius*. Johannesburg: Witwatersrand University Press, 1959.

Home, Marko, and Mika Taanila. *Futuro: Tomorrow's House from Yesterday*. Helsinki: Desura, 2002.

Hyman, Isabelle. *Marcel Breuer, Architect: The Career and the Buildings*. New York: Harry N. Abrams, 2001.

Jackson, Neil. "Metal-frame Houses of the Modern Movement in Los Angeles: Part I: Developing a Regional Tradition." *Architectural History* 32 (1989): 152–72; "Part 2: The Style that Nearly…." *Architectural History* 33 (1990): 167–87.

Jacobs, Karrie. *The Perfect $100,000 House*. New York: Penguin Group, 2006.

Junghanns, Kurt. *Das Haus für Alle: Zur Geschichte der Vorfertigung in Deutschland*. Berlin: Ernst & Sohn, 1994.

Jennings, Jan. *Cheap and Tasteful Dwellings: Design Competitions and the Convenient Interior, 1879–1909*. Knoxville: University of Tennessee Press, 2005.

Kelly, Brunham. *The Prefabrication of Houses: A Study by the Albert Farwell Bemis Foundation of the Prefabrication Industry in the United States*. New York: John Wiley and Sons, 1951.

Kieran, Stephen, and James Timberlake. *Refabricating Architecture*. New York: McGraw-Hill, 2004.

Knerr, Douglas. *Suburban Steel: The Magnificent Failure of the Lustron Corporation, 1945–1951*. Columbus, Ohio: Ohio State University Press, 2004.

Koch, Carl, and Andy Lewis. *At Home with Tomorrow*. New York and Toronto: Rinehart + Company, 1958.

Kolarevic, Branko, ed. *Architecture in the Digital Age: Design and Manufacturing*. New York and London: Taylor and Francis, 2003.

Krausse, Joachim, and Claude Lichtenstein, eds. *Your Private Sky: R. Buckminster Fuller, The Art of Design Science*. Baden: Lars Müller Publishers, 1999.

Kronenburg, Robert. *Flexible: Architecture that Responds to Change*. London: Laurence King Publishing, 2007.

McArthur, Shirley DuFresne. *Frank Lloyd Wright: American System-Built Homes in Milwaukee*. Milwaukee: North Point Historical Society, 1985.

McCoy, Esther, et al. *Blueprints for Modern Living: History and Legacy of the Case Study Houses*. Cambridge, Mass.: MIT Press, 1989.

Meyer-Bohe, Walter. *Vorgefertigte Wohnhäuser*. Munich: Callwey, 1959.

Nerdinger, Winfried. *The Architect Walter Gropius: Drawings, Prints, and Photographs from Busch-Reisinger Museum, Harvard University Art Museums, Cambridge, Mass. and The Bauhaus-Archiv Berlin*. Berlin: Mann, 1985.

Neuhart, John, and Marilyn Neuhart. *Eames Design*. New York: Harry N. Abrams, 1989.

Peter, John. *Aluminum in Modern Architecture*. New York: Reinhold, 1956.

Peterson, Charles E. "Early American Prefabrication." *Gazette des Beaux-Arts* 53 (1948): 37–46.

Ross, Michael Franklin. *Beyond Metabolism*. New York: Architectural Record Books, 1978.

Rubin, Robert M. *Jean Prouvé's Tropical House*. Paris: Centre Pompidou, 2007.

Schmal, Peter Cachola, Ingeborg Flagge, and Jochen Visscher, eds. *Kisho Kurokawa: Metabolism and Symbiosis*. Berlin: Jovis, 2005.

Sergeant, John. *Frank Lloyd Wright's Usonian Houses: The Case for Organic Architecture*. New York: Watson-Guptill, 1976.

Sheppard, Richard. *Prefabrication in Building*. London: The Architectural Press, 1946.

Sprague, Paul E. "The Origin of Balloon Framing." *Journal of the Society of Architectural Historians* 40 (1981): 311–19.

Stang, Alanna, and Christopher Hawthorne. *The Green House*. New York: Princeton Architectural Press, 2005.

Strauch, Dietmar. *Einstein in Caputh, Die Geschichte eines Sommerhauses*. Berlin: Philo, 2001.

Sulzer, Peter. *Jean Prouvé: Highlights: 1917–1944*. Baden: Birkhäuser, 2002.

Touchaleaume, Éric. *Jean Prouvé: Les Maisons Tropicales*. Paris: Galerie 54, 2006.

Von Vegesack, Alexander, ed. *Jean Prouvé: The Poetics of the Technical Object*. Weil am Rhein: Vitra, 2005.

Wachsmann, Konrad. *Building the Wooden House: Technique and Design*. Basel: Birkhäuser, 1995.

Wachsmann, Konrad. *The Turning Point of Building: Structure and Design*. New York: Reinhold, 1961.

Zellner, Peter. *Hybrid Space: New Forms in Digital Architecture*. New York: Rizzoli, 1999.

INDEX

ILLUSTRATION CREDITS

Every effort has been made to contact the owners of copyright for the photographs and illustrations herein. Any omissions will be corrected in subsequent printings.

© Peter Aaron/Esto: 176 [bottom right], 177; Akademie der Künste, Berlin, Konrad-Wachmann-Archiv: 80–85; Alaska Design Forum: 77; Markku Alatalo, courtesy Heikkinen-Komonen Architects: 173; The Alvar Aalto Museum, Drawings Collection: 28 [fig. 2]; Anderson Anderson Architecture: 172; © Archigram Archives 2008: 130–31; Architekturmuseum der TU Munich: 136–37; Courtesy Marcel Breuer papers, 1920–1986, Archives of American Art, Smithsonian Institution: 19 [fig. 13]; © Archives E. Touchaleaume-Galerie 54, Paris: 109; Archives Institut d'Histoire de l'Aluminium, Gennevilliers: 112, 115 [top right]; © Artists Rights Society (ARS), New York/ADAGP, Paris/Estate of Le Corbusier: 53, 98–99; © Artist Rights Society (ARS), New York/VG Bild Kunst, Bonn: 56–57; Excerpted from *Arts and Architecture*, 1944: 96; Excerpted from Audel, Theo, *Audel's Carpenter's and Builder's Guide* (1923): 41 [bottom left]; © Alain Banneel: 110; © C. Baraja, Archives Eric Touchaleaume, Paris: 115 [top left, bottom]; Barton Myers, FAIA: 138; Bauhaus-Archiv, Berlin: 18 [fig. 10], 19 [figs. 11, 12], 63, 65–66; Bauhaus-Archiv, Berlin/© ARS, New York: 17 [fig. 8]; Excerpted from Fetters, Thomas T. *The Lustron Home, The History of a Postwar Prefabricated Housing Experiment*. Jefferson, North Carolina: MacFarland Company, 2002, as attributed to collection of Mr. Morris Beckman: 102; Benthem Crouwel Architects: 164–65; Courtesy Barry Bergdoll, The Museum of Modern Art Imaging Services: 122; Courtesy Monica Garcia Brooks: 70–71; © Buckminster Fuller Institute 59–60, 90–93; Excerpted from *Business Week*, April 17, 1951: 104 [left]; Giacomo Castagnola and Alan Rosenblum: 183 [top]; © Centre Georges Pompidou: 111, 113; Chicago History Museum: 68–69; Excerpted from Fetters, Thomas T. *The Lustron Home, The History of a Postwar Prefabricated Housing Experiment*. Jefferson, North Carolina: MacFarland Company, 2002, as attributed to Clyde Foraker Files, Dan Foraker Collection: 105 [bottom left]; The Cinema Museum: 8 [fig. 1]; Columbia University, Avery Architectural and Fine Arts Library: 48; Excerpted from Le Corbusier. *Toward an Architecture*, trans. Frederick Etchells. London: Architectural Press, 1927: 12, [fig. 1]; Dell & Wainwright, EMAP/Architectural Press Archive: 41 [bottom right]; Jack Diamond for *Canadian Homes*: 139 [top left]; Excerpted from Knerr, Douglas, *Suburban Steel: The Magnificent Failure of the Lustron Corporation, 1945–1951*. Columbus, Ohio: Ohio State University Press, 2004, as attributed to Douglas Knerr Collection: 104 [bottom]; © Eames Office LLC: 95, 97; Eduardo Rodriguez Collection: 128–29; John Entenza, courtesy Eames Office: 97 [top left]; Eric Touchaleaume-Galerie 54: 116–19; floto+warner: 212–13; © Fondation Le Corbusier/Artist Rights Society (ARS), New York: 114; FRAC Centre: 120-121, 134-135, 170-171; © 2008 Frank Lloyd Wright Foundation: 51, 55, 72, 74; Excerpted from Freeland et al.: *Rude Timber Buildings in Australia*, London: Thames & Hudson, 1969, illustrator Wesley Stacy: 40 [top]; Courtesy Douglas Gauthier and Jeremy Edmiston: 204–13; Hans Jürgen Gerhardt: 66 [bottom right]; Courtesy Greg Lynn FORM: 174–75; Excerpted from: Gropius, Walter, Adolf Meyer, and Laszlo Moholy-Nagy. *Ein Versuchshaus des Bauhauses in Weimar. Zusammengestellt von Adolf Meyer*. Munich: A. Langen, 1925: 19 [fig. 9]; © Pedro E. Guerrero: 75; Kristian Gullichsen and Juhani Pallasmaa: 152–53 [bottom]; D. Gunning: 73; Zvi Hecker:159–60, 161 [top left, top right]; Heikkinen-Komonen Architects: 173; Hiroyuki Hirai, courtesy Waro Kishi + K. Associates/Architects: 168–69; Chad Holder, courtesy *Dwell*: 13 [fig. 2]; Horden Cherry Lee Architects/Haack + Höpfner Architects: 190, 192–93, 195, back cover; Richard Horden/Horden Cherry Lee Architects: 166, 167 [left]; Timothy Hursley: 125, 127; Osamu Ishiyama: 162–63; Michael Jantzen: 178–79; Lieselotte Junghanns on behalf of Kurt Junghanns: 16 [figs. 6, 7]; Juul & Frost Architects: 31 [fig. 4]; © Adam Kalkin: 176 [left]; © Akio Kawasumi: 35 [fig. 4]; Dmitri Kessel, courtesy The National Archives and Records Administration: 79; © Kieran Timberlake Associates: 224–31; G. E. Kidder Smith, Courtesy Kidder Smith Collection, Rotch Visual Collections, Massachusetts Institute of Techology: 156 [bottom]; Ken Kirkwood, courtesy Horden Cherry Lee Architects: 167 [right]; Rudolf Klein courtesy Zvi Hecker: 161 [middle left, bottom left, bottom right]; © Sascha Kletzsch: 191; Kengo Kuma & Associates: 187; Kisho Kurokawa Architects & Associates: 23 [figs. 17, 18], 144–46; Andrea Leiber: 194; Kaj G. Lindholm: 153 [top]; John Claudius Loudon: 40 [bottom left]; Excerpted from *South Australian Record*, November 27, 1837, illustration attributed to H. Manning: 40 [bottom right]; Marble Fairbanks: 185; Courtesy Massachusetts Institute of Technology School of Architecture and Planning/ Associate Professor Lawrence Sass: 197–203; Courtesy Mayekawa Associates, Architects & Engineers: 33 [fig. 2]; © Naomi Mizusaki: 2–3, 188–89; MUJI.net Co.: 180–81; © Museum of Finnish Architecture, Matti Suuronen: 140–43; The Museum of Modern Art: 61, 67, 123; Courtesy The Gilbert and Lila Silverman Fluxus Collection, Detroit, The Museum of Modern Art Imaging Services: 132–33; The Museum of Modern Art, Photographic Archive: 9 [fig. 2], 10 [fig. 4]; Courtesy The National Archives and Records Administration: 105 [right column], 106; The National Building Museum: 54; © John and Marilyn Neuhart, 94; © Arnold Newman/Getty Images: front cover; Eamonn O'Mahony, courtesy Rogers Stirk Harbour + Partners: 149, 151 [top left, middle left]; Tomio Ohashi courtesy Kisho Kurokawa Architects & Associates: 147; Gregorio Ortiz: 183 [bottom]; Oskar Leo Kaufmann + Albert Rüf: 214–23; The Paul Rudolph Foundation and the Library of Congress, Prints & Photographs Division: 154–55, 156 [top], 157; Excerpted from: Walter Prigge. *Ernst Neufert Normierte Baukultur im 20.* New York: Campus Verlag GmbH, 1999: 25, [fig. 20]; Ali Rahim and Hina Jamelle/ Contemporary Architecture Practice: 184; reiser + umemoto, RUR Architecture: 13 [fig. 3], 186; Gennady Revzin: 101; Courtesy Rhode Island Historical Society: 78 [left]; © H. Armstrong Roberts: 21 [fig. 15]; Rogers Stirk Harbour + Partners: 148, 150, 151 [bottom left, right]; Courtesy The Royal Museum, Scotland: 27 [fig. 1], 30 [fig. 3]; Moshe Safdie: 126 [middle]; Moshe Safdie and David, Barott, Boulva, Associated Architects: 124, 126 [left, middle]; Excerpted from Koch, Carl and Andy Lewis, *At Home With Tomorrow*, New York: Rinehart & Company, 1958, as attributed to Ben Schnall: 23 [fig. 16]; Sears, Roebuck and Company: 49; Sekisui Chemical Co.: 33 [fig. 3]; Karl Sliva: 139 [top right, bottom]; © Ernest Sisto/*The New York Times*: 32 [fig. 1]; © Ezra Stoller/Esto: 9 [fig. 3]; Syracuse University Library, Special Collections Research Center, Marcel Breuer Papers: 21 [fig. 14], 86–89; Sam Tata: 126 [right]; Courtesy Thomas Edison Archives: 43–45; Tijuana Workshop/Ana Aleman: 182; Excerpted from Fetters, Thomas T. *The Lustron Home, The History of a Postwar Prefabricated Housing Experiment*. Jefferson, North Carolina: MacFarland Company, 2002, as attributed to Vince Trunda: 103, 105 [top left, middle left], 107; United States Patent and Trademark Office: Endplates, 15 [fig. 5]; United States Printing Office: 76; Excerpted from: Viollet-le-Duc, Eugene-Emmanuel. *The Foundations of Architecture*, New York: George Braziller, 1990: 14 [fig. 4]; Courtesy Fürst zu Wied: 64; © Makoto Yoshida courtesy Atelier Tekuto, Co. Ltd. 36 [fig. 5]

ACKNOWLEDGMENTS

An exhibition of this scope is, needless to say, reliant on a small army of collaborators, and, in my efforts to enumerate all the individuals and their myriad contributions to this project, no doubt there are oversights. First and foremost, thanks to Glenn D. Lowry, Director of The Museum of Modern Art; Jennifer Russell, Senior Deputy Director of Exhibitions, Collections, and Programs; and Jerry Neuner, Director, Exhibition Design and Production, for their enthusiastic support of an historically ambitious undertaking brought together in a very short time.

Peter Christensen, Curatorial Assistant, and I are grateful to the participants of the two-day brainstorming session that brought together architects, critics, historians, and manufacturers. Elizabeth Alford, Allison Arieff, Andrew Blauvelt, Jason Coomes, Teddy Cruz, Colin Davies, Jeremy Edmiston, Kenneth Frampton, Douglas Gauthier, Karrie Jacobs, Adam Kalkin, Ray Koh, Giuseppe Lignano, Scott Marble, Mike Pitt, Max Risselada, Robert Rubin, Joel Sanders, Jennifer Siegal, Avi Telyas, and Ada Tolla provided valuable insight in the formative planning stages.

In addition to the hundreds of architects who generously and graciously shared their work with us, a number of architects were specifically asked to prepare a proposal for inclusion in the full-scale segment of the exhibition. They thoughtfully crafted a range of diverse and imaginative projects that presented us not only with tough decisions but also a lingering frustration of wanting to build even more. Proposals came from Anderson Anderson Architects (Seattle/San Francisco), Atelier Tekuto (Tokyo), Shigeru Ban (Tokyo) with Dean Maltz Architects (New York), Barkow Leibinger Architekten (Berlin), Estudio Teddy Cruz (San Diego), Neil M. Denari Architects (Los Angeles), Sean Godsell Architects (Melbourne), Gramazio Kohler (Frankfurt), Heikkinen Komonen Architects (Helsinki), Adam Kalkin (Bernardsville, New Jersey), Kennedy & Violich Architecture (Boston), Kengo Kuma Associates (Tokyo), César Augusto Guerrero Rodríguez (Monterrey), Rural Studio (Newbern, Alabama), and SANAA (Tokyo).

Critical insights and counsel in selecting five commissions from this rich list were provided by an advisory group comprised of Robert Beyer, Kenneth Frampton, Barbara Jakobson, Jerry Neuner, Guy Nordenson, Peter Reed, and Jennifer Russell. The five teams selected for this exhibition's full-scale component have given of themselves in ways not typical for a living artist or architect selected to participate in a MoMA exhibition. They have been on call for an entire year to negotiate contracts, submit and modify drawings, document their process in arduous detail, help raise funds, and handle countless tasks within a short time frame. All of them have executed their duties with aplomb, grace, and, of course, enormous design talent. Along with Richard Horden of Horden Cherry Lee Architects and Lydia Haack and John Höpfner we are grateful to Ulrike Fuchs, Yvonne Baum, Marijke de Goey, Vanessa Blacker Sturm, Burkhard Franke, Veronica Gruber, Claus Hainzelmeier, Walter Klasz, Stefan Koch, Christian Krauss, Bianca Matern, Hendrik Muller, Daniel Oswald, Miroslav Penev, Wiebke Seidler, Taisi Tuhkanen, Andreas Vogler, Tim Wessbecher, Nicole and Rupert Gatterbauer, Tim Brengelmann, and Stephen Cherry. Along with Lawrence Sass we would like to thank Daniel Smithwick, Dennis Michaud, Laura Rushfeldt, Anna Kotova, Christopher Dewart, Bill Young, Patricia Gay, Pam Bryan, Regina Dugan, and Jennifer Ponting. Along with Oskar Leo Kaufmann and Albert Rüf we are grateful to Jochen Specht and to the producers, Michael Kaufmann, Doris Kaufmann, and Reinhard Goggele of Kaufmann Zimmerei in Bregenzerwald, Austria. Along with Stephen Kieran and James Timberlake we are particularly grateful to David Riz, Steven Johns, Bradley Baer, Alex Gauzza, David Hincher, Matthew Krissel, Jeremy Leman, Richard Maimon, Chris MacNeal, Ryan Meillier, Dominic Muren, Sarah Savage, Andrew Schlatter, Carin Whitney, Avi Telyas, Geoff Crossman, Joseph Mizzi, Jay Gorman, Jon Morrison, Vassil Dragonov, and Brian Stacy. Jeremy Edmiston and Douglas Gauthier have carried out the duties in their complex project with a strong design and production team: Amber Lynn Bard, Henry Grosman, Joseph Jelinek, Sarkis Arakelyan, Ayat Fadaifard, Sara Goldsmith, Kobi Jakov, Ginny Hyo-jin Kang, Gen Kato, Katherine Keltner, Yarek Karawczyk, Ioanna Karagiannakou, Charles Kwan, Philip Lee, Christian Prasch, Megan Pryor, Troy Therrien, Anthony Rosello, Tony Su, Brian Osborn, Craig Schwitter, Cristobal Correa, and Byron Stigge.

The Museum's administration has provided stalwart support for and crucial guidance in the organization of this logistically unprecedented and labyrinthine project. Glenn D. Lowry provided crucial support for this project from the very beginning in addition to contributing a thoughtful foreword to this publication. Jennifer Russell has guided this exhibition to port with her unparalleled expertise and has taken an active role in figuring out just how to make this ambitious project work. Nancy Adelson, Deputy General Counsel, has stayed on top of all legal matters surrounding the exhibition with a keen and watchful eye. Carlos Yepes, Associate Coordinator of Exhibitions, has skillfully managed the complex finances and logistics of this project.

MoMA's publications department, under the direction of Christopher Hudson and aided by Kara Kirk, has remained intimately involved with every aspect of this publication. David Frankel, Managing Editor, coordinated the efforts of two editors, Julie DiFilippo and Ron Broadhurst. We are deeply grateful for Ron's thoughtful edits, which brought this catalogue to its completion on a tight schedule. Hannah Kim, Marketing and Book Development Coordinator, trafficked all of the texts and kept the writing on schedule. Christina Grillo, Production Manager, has tenaciously ensured that the imagery and appearance of this publication is of the highest caliber. Naomi Mizusaki, this catalogue's designer, has interpreted the subject matter wonderfully and has laid out an elegant book whose many design challenges have been rendered effortless by her deft eye.

Jerry Neuner has adroitly orchestrated his team to design a complex yet stunning exhibition. Betty Fisher, Exhibition Designer, was charged specifically with the installation of the houses on the vacant lot, a daunting task that she has executed with initiative and expertise at every stage. Lana Hum, Exhibition Designer, has similarly executed the interior installation with enthusiasm and creativity, melding everything from LEGO to a Lustron House seamlessly. Eric Meier provided valuable additional assistance to the whole team. Ingrid Chou, Assistant Director, Department of Graphic Design; Bonnie Ralston, Senior Graphic Designer; Claire Corey, Production Manager, Department of Graphic Design; and numerous others helped shape the visual identity of this exhibition. Richard Mawhinney, Director, and Nelson Nieves, Assistant Director, Operations, helped with crucial planning in the maintenance of this complex project.

Cooper, Robertson & Partners, based here in New York, have provided much-needed assistance in having the five houses delivered, coordinating with the city's Building Department and reviewing the drawings submitted by the architects. We are particularly grateful to Eric Boorstyn who, along with Scott Newman and Peter D'Andrilli, instilled complete confidence that this exhibition would not only happen but that it would look as good as we imagined. Joseph Mizzi and Jay Gorman of F. J. Sciame Construction have also been crucial in helping the museum with the vital site work and subcontracting necessary for carrying it off.

Eliza Sparacino, Manager, and Ian Eckert, Assistant, Collection & Exhibition Technologies, helped with the registration of scores of loans. Jennifer Wolfe, Associate Registrar, and Corey Wyckoff, Senior Registrar Assistant, coordinated the safe transport of those loans from dozens of lenders on three continents. Roger Griffith, Associate Conservator, and Erika Mosier, Associate Paper Conservator, have worked closely with us.

Todd Bishop, Director of Exhibition Funding; Mary Hannah, Associate Director of Exhibition Funding; Lauren Stakias, Associate of Exhibition Funding; and Becky Stokes, Director of Campaign Services, under the overall direction of Michael Margitich, Senior Deputy Director, External Affairs, deserve recognition for the orchestration of efforts related to raising the funds supporting this exhibition. Kim Mitchell, Director of Communications, Advertising, and Graphics; Margaret Doyle, Assistant Director, Communications; and Meg Blackburn, Senior Publicist, also deserve recognition for their wonderful efforts that generated so much excitement about this project, even before the fabrication of the houses began.

Diana Simpson, Director of Visitor Services and Government and Community Relations, and Lynn Parish and Melanie Monios, Assistant Directors of Visitor Services, helped plan and maintain a positive and safe museum-going experience. Allegra Burnette, Creative Director, and David Hart, Associate Media Producer, Digital Media, both coordinated with Maureen Costello, Petter Ringbom, Tsia Carson, Matt Kosoy, and Bryan Winters from Flat, a New York–based design firm, to create the exhibition's Web site, www.moma.org/homedelivery, a crucial element of the curatorial vision of this display not only of prefabricated architecture but the process of off-site fabrication.

In the Museum's Department of Education, a number of committed educators creatively interpreted the exhibition's curatorial material in both programs and materials meant for the museum's broad range of visitors. Led by Wendy Woon, Deputy Director for Education, the team includes Pablo Helguera, Director, and Laura Beiles, Associate Educator, Adult and Academic Programs; Sarah Ganz, Director of Educational Resources; Sara Bodinson, Associate Educator; and many others we are unable to mention at the time of writing. In the Museum's Library and Archives, Milan Hughston, Chief of Library and Museum Archives; Michelle Elligott, Museum Archivist; and Jennifer Tobias, Librarian, provided crucial research assistance.

Over the past year and a half the welcome burden of gathering films, drawings, models, images, support, and information from various corners of the globe has been all the more easy and enjoyable with the generosity of time and effort from the following people: Nakai Akari, Paul Andersen, Richard Anderson, Paola Antonelli, Allison Arieff, Alain Banneel, Candace Banks, Dr. Eva-Maria Barkhofen, Daniel Bauer, Gerald Beasley, Eve Blau, Jean-Claude Boulet, Marie-Ange Brayer, Florian Breiphol, Chrysanthe Broikos, Chris Chiei, Olivier Cinqualbre, Neil Cook, Teddy Cruz, Maria DeMarco Beardsley, Nicolette Dobrowski, Evan Douglis, Karen Fairbanks,

John Ferry, Belmont Freeman, Claudia Funke, Paul Galloway, Carey Gibbons, Dorothy Globus, Joan Harris, Zvi Hecker, Mikko Heikkinen, Jon Hendricks, Bjarke Ingels, Hina Jamelle, Päivi Jantunen, Trish Jeffers, Mina Kawakwami, Timo Keinanen, Dara Kiese, Waro Kishi, Michael Krichman, Petterri Kummala, Erik Landsberg, Hugo Laquerbe, Christian Larsen, Andres Lepik, Michael Leventhal, Cynthia Liccese-Torres, Patty Lipshutz, Bonnie Mackay, Dorte Mandrup, Scott Marble, Albert Marichal, Ed Moore, Tanja Morgenstern, Anne Morra, Susan Morris, Fréderic Migayrou, Laura Muir, Peter Nisbet, Michelle Ortwein, Ken Oshima, Curbie Oestreich, Atsuko Ota, Juhani Pallasmaa, C. Ford Peatross, Pamela Popeson, Ali Rahim, Shaparak Rahimi, Jesse Reiser, Gennady Revzin, Max Risselada, Eduardo Luis Rodriguez, Robert Rubin, Moshe Safdie, Rafi Segal, Patrick Seguin, Joshua Siegel, Howard Shubert, Charles Silver, Camille de Singly, Lauren Solotoff, Sabine Spähn, Elina Standertskjöld, Margo Stipe, Scott Stover, Nina Stritzler-Levine, Elizabeth Thompson, Kathy Thornton-Bias, Eric Touchaleaume, Fleur Treglown, Dana Twersky, Nanoko Umemoto, Marieke van't Hoff, Carina Villinger, Friedrich von Borries, Rasmus Wærn, Karin Äberg Wærn, Darren Walker, Alex Ward, Tessa Wijtman-Berkman, Todd Zeiger, and countless others who go unmentioned.

Joey Foryste, of Velocity Filmworks, joined us to spearhead the research and production of the exhibition's prominent film aspects. Carefully bringing together over sixty minutes of diverse footage, she has helped animate the interior portion of this exhibition with a stunning array of both generic and checklist-specific footage. Offering her expertise generously, the films that she has produced reflect her enthusiasm for the subject as well as her ability to translate the curatorial vision into a narrative of moving images.

Within the Museum's Department of Architecture and Design and Department of Publications, we have been blessed with the utterly invaluable assistance of eight multitalented interns including Heather Cleary, Elissa Jo-Hsun Huang, Alyson Liss, Jay Manzi, Jennifer Rector, Francesca Sonara, Aurélien Vernant, and Rodrigo Zamora. The title "intern" only begins to reflect the contributions each has made to this project. Matthew Schum joined temporarily as a Research Assistant at a crucial moment and helped coordinate many of the loans. Linda Roby, former Department Coordinator, and Colin Hartness, Assistant to the Chief Curator, managed a complex exchange of correspondence and appointments with vigor and diligence. Priscilla Fraser, Research Assistant, was charged with the tall task of researching all four hundred plus images in this publication, acquiring production-quality sets.

Andrea Lipps, Research Assistant, joined the team in the final stages, managing the exhibition's Web site and many other tasks with remarkable organization and efficiency.

Last, and anything but least, I owe an entirely inestimable debt of gratitude to Peter Christensen, Curatorial Assistant in the Department of Architecture and Design. His enthusiasm, zeal, dedication, intelligence, and creativity are reflected in every aspect of this double exhibition of astounding complexity, not least of which includes the vast majority of descriptive projects texts authored for this publication. He has been the most energetic and talented collaborator imaginable.

Barry Bergdoll
The Philip Johnson Chief Curator
Department of Architecture and Design

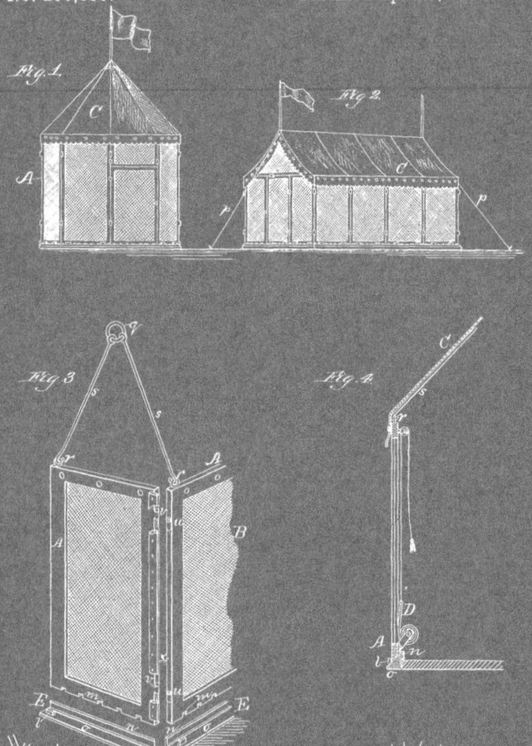

Fig. 1.
Fig. 2.

Fig. 3.
Fig. 4.

WITNESSES   INVENTOR —
F. B. Townsend   Netta G. Rood.
Thomas H. Banning   By P. C. Dyrenforth
                               Attorney

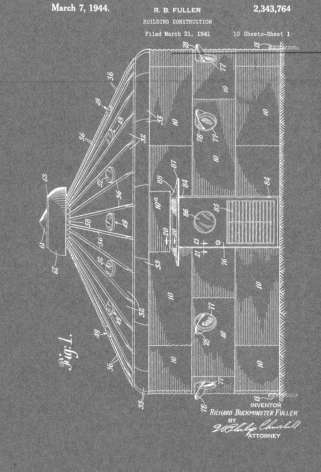

Fig. 1.

                        INVENTOR
                Richard Buckminster Fuller
                          BY
                                    ATTORNEY

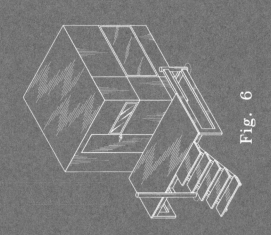

Fig. 6

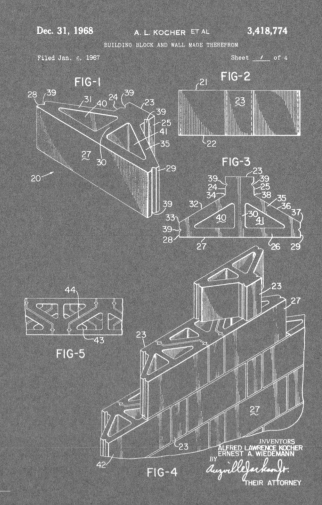

FIG-1

FIG-2

FIG-3

FIG-5

FIG-4

                        INVENTORS
                ALFRED LAWRENCE KOCHER
                ERNEST A. WIEDEMANN
                          BY
                                    THEIR ATTORNEY